Text designed by Robbie Adkins, www.adkinsconsult.com

Cover designed by Bunky Runser

Printed in the United States
Published by BearManor Media
P.O. Box 71426
Albany, Georgia 31708
books@benohmart.com

Library of Congress Cataloguing-in-Publication Data
Rhodes, Gary D.
Son of Dracula / Gary D. Rhodes and Tom Weaver
p.   cm.
ISBN 978-1-62933-431-8 (Hardback)
ISBN 978-1-62933-430-1 (Paperback)

1. Son of Dracula.   2. Horror Film Scripts.   I. Rhodes, Gary D.   II. Weaver, Tom.   III. Title.
PN1997.S5335.R11 2019

Dedicated to
Phillip Fortune, Oklahoma's greatest film and music collector,
and
John Antosiewicz, because, as so often happens, most of the illustrations in this book are from...

TABLE OF CONTENTS

"No, no, don't read me *that* book. Read me *Son of Dracula* again!"

FOREWORD
By Donnie Dunagan

MONSTERS and their Friends must stay in the Family...... and with *you*!

As the Grandson of Frankenstein, let me welcome you to *Son of Dracula*, a terrific new book by Gary Rhodes.

I am Donnie Dunagan, the little boy with all that curly blonde hair in the class monster film *Son of Frankenstein* (1939). I was the Monster's little friend—until he wanted revenge. Then he kidnapped me and placed me in great danger.

Even now at a fit age of 84, I keenly remember playing that role at Universal Studios. I'm asked about that unique event all the time. Folks like you readers are interested in those all-time classic monsters. New audiences today are re-discovering those spooky adventures.

Four years after *Son of Frankenstein*, in 1943, Universal gave us the Son of Dracula. The "sons" were doing very well in those days!

An unmatched actor, Lon Chaney Jr. was the new Dracula in this classic. Perhaps because the Second World War was battering Europe, the Son of Dracula pulled up stakes and came to the States. He moved into a real creep joint, an estate of his secret evil, in the South of our America. The locals had no idea who and what such a smart monster he was, or any clue except the fear he left in his Monster wake.

Armed with exciting memories of being a child co-star in *Son of Frankenstein*, I still tell my stories to large groups of people today, and that's a joy for all. That makes it easy for me to relate to Dracula and his Son. Author Gary Rhodes can share with you more of their exploits in this new book.

Enjoy the adventure of reading this book. There'll be some surprises. Gary helps keep the Monster Families born in Universal Studio alive and exciting, as they deserve.

Watch out! What was that noise behind the wall over there? Well, *hellll-looo*!

—Donnie Dunagan
September 2018

Son of Dracula (Universal, 1943)

80 minutes
Associate Producer: Donald H. Brown
Produced by Ford Beebe
Directed by Robert Siodmak
Screenplay: Eric Taylor
Original Story: Curtis [Curt] Siodmak
Photography: George Robinson
Art Directors: John B. Goodman and Martin Obzina
Sound Director: Bernard B. Brown
Technician: Charles Carroll
Set Decorators: R.A. Gausman and E.R. Robinson
Editor: Saul Goodkind
Music Score: Hans J. Salter
Assistant Director: Melville Shyer
Gowns: Vera West

Uncredited:

Executive Producer: Jack J. Gross
Tracked Music: Jimmy McHugh (the Universal fanfare), Hans J. Salter, Frank Skinner, Charles Previn, Jean Le Seyeux and Werner R. Heymann
Assistant Director: F.O. Collings
Second Unit Director: Ford Beebe
Special Effects: John P. Fulton
Camera Operator: Eddie Cohen
Assistant Camera: Walter Bluemel
Still Photographer: Bill Fildew
Gaffer: Max Nippell
Grip: Roland Smith
Floorman: Roger Parrish
Recorder: John Kemp
Women's Wardrobe: Ann Fielder
Men's Wardrobe: Tom Clark
Makeup: Bert Hadley
Hairdresser: Emmy Eckhardt

Assistant Cutter: Carl Himm
Script Clerk: Mary Chaffee
Prop Man: Wally Kirkpatrick
Robert Paige's Stand-in: Bob Pepper
Louise Allbritton's Stand-in: Frances Miles
Evelyn Ankers' Stand-in: Marjorie Grant
Frank Craven's Stand-in: Rex DeWitt
J. Edward Bromberg's Stand-in: Bert Rose

Publicity Photo Snipe:

Louise Allbritton's Makeup: Jack P. Pierce

Cast:

Robert Paige (*Frank Stanley*)
Louise Allbritton (*Katherine Caldwell*)
Evelyn Ankers (*Claire Caldwell*)
Frank Craven (*Dr. Harry Brewster*)
J. Edward Bromberg (*Prof. Lazlo*)
Samuel S. Hinds (*Judge Simmons*)
Adeline DeWalt Reynolds (*Queen Zimba*)
Patrick Moriarity (*Sheriff Morley Dawes*)
Etta McDaniel (*Sarah*)
George Irving (*Col. William Geddes Caldwell*)

And LON CHANEY As COUNT DRACULA

Uncredited:

Charles Moore (*Mathew*)
Jess Lee Brooks (*Steven*)
Sam McDaniel (*Andy*)
Emmett Smith (*Servant*)
Robert Dudley (*Jonathan Kirby*)
Jack Rockwell (*Deputy Sheriff*)
Cyril Delevanti (*Dr. Peters*)
Joan Blair (*Mrs. Land*)
Charles Bates (*Tommy Land*)
Walter Sande (*Mac—Jailer*)
Ben Erway
Robert Hill

SYNOPSIS

At their plantation, Dark Oaks, Colonel Caldwell (George Irving) and his daughter Katherine (Louise Allbritton) are entertaining Count Alucard (Lon Chaney) and Katherine's fiance Frank Stanley (Robert Paige). The Caldwell's friend Dr. Brewster (Frank Craven) suspects Alucard, whose name is "Dracula" spelled backward, of relationship to the infamous vampire.

Katherine's father dies and she marries Alucard. Firing a gun at his rival, Frank sees the bullet pass through him and kill Katherine. Dr. Brewster, thinking that the Colonel died in a strange manner, calls in Professor Lazlo (J. Edward Bromberg) for consultation. They agree that Alucard is a vampire.

Katherine, who is now a vampire tells Frank to destroy Alucard and join her in "immortality." After a desperate struggle, Alucard is destroyed. Frank decides that the best course is to destroy Katherine as well. He sets fire to Dark Oaks and she is cremated in the smouldering ruins.

"HORROR PICTURES"

By Robert Siodmak

(from *The Hollywood Reporter*, November 1943)

When I returned to the United States after ten years directing and producing pictures in France and Germany, I was struck by the tremendous interest of Americans in so-called "horror" pictures.

It was in 1938 that I left France (just one day before the country declared war on Germany) and at that time, European audiences were finding their "escape" in heavy dramas like *Hatred*, starring Harry Bauer (one of the last French pictures I directed), or in American-produced light comedies.

True, when films like *Frankenstein* and *Dracula* were first presented here, a great many moviegoers were inclined to scoff at them. but as war came closer, there was less scoffing and more genuine interest in this type of picture.

Whatever the cause of this, I don't know. Perhaps it was because the atrocities committed in Nazi Europe made Americans almost willing to believe in the existence of inhuman monsters, or perhaps, though they didn't believe in them at all, they wanted entertainment that would lift them entirely out of reality.

Anyway, for some reason, these films became a preferred form of escape for theater patrons.

Nor was this increase in interest and appreciation confined only to children and sub-normals. On the contrary, some of the most enthusiastic followers of the "chillers" (and President Roosevelt is among them) were persons of outstanding mentality. Inevitably this induced producers and directors to the realization that horror films could stand a touch of "adultness."

Thus the cycle came full turn.

Two schools of "mysterioso" motion pictures evolved: One, the classical school, followed the conventional pattern from which all films of that type had hitherto been made; the other, the modern school of "horror," achieved its grip and weirdness more by suggestion and implication than by outright scariness.

Director Robert Siodmak and Charles Laughton, the star of Siodmak's 1944 melodrama *The Suspect*.

This led to an interesting contest between the "goon" type of "horror" characters (like Frankenstein, Dracula *et al*.) and the "new" perpetrators of deviltry like those in Val Lewton's *Cat People*, *The Leopard Man* and others. Exhibitors, the final judges, continue to find room for both.

I should say here that no matter what school a director follows—and there is merit in both of them—he cannot hope to turn out a good "spine-tingler" unless he can visualize situations that set his hair (or a reasonable facsimile thereof) on end.

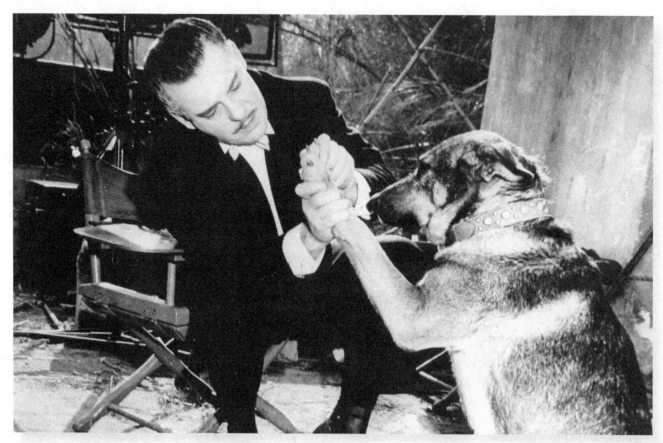

Androcles and the Lon? On the set of Robert Siodmak's *Son of Dracula*, Lon Chaney Jr., in vampire raiment, checks out his dog Moose during a paws in the day's activities.

But, of course, to ask this, is to ask only the same integrity that is required of a director for any type picture. And right here is a good place to point out that a good director should be as flexible in his handling of films as a good actor. Also, he should not run the risk of being typed.

I like to think that, when a competent director considers the pulling power of a horror film to which he is devoting himself, he imagines it as a candle to which thousands of "moths" (moviegoers) will be drawn, attracted in spite of themselves by the flame of his weird and diabolical demonstration.

I don't know whether this would hold in court, but it occurs to me that it is a great help to a "horror" director if he has been raised in a gentle atmosphere. Take my case: Though I was born in this country [editor's note: Siodmak was actually born in Germany], I spent a good many years in Europe, where my father's business took him. Yet, despite being transplanted, we were an average American family.

Thus, with so little actual "horror" in my own life, I'm essentially a mild-mannered, gentle fellow, who feels genuinely sorry for the "condemned souls" characterized in films like *Son of Dracula*.

But there is no doubt that I have also absorbed a great part of my susceptibility to the weird and unnatural from my brother, Curt Siodmak, a most prolific writer (I almost said "a most horrible") of such screen material. Many of the theories I've expressed here have come out of sessions we've had together and though we disagree in some instances, we do agree that "horror" pictures, like the politicians, are here to stay.

DEATH COMES TO DARK OAKS
Son of Dracula as Film "Noird" (and Other Occult Matters)
By Robert Guffey

In February 2012, within the pages of *The New York Review of Science Fiction*, I published a lengthy article entitled "Film Noird and the Multiple Realities Thereof" in which I analyzed a trio of Golden Age films, ranging from the early 1940s to the mid–1950s, in the context of a rapidly growing subgenre that bestselling novelist China Miéville has christened "noird."[1] I began the article as follows:

> In 2009, novelist China Miéville published a semi–tongue-in-cheek essay entitled "Neither a Contract Nor a Promise: Five Movements to Watch Out For" in which he predicted the emergence of several new subgenres in the near future. They included what he called "noird," i.e., "weird noir." He defined the term as follows: "Crime novels, particularly of a hard-boiled variety, infused with and riffing off the strange. Detective fiction with a deeply skeptical relationship to the supposedly everyday, whether it eschews morality or not."

Dark Oaks opens its doors to death: The Caldwell family's ballroom reception for Count Alucard is spoiled when he apparently no-shows. Actually, he's just upstairs, putting the bite on patriarch Col. Caldwell.

…Noird might be further defined as the melding of various genres with that of the traditional crime noir narrative, and often involves some aspect of the paranormal intruding on that narrative in ways that are unexpected. But the presence of the supernatural is not the only criteria, nor even a necessary one. If it was, then Seabury Quinn's occult detective series about the exploits of Jules de Grandin (which appeared in the pages of *Weird Tales* magazine between 1925 and the early 1950s) would be considered noird, and yet clearly it is not, for Quinn's stories belong to an older, quasi–Gothic tradition that includes Algernon Blackwood's tales of "John Silence" in which Sherlock Holmes–like detectives match wits with supernatural beings. Richard Kadrey's *Sandman Slim* novels could be considered the most recent examples of noird, as these urban thrillers combine the tradition of Seabury Quinn with a genuine crime noir sensibility, à la Cornell Woolrich or Jim Thompson.

The three films I analyzed in this specialized context were Wallace Fox's *Bowery at Midnight* (1942), Arthur Ripley's *The Chase* (1946) and Robert Aldrich's *Kiss Me Deadly* (1955). Robert Siodmak's debut film produced for Universal, *Son of Dracula* (1943), would not have been out of place on this list. Siodmak, of course, is most well-known as the director of such hard-hitting classic films noir as *Phantom Lady* (1944), *The Killers* (1946), *The Dark Mirror* (1946) and *Criss Cross* (1949). Based on the Ernest Hemingway short story, *The Killers* is often cited as one of the most important films noir ever made. In his 1988 book **The Devil Thumbs a Ride** *& Other Unforgettable Films*, novelist Barry Gifford calls it "[p]robably the best movie version of a Hemingway story."[2] Its expressionist lighting, non-linear structure and existentialist characterizations often invite comparisons to Orson Welles' *Citizen Kane* (1941). In fact, it's not uncommon to hear Siodmak's *The Killers* referred to as "the *Citizen Kane* of film noir."[3] Siodmak, however, did not develop this ambitious approach for *The Killers* alone. Expressionist stylings, artful camera angles and bleak fatalism also pervade his turn at directing a crowd-pleasing Universal horror film in the form of *Son of Dracula*.

In mid–1942, Siodmak's brother Curt wrote the screenplay for what would eventually become *Son of Dracula*. When Robert Siodmak received the assignment to direct it, his first decision was to fire his brother and replace him with screenwriter Eric Taylor. According to *Universal Horrors: The Studio's Classic Films, 1931-1946* by Tom Weaver, Michael Brunas and John Brunas, Curt Siodmak blamed his dismissal on a "sibling rivalry" with his older brother that persisted until Robert's death in 1973.[4]

In *Universal Horrors*, Michael Brunas succinctly assesses the merits of *Son of Dracula* in relation to other Universal horror films of the 1940s:

> [O]ften lumped together with the rest of the Universal monster pictures of the '40s in the early years of horror movie scholarship, [*Son of Dracula*] has incrementally been seen as the product of a more sophisticated mindset.... Still, in the canon of Robert Siodmak's career, *Son of Dracula* is...regarded as a footnote, a stepping stone to his later, highly regarded film noir works.

Eric Taylor deserves as much credit as Siodmak for elevating *Son of Dracula* above the standard B level, working an adult sensibility into the material and underscoring character development and motivation to a greater extent than the recent run of Universal shockers. Indeed, Siodmak's most important contribution to the film, along with his polished direction, might very well be his dismissal of his brother Curt from the movie. While there may have been a family dynamic at play, as Curt suggested, it's possible it could have been a case of Robert being underwhelmed by some of his sibling's recent horror assignments. Surely if [Curt's] script of *Frankenstein Meets the Wolf Man*, with its action-driven plot and comic book ruminations on the nature of life and death, were any indications of how Curt would have handled the Bram Stoker character, who could blame [Robert]? In comparison, Taylor's brew of film noir, Gothic romance and traditional horror was probably a lot closer to Robert's temperament.[5]

When one examines the film in detail, it becomes clear that the "adult sensibility" mentioned in the previous passage emerges directly out of the screenwriter's fatalistic approach toward the characterizations, an approach that marks the director's far more famous films noir. Given the fact that this approach is absent, for the most part, in Taylor's other Universal screenplays (*The Ghost of Frankenstein* [1942] and *Phantom of the Opera* [1943])—it's reasonable to conclude that this approach might have been suggested by Robert Siodmak himself.

It's possible that the dismissal of Curt Siodmak as the writer led to an equally crucial—and perhaps the most damaging—absence in the film, that of the actor Bela Lugosi. According to Curt, he wrote the character of Dracula with Lugosi in mind. In his 2001 autobiography *Wolf Man's Maker: Memoir of a Hollywood Writer*, Siodmak explicitly states, "Bela Lugosi should have played the part."[6] The troubles Lugosi experienced while filming *Frankenstein Meets the Wolf Man* in October 1942 may have given Universal executives second thoughts about casting him in a lead role. Not only did Lugosi collapse on the *Frankenstein Meets the Wolf Man* set on October 5 (no doubt due to the fact that a 60-year-old man was wearing layers of makeup and a costume weighing 35 pounds in order to enact the role of Frankenstein's Monster), but all of his lines were subsequently cut from the final edit of the film due to the producers' belief that Lugosi's performance

Lon Chaney as Alucard and Louise Allbritton as Katherine in a pair of incongruous sunlit shots.

as a speaking Monster would strike audiences as unintentionally humorous. Lugosi would not make another film for Universal until six years later, when he reprised the role of Dracula in *Abbott and Costello Meet Frankenstein* (1948).

Since Siodmak has stated that he wrote the title role of *Son of Dracula* with Lugosi in mind, it's logical to conclude that the original intention of the project was not to feature Dracula's progeny in the film, but the original count himself. Given the plot of *Son of Dracula*, in which Alucard murders a wealthy old Southerner named Col. Caldwell (George Irving), then weds one of the colonel's daughters, I've always suspected that the studio's original intent might have been to title the film *The Bride of Dracula* as a strategic nod to *Bride of Frankenstein* (1935), James Whale's successful sequel to *Frankenstein* (1931). When the studio grew skeptical about Lugosi's ability to handle a starring role in a major studio production, these original plans were no doubt scrapped and a replacement hurriedly found for Lugosi. Since Lon Chaney Jr. was already under contract to Universal, and had portrayed the Wolf Man, Frankenstein's Monster and the Mummy in commercially successful films, it made sense to let the studio's resident boogeyman continue his streak. To distinguish

Getting ready to…neck? *The Bride of Dracula* might have been a better title for the movie, given that Katherine Caldwell is a more pivotal character than Count Alucard.

Lon Chaney as the "poor, doomed" Larry Talbot in a moody shot from *Frankenstein Meets the Wolf Man* (1943).

Chaney as Alucard

Once we accept Lugosi's absence from the film, we can move on and appreciate Chaney's performance. To this day, even among devoted horror fans, Chaney is castigated as an actor of limited range. And yet how many actors of "limited range" could deliver a performance that still has the impact of Chaney's turn as Lennie Small in Lewis Milestone's 1939 film adaptation of John Steinbeck's *Of Mice and Men*? It's hard to imagine any other 1940s Hollywood leading man capable of bringing to the screen the gravitas necessary to make Lawrence Talbot's phantasmagoric predicament as a cursed outsider believable and sympathetic, as Chaney does in George Waggner's *The Wolf Man* (1941). Producer-director Stanley Kramer clearly respected Chaney's acting skills very much, as he cast him in key supporting roles in *High Noon* (1952), *Not as a Stranger* (1955) and *The Defiant Ones* (1958). Regarding the latter: In the 2015 essay "Evolution of a Horror Star," Greg Mank insists that Chaney's interpretation of ex-convict Big Sam, who dissuades a mob from lynching protagonists Tony Curtis and Sidney Poitier, was worthy of a Best Supporting Actor Oscar nomination.[7] It's hard to disagree with that assessment.

Chaney's style was not Lugosi's style. Lugosi's over-the-top, quasi-surreal acting techniques could often make his horror films even more dreamlike than intended. Chaney's approach was the reverse. In his horror films, Chaney operated as a ballast for the High Weirdness that surrounded him. To appear believable and relatable, no matter how outlandish or garish the situation, was Chaney's main talent.

Chaney's Midwestern, down-to-earth persona; his overpowering physique; his weathered road map of a face that so often seemed to bear permanent, unseen scars lurking just beneath the surface: All of these elements combined to create a necessary anchor for the carnival-esque strangeness that surrounded his own personal cinematic universe. His ability to impart gritty realism to even the nuttiest and most melodramatic scenarios is evident in his most memorable roles: not just the aforementioned man-child Lennie in *Of Mice and Men*; not just poor, doomed Lawrence Talbot in that quintet of classic horror films, i.e., *The Wolf Man*, *Frankenstein Meets the Wolf Man*, *House of Frankenstein* (1944), *House of Dracula* (1945) and *Abbott and Costello Meet Frankenstein*; not just the tired, fatalistic Martin Howe in *High Noon*, but also in less appreciated works such as Jack Hill's *Spider Baby* (1967), Roger Corman's

Chaney's interpretation of the immortal count from the version Lugosi had so indelibly burned into the memories of moviegoers, someone involved in the production—perhaps Robert Siodmak or Eric Taylor—decided to present Chaney as Dracula's descendant rather than as the count himself. I suspect this change came very late in the production. Aside from the title itself, there's only a single reference in the script to Chaney being Dracula's descendant and not the count himself, and even that one comment (made by J. Edward Bromberg's Prof. Lazlo) is presented as speculation, not fact.

Chaney's *Son of Dracula* performance is the one element in Siodmak's film that has elicited the most ire from critics and fans. If Lugosi had been awarded the starring role, I suspect that *Son of Dracula*'s reputation as a genuine classic of horror cinema would have been assured. Alas, this was not the case. As a result, *Son of Dracula* is rarely discussed by film scholars and mavens except as a minor prologue to Siodmak's later career. Instead of bemoaning the film that might have been made, let's instead assess the merits of what Robert Siodmak and company actually did accomplish with the relatively limited resources available to the directors of Universal's B horror films during the Second World War.

The residents of Dark Oaks better be ready for Hell because Alucard is bringing it with him.

With his gray temples and pencil mustache, Lon looks more like one of his Inner Sanctum brainiacs than the King of Vampires. According to the pressbook, his makeup also included bluish-gray greasepaint.

The Haunted Palace (1963), Roy Del Ruth's *The Alligator People* (1959), Bert I. Gordon's *The Cyclops* (1957), Jack Pollexfen's *Indestructible Man* (1956), Roy Kellino's TV episode "The Golden Junkman" (1956), John Hoffman's *Strange Confession* (1945), Reginald LeBorg's *The Mummy's Ghost* (1944) and George Waggner's *Man Made Monster* (1941). Some of these films are genuine masterpieces of cult cinema (e.g., *Spider Baby*); others boast significant historical importance (e.g., *The Haunted Palace* is the first cinematic adaptation of H.P. Lovecraft's work, now a veritable cinematic subgenre of its own); some showcase sincere, master-class performances within a modest budget (e.g., "The Golden Junkman"); some feature a wonderful starring performance despite the low-budget madness that threatens to overwhelm even Chaney's considerable presence. (The next time you watch *Indestructible Man*, ask yourself, "Who else but Chaney could hold an entire film together with little more than close-ups of his pained eyes?") Others demonstrate that the actor was eminently capable of transmitting genuine emotion even with one hand tied not behind his back, but to his chest (the Mummy movies).

Note how Chaney is able to suggest thousands upon thousands of years of frustrated sexual desire with nothing more than subtle body language in *The Mummy's*

Ghost during the pivotal scene in which Kharis' long-lost lover, Ananka, dissolves into dust seconds before he's about to hold her in his arms once more. Remember *Man Made Monster* and Lon's "Dynamo" Dan McCormick, a carnival performer with boyish charm who becomes an unwitting guinea pig in an illicit scientific experiment involving electrophysiology and mind control.

When I first saw *Son of Dracula*, my immediate reaction was that the eerie atmosphere Robert Siodmak had painstakingly created seemed to sputter out like a dying flame every time Chaney opened his mouth. As Michael Brunas writes in *Universal Horrors*, "His brawny, outdoorsy personality would serve him well in various roles over the years but, as a creature of the night, he was hardly in the same league as Lugosi, Max Schreck or even his own father. To his credit, Chaney puts out a damned good effort though his best moments are, unsurprisingly, non-verbal...."[8] Chaney's Midwestern accent might seem an insurmountable detriment when attempting to portray a Transylvanian count; however, this apparent discrepancy can actually be seen as a character point. In Stoker's novel, Dracula suggests that he's visiting the shores of England because he's curious about certain aspects of the modern world. Eric Taylor

Too haute to handle: Kay wants it all, a Southern plantation, a titled husband—and life everlasting.

In the wee hours, Frank barges into Dark Oaks and is met with its new master's wrath.

appears to have done his homework, as the Dracula we see here offers a similar explanation for his interest in the United States: "My land is dry and desolate. The soil is red with the blood of a hundred races. There is no life left there. Here you have a young and vital race." Therefore, one could conclude that the count's distinctly American accent reflects his desire to blend in with this "younger...and more virile" country.

Rather than focusing on the qualities Chaney does not share with Lugosi, Schreck or his own father, let's instead analyze attributes that are unique to him and his performance in *Son of Dracula*. One of the most arresting moments in the film, and in 1940s horror in general, is the scene in which our young hero, Frank Stanley (Robert Paige), confronts Alucard and his new bride Katherine Caldwell (Louise Allbritton) in the Caldwell home, also known—somewhat more ominously—as Dark Oaks Estates. Frank is in love with Katherine, and has been ever since he was a child. From his perspective, it was inevitable that he and Katherine would eventually wed. Suddenly, this weird Transylvanian count with an incongruous Midwestern accent swoops in and marries Frank's fiancée right out from under him. Frank can't handle this abrupt shift in his reality; he cracks and pulls a revolver on the count.

Here Siodmak uses Chaney's intimidating physique to considerable advantage. When Alucard casts Frank aside, we see an aspect of Dracula's personality (as con-

ceived by Stoker) that we have not seen in the cinema before: his pure animal ferocity. In Stoker's original novel, as well as in the posthumously published short story "Dracula's Guest," the count can unleash this unrestrained viciousness and assume the form of a wolf whenever he deems it necessary. For example, the unnamed narrator of "Dracula's Guest" relates his fearful experience with the count while lost in a Munich cemetery late at night during a powerful snowstorm:

> I felt a warm rasping at my throat, then came a consciousness of the awful truth, which chilled me to the heart and sent the blood surging up through my brain. Some great animal was lying on me and now licking my throat. I feared to stir, for some instinct of prudence bade me lie still; but the brute seemed to realize that there was now some changes in me, for it raised its head. Through my eyelashes I saw above me the two great flaming eyes of a gigantic wolf. Its sharp white teeth gleamed in the gaping red mouth, and I could feel its hot breath fierce and acrid upon me.[9]

Before Siodmak's *Son of Dracula*, American audiences had never seen Dracula transform into an animal before their eyes. Thanks to special effects, near the beginning of the film we watch as Chaney transforms into a bat. In the aforementioned scene in which Alucard attacks Frank Stanley, with no special effects, with little more than moxie and pure Lon Chaney method acting, we witness Alucard transforming into an animal not physically, but *emotionally*. We get the sense that Alucard could, if he wanted, tear Frank to pieces with minimal effort and no remorse whatsoever. This version of Dracula, portrayed as raw animal energy manifested in what appears to be human form, is completely new to the silver screen. Chaney's performance here points the way toward Christopher Lee's far more violent portrayal of Dracula in Terence Fisher's classic Hammer film *Horror of Dracula* (1958). The way in which Chaney lunges at Paige in this scene prefigures later cinematic interpretations of the vampire, such as the unforgettable moment in *Count Yorga, Vampire* (1970) in which Yorga (Robert Quarry) hurtles toward the camera with an animalistic expression distorting his pale, nightmarish face. Chaney's Dracula is a predatory beast whose ferocity is always simmering mere centimeters beneath an ersatz civilized veneer. When Chaney's Dracula allows this rage to explode at last, it's truly frightening. Chaney's overall performance throughout Siodmak's film can be, in this sense at least, considered prescient.

Dead man walking: Will Frank's life ever be the same after the series of shocks he receives in *Son of Dracula*?

The Blind Fool

Chaney is not the only actor in the film to deliver a memorable performance. Robert Paige as Frank Stanley is perhaps the most tragic hero of any of the Universal horror films. How many other handsome leading men in these films are unfortunate enough to get caught in the web of an occult con job? Frank's One

Frank needs to start pinning his hopes on Brewster and Lazlo, not Smith and Wesson.

True Love betrays him, he shoots her accidentally, she dies, resurrects, reveals to him that she betrayed him because she really *does* love him, and compels him to break out of jail and kill the count. Then poor Frank is forced to torch her corpse to prevent her from rising from the grave (yet again). Fade out. The final shot of the film, in which we see an empty, haunted look in Paige's eyes, tells us everything we need to know about this man's future. He doesn't have one. He's seen too much. His worldview has collapsed far too quickly and irreversibly.

In most modern horror stories, the status quo is somehow maintained despite an onslaught of demons, the undead, werewolves, ghosts and the like. Even though the neighborhood has been turned upside down and the severed head of the Nice Old Woman down the street is now decorating a flagpole on the Johnsons' lawn and the neighbor's dog is leaking entrails all over the fire hydrant on the corner, somehow, after all is said and done, everybody is ready to resume church on Sunday morning and go about life again as if everything's normal. The truth is that the status quo could never withstand such a catastrophic onslaught. Reality cannot be twisted in upon itself and inside out and backwards and forwards without leaving permanent psychic scars. Nobody who ever survived a war just brushed off the experience as if nothing happened. Nobody who thinks they've seen a ghost for even a single moment walks away totally unchanged. And yet, in the vast majority of these Hollywood horror flicks, that's exactly what occurs. At the end of the day, after the final battle has been won, it's often implied that the leading man and the leading lady are ready to return to Life as Usual and Live Happily Ever After. This happens in Tod Browning's *Dracula* (1931), Karl Freund's *The Mummy* (1932), Merian C. Cooper and Ernest B. Schoedsack's *King Kong* (1933), James Whale's *Frankenstein* (1931) and *Bride of Frankenstein* (1935), Lambert Hillyer's *Dracula's Daughter* (1936), Rowland V. Lee's *Son of Frankenstein* (1939), on and on.

Son of Dracula, however, does not do that at all.

True, Reginald LeBorg's *The Mummy's Ghost* concludes on a down note when the young hero's girlfriend, Amina (Ramsay Ames), ages rapidly into a withered corpse while being dragged into a swamp by an Egyptian mummy, but what could have been an extremely emotional moment is diminished by relatively substandard writing and inadequate acting on the part of the supporting players. The bystanders watching the girl dying before their eyes seem almost unaffected by this mind-blowingly strange tragedy. The second that Amina's head sinks below the surface, the villagers just shrug and trudge away, perhaps returning home to resume whittling.

Son of Dracula operates on a level that's much more subtle and sophisticated. Robert Siodmak's direction, coupled with Paige's non-verbal acting, wrings much emotional power out of *Son of Dracula*'s final scene. The empty expression in Frank Stanley's eyes suggests that nothing will ever be the same for him; in fact, one can conclude that Frank's spirit is just as lifeless as that of his fiancée Katherine.

When Reginald LeBorg directed films such as *The Mummy's Ghost*, I suspect he assumed he was making a B-film and nothing more. Siodmak, on the other hand, seems to believe he's making a classic Greek tragedy, and this sincerity raises the quality of the production.

On some level, Robert Siodmak and Eric Taylor knew they were playing with larger-than-life Jungian archetypes. Frank is a Reluctant Hero who's perceived to be little more than a fool by those around him. His fiancée's sister Claire (Evelyn Ankers) explicitly states that Frank is "living in a fool's paradise." As literary scholar Joseph Campbell has pointed out at great length in such works as *The Hero with a Thousand Faces*, the fool's journey is a painful odyssey that often begins in the darkness of ignorance and ends in the illumination of pure, unadulterated Gnostic awareness. As in the classic myths, awareness occurs only after the artificial layers of the everyday world are swept away, laying naked the ugly, disturbing realities underneath. In *Son of Dracula*, Katherine initiates her lover into the dark mysteries of the netherworld in the most jarring

Want to be immortal? Glampire Kay hard-sells the perks of an undead existence to a hapless, horror-stricken Frank.

manner possible. Her death-in-life is what psychologist Timothy Leary called a "circuit breaker," a turning-point moment during which one's reality tunnel is suddenly expanded and turned upside down in such a way that one's consciousness must either evolve or collapse in upon itself. Like many an initiate before her, Katherine can't wait to share her illumination with those closest to her, so she chooses to drag Frank through the rabbit hole, not caring how much chaos this will cause within his eggshell-thin psyche. Too much illumination too soon can be a dangerous prospect.

Because of Frank's rigid worldview, forged among the conservative traditions of the American South, Katherine decides she has to shatter his defenses without his consent. She's clearly obsessed with the notion of forcing him to see the world through her eyes. Rather like Nada (Roddy Piper), the hero of John Carpenter's science fiction Gnostic parable *They Live* (1988), Katherine is intent on waking up those around her to the secrets of the occult (and we must keep in mind that the word "occult" simply means "that which is hidden") through the most violent means possible. Nada uses his fists and firearms. Like a classic femme fatale in a 1940s film noir, Katherine uses her wits and feminine wiles. But *un*like a typical film noir dame, Katherine is not after money. What she wants is eternal life and, perhaps even more importantly, vindication. Recognition. Undeniable proof that her unorthodox metaphysical beliefs are not the mere product of naïve wish fulfillment. She craves the simple satisfaction of saying, "I told you so" to her lover Frank, her sister Claire and the other naysayers in her simple, Christian surroundings. Frank is a hardheaded rationalist with a worldview that couldn't be more beholden to the mainstream. Katherine has decided to change that worldview by boldly attempting to double-cross the Devil—or his closest equivalent on Earth, i.e., Alucard. Clearly, Katherine has never read the Edgar Allan Poe story "Never Bet the Devil Your Head." Such deals rarely end up well for she whose head is on the block.

Katherine's scheme to wrest eternal life from the count is curiously similar to the complex plots and counterplots dreamed up by such film noir femme fatales as Phyllis Dietrichson (Barbara Stanwyck) in Billy Wilder's adaptation of James M. Cain's 1943 novel *Double Indemnity* and the equally manipulative Cora Smith (Lane Turner) in Tay Garnett's adaptation of Cain's 1934 novel *The Postman Always Rings Twice*. The former film was released in 1944 and the latter in 1946. *Son of Dracula* predates both films by a full year in the first case and three years in the second, but it's possible that one of the writers decided to draw upon Cain's popular crime novels when constructing the *Son* storyline. Curt Siodmak had already blended noirish elements with the phantasmagoric in his screenplay for Arthur Lubin's *Black Friday*, which enmeshed Boris Karloff and Bela Lugosi in a science fiction–horror crime drama involving brain-switching, $500,000 in stolen cash and New York gangsters.

It was a rather clever idea to flip audience expectations and make Alucard's bride *Son of Dracula*'s true villain. Rather than falling victim to the vampire's hypnotic wiles, Katherine turns the tables and lures him into *her* web. This is why *Son of Dracula* had to take place in the United States and not in Transylvania. Katherine is on her home turf, and thus in a position to control Alucard's movements, not the other way around. At one point we watch Alucard float across the surface of a body of swamp water to meet his co-conspirator on the bank, only to be led into an automobile driven by Katherine. He seems out of place in such a uniquely twentieth century conveyance … because he *is* out of place. He's out of place, he's out of time, and Katherine is in the driver's seat. In the United States, deep in the South, he needs Katherine more than she needs him. Once Alucard grants Katherine eternal life, his dark allure means nothing to her at all. He was merely

Count Cuckold!: Poor Alucard is about to tie the knot with Katherine, unaware that it will be a marriage steeped in feminine deceit.

a means to an end. Like many an older man, he believes his young lover is under his thumb. He's convinced that he's manipulated Katherine into a conspiracy to murder her father, marry, then inherit the dead man's estate from which to establish a base of operations for the count's vampiric activities. In truth, Katherine has used her father, as well as her estate, as bait to involve Alucard in her own scheme. Perhaps the count's spent far too much time in the Old Country and does not realize quite how independent these modern American women can be. Alucard never even suspects that Katherine will betray him. After all, young brides do not betray their husbands, do they?

This one does. Frank is jailed for having shot Katherine to death—not at all dissimilar to how Al Roberts (Tom Neal) unintentionally kills Vera (Ann Savage) in Edgar G. Ulmer's *Detour* (1945), yet one more noirish trope on full display in *Son of Dracula*. The undead Katherine materializes in Frank's cell to describe to him her entire scheme. She doesn't love Alucard at all. She only wanted the gift of eternal life so she could then share that gift with Frank: any true lover's ultimate gift. Frank seems paradoxically relieved and horrified at once—relieved that Katherine is still alive, at least in some form, and horrified that she believes he would ever have wanted her under these circumstances. Frank must fight every instinct in his mind and body to do what has to be done.

Paige's performance is so multilayered that we sense how conflicted his spirit really is without it having to

In *Son of Dracula*, fire is added to the list of things that can destroy a vampire. Well, piss him off, anyway. (At the end, fire *does* destroy Kay.)

Alucard accosts Dr. Brewster on the cellar staircase. In 1943, the *Minneapolis Sunday Tribune* reviewer opined, "Chaney makes a satisfactory ghoul, although you get the impression he couldn't have become such a stalwart physical specimen on a diet of corpuscles." Years later, film historian William K. Everson was in agreement, calling Chaney's Alucard "far too robust and healthy."

be spelled out for us. Part of him wants to accede to Katherine's wishes, to give up and slip away forever into her arms. Instead, he forces himself to do what's right. Not only does he destroy Alucard, exactly as Katherine wished, but he forces himself to destroy *her* as well. He's given up everything he ever wanted, and the tortured expression on his face in the final scene tells us that

he'll examine this decision for the rest of his blighted existence. The hollow look in his eyes is completely at variance with the triumphant music that blares at us. There is no triumph here. After all, what's left for Frank in this world? Realistically, he is going to be arrested for shooting Katherine, stealing her corpse, then setting it on fire. If he tries to convince a jury what really happened, he'll be tossed into a mental asylum. Ironically, he would be in the same position in which Katherine found herself when she was fruitlessly attempting to convince "blind fools" like Frank and Claire of the importance of "occult matters." But "blind fools" can't be convinced of anything so unorthodox as the occult… unless, of course, the Unorthodox Idea in question is grabbing them about the throat and effortlessly flinging them across a room. You can't deny the existence of the supernatural when it's stealing your girlfriend.

Death is coming to Dark Oaks according to the old Hungarian gypsy Queen Zimba (Adeline DeWalt Reynolds), only moments before Zimba herself is killed by Alucard. Col. Caldwell and Katherine soon follow Zimba into the grave. But perhaps Frank Stanley should be included on this necrology as well. Though he's not physically deceased, he's no less dead inside by the time the end credits roll. The reason for Frank's spiritual death will no doubt remain a mystery to the law enforcement and medical officials who attempt to get to the bottom of his case. No amount of conventional detective work could ever uncover the bizarre truths lurking below the bloody loam of Dark Oaks Estates.

Like many other entries in the "film noird" subgenre, *Son of Dracula* is ultimately a story about hidden realities, about the exoteric vs. the esoteric. As in many crime noir tales, the naïve young hero discovers the hardest way possible that a much darker and harsher world than the one we see exists just beneath the surface of everyday life. Robert Paige's committed performance as the "blind fool" drives home this underlying theme—the rarely acknowledged truth that it would be almost impossible for even the purest of us to withstand a true encounter with the transgressive, the supernatural, the zero point Unorthodox Idea that turns one's world upside down…unless, of course, one is willing to ride the mindquake and transform along with it, to join the uncertain darkness on the other side. Frank is not willing to make that transition. As a result, his lover is in ashes at the end of his fool's journey. Happy Wedding Day, Frank.

Death comes to Dark Oaks in more ways than one, as the "death" of this particular Blind Fool transcends the mere physical.

UNHOLY OFFSPRING: A PRODUCTION HISTORY OF SON OF DRACULA

By Gary D. Rhodes

Choosing where to begin a story is not always easy. "In the beginning" or "Once upon a time" are appropriate phrases, but they don't bring with them dates etched in stone. Consider, for example, World War II. When did it begin? If writing a book on the subject, where should we start? Some of us might consider December 7, 1941, and the bombing of Pearl Harbor. But others could point to earlier events, whether Germany's invasion of Poland in 1939 or Hitler's rise to power in 1933. Others might suggest World War I and the notion that its conclusion was so problematic that World War II was the horrible result.

The same question is true of a wartime film like *Son of Dracula* (1943). The notion of a sequel to the "horror film" – meaning those produced after that term became common in 1931 and 1932 – dates to *Bride of Frankenstein* (1935). But, even earlier, there were for example *The Return of Dr. Fu Manchu* (1930) and *Daughter of the Dragon* (1931), two films that brought Sax Rohmer's villain back to the screen as sequels to *The Mysterious Dr. Fu Manchu* (1929). For that matter, it is clear that the same devil costume appeared in American Mutoscope & Biograph's *The Prince of Darkness* and *A Terrible Night*, both filmed in America by Frederick S. Armitage in approximately April of 1900. The identical character returned, as later characters ranging from Frankenstein's Monster to Jason Voorhees would do, along with some of their family relations.

The kinship of horror dates to an earlier period, to be sure. That specific demons were hell-spawned, all part of Satan's ex-

tended family, his comrades in the Inferno, has been discussed for centuries. Some of them, like Beelzebub, have names that are also used as synonyms for the Devil. The lines between these characters blur. As a demon tells Jesus in Mark 5:9, "My name is Legion ... for we are many." Here we should also consider that the very name "Dracula" explicitly invokes a father-son relationship, given it translates literally as "Son of the Dragon."

Son of Dracula was hardly the only time that World War II and vampires converged. Here is nose art painted on an American B-24 Liberator, a heavy bomber that saw much action.

The familial instinct guided Universal Pictures, which learned that the death of a financially successful horror movie character could be handled in different ways, ranging from disregarding earlier film narratives (as *Son of Frankenstein* would do in 1939, ignoring the fact that the Monster had been blown to atoms in 1935) to shifting the emphasis to another branch of the same genealogical tree. Rather than revive Dracula in 1936, given that he had been destroyed in 1931, the studio birthed *Dracula's Daughter* (1936) in the form of actress Gloria Holden.

Son of Dracula (1943) presents a unique situation, its production history complicated by various factors. Within three weeks of the 1931 premiere of Tod Browning's *Dracula*, Universal presented titles for follow-ups to the Hays Office: *The Modern Dracula*, *The Return of Dracula* and – notably, for this discussion – *The Son of Dracula*. Though no notes exist regarding possible story content, if any ever existed, each of the three titles underscore the problem intrinsic to the ending of Browning's film. Should the original Dracula reincarnate, return (somehow) or reappear in the form of a descendant?

Over a decade later, *Son of Dracula* provided an answer, perhaps more than one, to that question from 1931. It did so by drawing on a lengthy history of what film scholar Tony Williams has called "hearths of darkness," meaning the family in the horror film. *Son of Dracula* arguably became Universal's most atmospheric horror movie of World War II, a minor achievement that deserves to be reconsidered as a major classic, one of the best of its era.

Progeny

The Universal that produced Browning's *Dracula*, controlled as it was by Carl Laemmle and his son, was very different from the Universal that produced *Dracula's Daughter*, a company in transition towards what the industry called the "New U." The same could be said of the Universal that produced *Son of Dracula*, it having undergone various changes from the '30s, not least of which was the resumption of horror film production in late 1938, the offspring *Son of Frankenstein* at the vanguard.

The timeline of 1941 is important in this context. Universal's Chairman of the Board J. Cheever Cowdin had been heavily involved in the formation of the New U. In the years that followed, he solidified his power, a process that has unfortunately been ignored by most film historians. In April 1941, for example, he reported profits for late 1940 and early 1941 that were noticeably larger than the same period for the prior year. On June 26, 1941, Universal reported a staggering 50 percent gain in domestic film sales. That same day, the studio claimed to be "entering the busiest period of production in the history of the company."

By mid–July 1941, Universal announced it had half of the films for its 1941-42 either completed or in progress, meaning 24 of 47 films. The new season inspired hope, particularly when investors learned in mid–September that gross studio profits for the prior 39 weeks had soared to $2,751,864, as compared to $1,771,805 for the same period in 1940. The difficult years of the Great Depression were now in the past. And the future would include such hit films as *The Wolf Man* (1941) with Lon Chaney Jr., billed on-screen simply as **Lon Chaney**. These events proved crucial in the road to *Son of Dracula*.

Son of Dracula draws on the history of horror at Universal, to the extent that the gloved hands wiping away cobwebs to reveal its title is a lift from the 1927 *The Cat and the Canary*.

And then there was the famous vampire himself. Cowdin's Universal had made recent profits from *Dracula*, which played on a double bill with *Frankenstein* (1931) in Chatham, Ontario, in early 1942. A theater manager's report, published in *Motion Picture Herald* in March of that year, excitedly endorsed the duo: "A special horror show reissue that did outstanding business. Would advise it for any situation."

Following standard practice, Universal announced its initial plans for the 1942-43 season in February 1942: 53 features, one being *The Ghost of Frankenstein* with Chaney. Increased profits altered the larger strategy in June 1942, with the studio planning 55 features, five of them being "specials" and two in Technicolor. Universal had not produced any color features since *King of Jazz* in 1930, so the latter announcement was major news. And one of the them would be a remake of *The Phantom of the Opera*, to be produced and directed by Henry Koster. On June 5, 1942, *Daily Variety* detailed other plans:

> "Horror" product will be represented on the new schedule by two pictures, *Frankenstein Meets the Wolf Man*, with Lon Chaney playing both title roles, and *Son of Dracula*. George Waggner will be associate producer on the two pictures....

The trade paper did not specify Chaney's name for *Son of Dracula*, or for *The Mummy's Tomb*, which was mentioned elsewhere in the same article. No other trades connected Chaney's name to the films either.

Within two more weeks, Universal released updated plans, which upped the number of Technicolor features to five. Chaney was now to star in two Inner Sanctum films. Other titles listed included *The Invisible Man's Revenge*, *The Mad Ghoul*, *The Mummy's Ghost* and *Son of Dracula*. Chaney's name was not connected to any of them.

Nevertheless, the original intention for him to play both the Monster and the Wolf Man in the same film suggests the studio's emphasis on him (which seems all the more stark since none of the announcements referred to plans for Bela Lugosi or Boris Karloff), their apparent faith in his acting ability, and a reason beyond mere publicity for referring to him without the "Jr." Here was an offspring that could assume his father's place by name, as well as by varied roles that required fantastical makeup.

Son of Dracula

Audiences had been exposed to the notion of a "Son of Dracula" as early as March 1937, when R. Alfred Hassler's short play *Son of Dracula* appeared as part of an annual event in Brooklyn, one presented by the Counselors Alumni of the Young People's Baptist Union of Brooklyn and Long Island. Over the course of a prologue and two acts, this *Son of Dracula* "portray[ed] the trials of Dracula Jr., when the sheltered life he has led for 1000 years of being a vampire is rudely disturbed by the 'spikeing' [*sic*] of his father, Count Dracula." According to one critic, its funniest scene featured Junior "learn[ing] the first principles of biting mortals while his invisible father 'kibitzes.'"

By January 1941 (if not earlier), the team of King and Roche, formerly of the Club Montmartre in Paris, presented a "weird" dance called *Son of Dracula*. Staged in vaudeville and at nightclubs, their act was well-received. One critic called it a "realistic dance on their conception of the Dracula theme"; another said it was an "impressive interpretation." They continued performing it until at least the spring of 1942.

As for the Universal feature film, moviegoers began to read about *Son of Dracula* as early as June 8, 1942, when the *Los Angeles Times* revealed that Curt Siodmak was writing the screenplay. His connection to horror and science-fiction had deep roots, dating to the novel and screenplay for *F.P.1 antwortet nicht* (*F.P.1 Doesn't Answer*) in 1932, and continuing through screenplays for such Hollywood films as *Black Friday* (1940), *The Invisible Man Returns* (1940), *The Ape* (1940) and *Invisible Agent* (1942). But Universal most likely entrusted *Son of Dracula* to Siodmak – who had just sold his novel *Donovan's Brain* in the summer of 1942 – due to the success of *The Wolf Man*, produced from what remains his most famous script.

More news soon appeared in newspapers and the trade publications. On July 14, 1942, for the first time, the press reported that Chaney would star in *Son of Dracula*. Its production would "start in September."

The choice seems evident: Universal was pushing its new horror star in several projects, *Son of Dracula* being one of them. Months later, on November 25, 1942, Edwin Schallert reiterated the casting in the pages of the *Los Angeles Times*:

> Lon Chaney is certainly going the rounds of horror characters, for he is now spoken of in connection with *Son of Dracula*, which is being prepared by George Waggner.... This is the first

Curt: Coming to America.

"Dracula" film with which Chaney has been associated, by the way. He played the Wolf Man in the film of that title and in *The Wolf Man and Frankenstein* [*sic*], and he did the monster in *The Return of Frankenstein* [*sic*]. In *The Wolf Man and Frankenstein*, Lugosi, who created Dracula on stage and screen, enacted the monster. So it's a "your move next" situation when it comes to these shiver delineations, apparently.

Schallert mangled the titles cited in his film history, having meant *Frankenstein Meets the Wolf Man* (1943) and *The Ghost of Frankenstein* (1942), respectively. But his basic point was well stated. Earlier that same month, Hedda Hopper's column had told readers that Universal was finally proceeding with its *Phantom of the Opera* remake, with "none other than Lon Chaney Jr. in the role that his father created." Much to Chaney's disappointment, which Hopper described as "bitter" in January 1943, the studio replaced him with Claude Rains.

What does this mean? For one, there is certainly no evidence of a studio conspiracy against Bela Lugosi, the actor most associated with the Dracula role. His absence from *Son of Dracula* says a great deal more about the studio's interest in Chaney than its alleged *lack* of interest in Lugosi. At any rate, by August 20, 1942, Lugosi was on a train to Chicago to star in a stage version of *Dracula*. (For reasons unknown, that production folded.)

Progress on *Son of Dracula* continued. On July 25, *Motion Picture Herald* reported that Universal had "purchased" Siodmak's script, language that implies he had finished his draft. According to the August 24, 1942, *Daily Variety*, Universal assigned Eric Taylor the task of writing the final script. He had worked on the screenplays for *Black Friday* (along with Siodmak) and the new *Phantom of the Opera*, as well as on the stories for *The Black Cat* (1941) and *The Ghost of Frankenstein*. On September 30, 1942, the same trade reported, "Eric Taylor has completed [his] script on Universal's *The Son of Dracula*, and has checked off the lot."

Why turn to Taylor? Presumably Universal did not find Siodmak's script acceptable. Perhaps they knew it was too horrific to be approved by the Production Code Administration (PCA). Perhaps they believed it would prove too costly to film. Or perhaps, given the decision to cast Lon Chaney, the studio did not find his version of the Dracula character appropriate.

Curt Siodmak believed his brother Robert, the director of *Son of Dracula*, was to blame. In 1984, Curt told interviewer Tom Weaver:

We had a sibling rivalry. When we were in Germany, Robert had a magazine and when I wrote for it, I had to change my name. He only wanted one Siodmak around. This lasted 71 years, until he died.

In this case, though, Curt might have been wrong, as there is no indication that brother Robert was assigned to *Son of Dracula* when Taylor was hired. At any rate, Taylor received on-screen credit for the screenplay, and Siodmak for "Original Story."

Regrettably, no copies of any screenplays dated from July to September 1942 have surfaced. The earliest known information comes not from a script, but rather the PCA's response to one, as recorded in a lengthy December 16, 1942, letter from Joseph H. Breen to Universal. It specifically refers to a script dated December 12, 1942. In general, letters from the PCA to studios make reference to earlier drafts, if they had been submitted, but Breen's does not. While in no way definitive, his letter reads as if the office had not received any draft prior to the December 12.

Overall, Breen indicated that its "basic story" was "acceptable under the provisions of the Production Code," but he urged that Universal "minimize the gruesomeness and the horror angles throughout, since such angles seem overdone in the present story." He added:

You will have in mind, further, that political censor boards and private reviewing groups are

"Don't cross me!": Alucard gets rough with the movie's bush-league Van Helsing, Prof. Lazlo. (In this scene in the movie itself, the count chokes Dr. Brewster, not Lazlo.)

particularly critical at this time about horror stories. You undoubtedly know, also, that the British Board of Film Censors has announced that they will not approve "horrific" stories until the end of the present war, so that it is unlikely that this picture will be acceptable at this time.

Breen's admonition is similar to advice he gave for many other horror film scripts of the period.

His specific concerns about the December 12 draft give important insight into plot points that appeared in it. For example, he advised:

[T]he showing of Zimba's death should be held to a flash.

[T]he business of the bat sucking blood from Frank's throat should be suggested rather than shown. This caution about the bat applies through-out the story, wherever this business is used.

[T]he showing of Katherine in her coffin should be held to a flash.

The business of the disintegration of Count Dracula should be suggested rather than shown in detail as now indicated. It will be acceptable to pickup his skeleton after his disintegration has been <u>suggested</u>.

In scene 99, you begin to characterize Frank as possibly insane. We believe such characteriza-tion is offensive to mixed audiences generally.

...We suggest that Frank be shown merely agitated, rather than mad, at all times.

In scene 117 (cont'd), you begin one of numerous "choking" sequences about which political censor boards are especially sensitive. We recommend that these either be changed to some other business or that they be masked from the audience.

In scene 173, we request that you omit the showing of the dead chickens, since this is an unnecessary suggestion of cruelty to animals.

In scene 280, the business of Frank slugging the jailer with a gun should be suggested out of frame.

Even in a fantastic story such as this, we feel that there should be some definite indication that the processes of law will function. With this thought in mind, we request you change the sheriff's speech, ending with "There isn't a judge in the state who'd question his word," to something to the effect that Frank's guilt is something for the courts to decide, and the sheriff should definitely have Frank in custody as they leave the burning mansion.

Breen also asked to see the lyrics to "all songs to be used in this production," a direct result of a scene on page 30 of the December 12 draft.

From the December 21, 1942, *Hollywood Reporter*:

Universal will launch the balance of its 1942-43 program, comprising 15 features, within the next 90 days to swell the already large backlog, heaviest in the company's history. Home office executives are coming to the studio early in January for product talks, to set release schedules and to look ahead to U's program for 1943-44.

The article continued by noting that "eight of the 15 new films will get under way shortly after the holidays." *Son of Dracula* was one of them, its start date set for January 4, 1943.

As part of an effort to make that deadline, Universal sent a new draft to the PCA on December 29, 1942. For reasons unknown, the script bore a new title, *Des-tiny*. Was the removal of Dracula's name an expedient effort to temper its "gruesomeness" in the eyes of the PCA? Or was it an effort to account for the fact that the script did not definitively state that the male vam-pire really is Dracula's son? Universal simply told the PCA the new script was "Formerly titled *Son of Dracula*

– and in which were material changes from the first script submitted to you."

Breen's December 31 response suggests that the new draft was not very new:

> The present script appears very similar to the one we read before, and about which we wrote you under [the] date of December 16, 1942. We direct your attention to that earlier letter, with especial reference to avoiding gruesomeness throughout, getting away from the choking scenes, or masking them so that they will not be subject to deletion by political censor boards, and the other matters contained therein.

Frank is shattered when he sees Kay's body in the vault. From the *Los Angeles Times'* *Son of Dracula* review: "Robert Paige is especially to be praised for his fine work. He is a fine emotional actor and should be given opportunity in a larger sphere."

> We call your attention again to page 125, where the sheriff's line, "There isn't a judge in the state who'd question his word…" should be changed, to suggest definitely that Frank is going to stand trial for his various actions throughout the story. An acceptable change would include something to the effect, "That's up to the courts to decide." It is important that Frank be in the custody of the sheriff at the end of the story.

These ongoing problems led Universal to submit another script to Breen on January 4, 1943, thus delaying the production's start date.

The script reproduced in this book is Robert Siodmak's personal copy, which included inscriptions to him on the backs of the first three pages. Used during pro-

duction, it includes amendments dated as late as January 14, 1943. It features "Changes" dated January 2, 1943, the direct result of Breen's December 31, 1942, letter. But it also retains a number of elements that the PCA found objectionable: the striking of the jailer, images of dead chickens and repeated references to insanity.

Destiny

On January 6, 1943, *Daily Variety* referred to *Son of Dracula* by its new title *Destiny*. Production finally commenced the following day. Its great German-born director Robert Siodmak began his career in Germany by helming (with Edgar G. Ulmer) 1930's *Menschen am Sonntag* (*People on Sunday*). The Nazis' rise to power caused him to move to France, where he directed a number of films before immigrating to the United States. His Hollywood career – best remembered now for his film noirs made after World War II – got underway in 1941.

Despite being originally attached to *Son of Dracula*, producer George Waggner was too busy with the new *Phantom of the Opera* to work on it. Ford Beebe assumed the *Son of Dracula* producer mantle; in mid–January he also became the film's second unit director, handling most or perhaps all scenes requiring process shots. Beebe had previously co-directed the serials *Flash Gordon's Trip to Mars* (1938), *Buck Rogers* (1939), *The Phantom Creeps* (1939) and *Flash Gordon Conquers the Universe* (1940), as well as such features as *Night Monster* (1942). After *Son of Dracula*, he directed *The Invisible Man's Revenge* (1944).

Melville Shyer was assistant director, having served in the same capacity on a large number of horror and mystery films, among them *The Secrets of Wu Sin* (1932), *Murder on the Campus* (1933), *The Ghost Walks* (1934), *Condemned to Live* (1935), *Death from a Distance* (1935), *A Shot in the Dark* (1935), *The House of Secrets* (1936) and *Murder at Glen Athol* (1936). He went on to do the same for *Frankenstein Meets the Wolf Man* (1943), *Captive Wild Woman* (1943), *Jungle Woman* (1944), *Pillow of Death* (1945) and *The Cat Creeps* (1946). He also directed seven films, including *Sucker Money* (1933) and *Murder in the Museum* (1934).

George Robinson was cinematographer. His genre credits were as expansive as his talent. He shot *The Charlatan* (1929), *Drácula* (1931), *The Mystery of Edwin Drood* (1935), *The Invisible Ray* (1936), *Dracula's Daughter* (1936), *Son of Frankenstein* (1939), *Tower of London* (1939), *The Mummy's Tomb* (1942) and – after working on *Frankenstein Meets the Wolf Man* and *Son of Dracula* – *Captive Wild Woman*, *Cobra Woman* (1944), *House of Frankenstein* (1944), *Murder in the Blue Room*

Evelyn Ankers, queen of the Universal shockers, as she appeared in *Son of Dracula*.

On stage and screen, Frank Craven specialized in small-town cracker-barrel types. He was also a playwright. He died in 1945 at age 70 after a three-month illness.

(1944), *House of Dracula* (1945), *The Cat Creeps* (1946), *The Creeper* (1948), *Abbott and Costello Meet the Invisible Man* (1951), *Abbott and Costello Meet the Mummy* (1955), *Tarantula* (1955) and *Francis in the Haunted House* (1956). Despite the praise often heaped on his cinematography for the Spanish-language *Drácula*, Robinson remains one of the most overlooked and under-researched creators of the classic horror film.

As much as anyone behind the camera, though, art directors Martin Obzina and John B. Goodman deserve particular praise for *Son of Dracula*. Along with having served as associate art director on *The Invisible Man Returns* (1940), and as art director for *Horror Island* (1941) and *The Strange Case of Doctor Rx* (1942), Obzina had worked on *The Flame of New Orleans* (1941), which might well have helped him evoke the Deep South atmosphere of *Son of Dracula*. He and Goodman teamed again as art directors on *The Mad Ghoul* (1943).

As for the on-screen talent, Louise Allbritton assumed the role of Katherine, or "Kay" as she's normally called in the film. Allbritton had earlier appeared with Abbott and Costello in *Who Done It?* (1942). Universal announced her for *Destiny* on January 7, 1943, which likely suggests she was cast at the last minute. Only weeks earlier, in November 1942, *Daily Variety* claimed she was one of a few "starlets" being "publicized for future stardom."

Evelyn Ankers played Kay's sister Claire. Based upon press accounts, she was attached to the project before most of the other actors, save Chaney. She was one of the greatest scream queens in film history, appearing in *Hold That Ghost* (1941), *The Wolf Man*, *The*

Ghost of Frankenstein, Captive Wild Woman, The Mad Ghoul, Weird Woman (1944), *Jungle Woman* (1944), *The Invisible Man's Revenge* and *The Frozen Ghost* (1945).

On January 12, 1943, Universal reported that Frank Craven and J. Edward Bromberg had joined the cast. Craven, who had earlier appeared in director Tod Browning's macabre *Miracles for Sale* (1939), played Dr. Brewster. Bromberg, who portrayed Prof. Lazlo, is now best remembered for being blacklisted in the McCarthy era.

Samuel S. Hinds, who had appeared in such films as *The Ninth Guest* (1934), *The Raven* (1935), *Man Made Monster* (1941) and *The Strange Case of Doctor Rx*, played Judge Simmons. And as Queen Zimba, Universal cast Adeline DeWalt Reynolds. Born in 1862, DeWalt Reynolds did not begin her acting career until she was 78 years old. (There's more on DeWalt Reynolds on pages 53 and 54.)

Filming Alucard

When shooting began on January 7, Alan Curtis had the role of Frank, the young male lead. On January 15, *The Hollywood Reporter* announced that Robert Paige would replace Curtis, who had suffered a knee injury during the filming of his last scene in *Flesh and Fantasy* (1943). (The knee injury not only kept Curtis out of *Son of Dracula*, it ended up keeping him out of the Army.) Given the shooting schedule reproduced herein, it is difficult to determine if Robert Siodmak directed any scenes with Curtis for *Son of Dracula*, or if he was replaced before he was ever needed on set.

When Queen Zimba tries to warn Kay, Dracula goes into winged action.

Few details about the production survive in the form of studio files or trade reports, but a comparison of the script to the final film reveals a number of changes, some large and some small. Consider the opening scenes, which begin in the script with an engraved invitation to a reception at Dark Oaks as well as Dr. Brewster's meetings with Frank and Tommy: Here are six pages in total, nowhere to be found in the film. Were they shot and not used, or never even filmed? The answer is unknown, save for the fact that the continuity breakdown refers to a shot of the invitation. At any rate, little of importance is lost, save for the fact that the reception is held on Friday the 13th.

Likewise, Scene 65 (two servants talking about the strange goings-on) does not appear in the film. Was it deleted in editing or never filmed? Either way, little of narrative importance is lost. Scene 66 is not in the movie but the existence of the still (see page 73) makes it seem likely that it was filmed.

Another change came with the telephone conversation between Dr. Brewster and Prof. Lazlo. In the script, the scene occurs immediately after Brewster leaves the train station. In the film, it does not unfold until after Count Alucard appears at Dark Oaks. The result: The first mention of the name "Dracula" is delayed until later in the film, keeping the tease of his name going for several more minutes. Was the re-ordering of sequences decided during production, or in post-production? It is tempting to believe the latter, but a minor dialogue change from script to screen is noticeable. Brewster

does not say that Alucard is "coming here," as in the former, but instead that he is already visiting a friend.

Other changes are relatively minor, but worth noting. Queen Zimba has no dead rooster, as the script suggests on page 17. On page 23, Frank mentions "dead chickens," but on-screen he says "stuffed toads" instead, thus limiting his mention of dead chickens to one occasion. Descriptions of mutilated chickens on pages 60 and 118 aren't visualized in the film, even though — according to the continuity breakdown — at least one of them was shot. The script's explicit suggestion on pages 23-24 that Kay might be blamed for Zimba's death is greatly diminished on screen. And while the script features Frank hitting the jailer with the gun, in the film it is only implied after the fact, after the jailer is helped up off the floor and rubs his head.

When Alucard first arrives at Dark Oaks, he "kindly" asks to be admitted entrance. Chaney does not speak that word in the film, making him more demanding. In the script, he tells Kay she will "be the Countess Alucard," but on-screen he says "become," which subtly invokes the process from human to vampire. And rather than telling Brewster he is the "head" of Dark Oaks, on-screen he calls himself its "master."

At times, the script is more evocative than the film. Kay's journey to Queen Zimba is more atmospheric as written on page 17 than as it appears on-screen. And Alucard's appearance as a "huge wolf-dog with frothing jaws" that "dissolves" in front of Frank's car on page 49 is entirely missing. This notion must have been discarded during the production phase, as Frank's dialogue on page 55 references "a wolf and a bat," but on-screen he doesn't mention the wolf.

And then there is the rainstorm referenced from Scene 180 on page 67, which continues until the sheriff, Frank and the others visit Dark Oaks, by which time the "ground and trees are wet." The atmospheric opportunities for a windy storm are obvious, and remained so until some point in the production, as the judge wears a raincoat on-screen in Scene 180 (though it isn't very wet). And dialogue referencing the continuing rain was altered once shot. The judge does not say it's "been pouring ever since" the previous evening, that line even crossed out in the script. When the sheriff discovers the front door open at Dark Oaks, he says, "Funny they'd leave the door open" before the same shot continues, making clear the rest of his original dialogue

Alucard levitates over the surface of the water toward Kay, unforgettable imagery not imagined in the script.

"on a day like this" was not filmed. Moreover, to maintain continuity in keeping with the change, the judge holds his raincoat over his arm in that scene and at the Dark Oaks graveyard, rather than continuing to wear it. Why limit such a wonderful addition to the film's atmosphere? The answer is unknown, but budgetary restraints seem to be the most logical reason.

In other cases, Robert Siodmak achieved a greater atmosphere on-screen than what appears in the script, including Kay's visit to Count Alucard at the swamp. On page 41, the script describes Alucard's hand lifting (from inside) the lid of the chest in which he lies, at the water's edge. It provided an opportunity to highlight the ring he wears, an important element given that it later helps Lazlo identify his skeleton. But the scene on film is far more surreal, the chest surfacing far from the bank where Kay stands. Alucard emerges in the form of vapor fog that forms into the vampire incarnate. He glides across the surface of the water toward her (see photos above).

Son of Dracula's production phase ended on February 2, only one day after the industry press reported, "Net earnings of Universal for 1942, after all taxes and depreciation, are estimated to be around $3,000,000, which is higher than the company's earnings for 1941." As J. Cheever Cowdin announced a few days later, that difference was nearly $300,000. The result meant that Universal's board sought recapitalization, which would allow them to pay off some loans, including to British interests that had a hand in the studio's financing since 1936.

The film thus moved into post-production at a financially happy studio. Saul Goodkind edited *Son of Dracula*. He had earlier edited the serials *Flash Gordon* (1936) and *Flash Gordon's Trip to Mars*, and would go on to edit *The Invisible Man's Revenge*, *The Mummy's Ghost* and *The Creeper*. Again, little is known of the process, but one line of Frank's dialogue in Scene 57 (pages 22-25) was not only added beyond what appears in the script, but almost certainly during post-production. Frank says, "Ever since you met this Count Alucard in Budapest, you've changed. I hardly know you." The audio sounds noticeably different than the rest of the

Continued on page 25

"Though lovers, straitlaced Frank and Kay fail to generate any smoldering passion…. Adding Chaney's low-libido Count Alucard into the mix makes a romantic triangle that barely simmers." – Michael Brunas, *Universal Horrors*

Robert Siodmak on *Son of Dracula* (*Sight and Sound* magazine interview by Russell Taylor, 1959):

In 1943 I had been in Hollywood for three years, doing what work I could get. Then Universal sent me the script of *Son of Dracula*: It was terrible—it had been knocked together in a few days. I told my wife I just couldn't do it, but she said to me: "Look, they've been making these films for 20 years, they know just what to expect from a director and just how much they're going to pay him," (I'd been offered $150 a week for the three weeks shooting) "so if you're just that little bit better than their other directors … then they'll see right away and it'll lead to better things." So I took the job, and on the third day of shooting they offered me a contract, with options, for seven years. I took it and our association was very happy: in fact, though my salary was supposed to rise gradually until I was earning $1100 a week in the seventh year, if I lasted that long, in fact they tore up the contract and by the third year I was earning about $3000 a week. As for *Son of Dracula*, we did a lot of rewriting and the result wasn't bad: It wasn't *good*, but some scenes had a certain quality.

In this publicity shot from 1943, Evelyn Ankers' "scepter" shows the titles of the Universal Horrors in which she's appeared; the top two, *The Mad Ghoul* (shot in May) and *Son of Dracula* (shot in January-February), were then her latest. She's flanked by *Mad Ghoul* director James Hogan and the Ghoul himself, David Bruce.

Continued from page 23

dialogue and the entirety of it is heard over a medium cutaway shot of Kay.

Also missing in the final film is Dr. Brewster's dialogue from page 88, when he can't believe anyone would choose to become a "thing so loathsome ... living on human blood ... as it comes from the body." In the film, his shot ends on the word "loathsome," the remaining dialogue missing. Given the timing of the edit, it was likely eliminated in post.

The biggest change that might have happened during post-production was the film's conclusion. As written, the confrontation between Frank and Alucard features more dialogue than heard in the scene, including a line in which Alucard suggests both characters might "plunge" together into (an unmentioned) Hell. As it unfolds on-screen, the action-packed scene is appropriately edited faster than most of the rest of the film. As a result, it is difficult to determine whether this exchange was filmed and then not used, perhaps as part of an effort to keep the scene moving, or whether it was never filmed.

Son of Dracula (Again)

On February 11, 1943, *Motion Picture Daily* reported that *Son of Dracula* had replaced the title *Destiny*. On February 25, the PCA awarded it certificate number 9194, which indicates Breen or his associates

had viewed the film. They accepted it, even if on sufferance, given the film's obvious rejection of some of Breen's recommendations, ranging from the repeated references to insanity, Alucard's hand transforming on-screen into a skeleton hand, and the bat biting Frank (though as filmed, we see only the shadow of the bat).

On March 31, 1943, *Variety* readers learned that the film was finished. But even as late as October, *over six months later*, it still did not have a formal release date. After an October 28 preview, *Son of Dracula* finally premiered on November 5. Why the delay, when the film was ready for months? The answer is unknown, but this late October *Daily Variety* item presents a possibility:

> With successful box office reaction in teaming pair of horror dramas during past year, Universal will release *The Mad Ghoul* and *Son of Dracula* as a chill-thrill dual package bill in tandem. In line with sales policy. Universal previewed the two pictures together.

"Trailers from Hell"'s Joe Dante: "This is one of Universal's best horror films of the '40s.... The treatment is stylized, impressively produced, and beautifully shot by the excellent George Robinson. ...It's a B that looks like an A."

An investigation of *Son of Dracula*'s release across the U.S. suggests that at roughly one-third of its screenings, it did share the screen with *The Mad Ghoul*. Had the studio held off on releasing *Son of Dracula* just so that it could pair it with another horror film?

The answer is unknown, but an important exception to the dual bill came at *Son of Dracula*'s premiere at New York City's Rialto on November 5, 1943. It opened without benefit of radio commercials on station WMCA, which refused to air a one-minute spot because it was "too gruesome."

The critics' reactions varied. The *New York Times* dismissed it as "often as unintentionally funny as it is chilling." The *New York Herald Tribune* declared, "This second try on the Dracula theme, like most of the metaphysical follow-ups, is disappointing." Likewise, the *World-Telegram* called *Son* a "new and vastly inferior version" of its forebear.

The New York *Post* said *Son* was "certainly guaranteed for goose-pimples – and, we might add, laughs." The *Mirror* reviewer, impressed with the crew, told readers, "Direction, lighting and good camera work make for some eerie effects." The *Journal-American* advised, "If this is what you want, the Rialto has it for you in a big, strong dose." Similarly, the *Daily News* wrote, "It's entirely up to you whether you can enter into the spirit of the thing and make like you're scared half to death by the supernatural happenings."

Overall, the critics at the industry trade publications were more positive about the new vampire movie:

Robert Siodmak directs with accent on the suspenseful angles of the plot, while photographer George Robinson turns in good job of low-key lighting. – *Daily Variety*, October 29, 1943

In the shocker horror field, *Son of Dracula* is a topline entry. ...Photography by George Robinson is invaluable in setting the low-key mood of the show. Its music score by H.J. Salter, art direction by John B. Goodman and Martin Obzina, and the uncredited special effects are of uniformly high order. – *The Hollywood Reporter*, October 29, 1943

It's a good entry of its type, and due for coinful box office reception from the thrill-inclined customers. – *Variety*, November 3, 1943

[O]ne of the best of its kind of late. – *Motion Picture Daily*, November 4, 1943

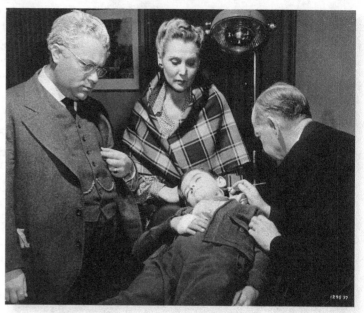

If Dr. Brewster *really* cared about little Tommy Land, he'd paint crosses on *both* sides of the kid's neck.

A well-paced successor to the original *Dracula* that has good timing, chills and suspense and can be top drawer in the eerie houses where horror pays off. – *Showmen's Trade Review*, November 6, 1943

Where supernatural horror melodramas are liked, *Son of Dracula* should prove acceptable program fare. ...Trick photography has been employed to good advantage. – *Harrison's Reports*, November 13, 1943

The direction of Robert Siodmak welds the complicated story structure into a smoothly-moving vehicle. ...For chills, thrills and spine-tingling sensations, the picture hits the mark. – *Motion Picture Herald*, November 13, 1931

All the ingredients on which horror gourmets sharpen their cinematic appetite are contained in *Son of Dracula*. ...The acting in general befits a tale of this sort. ...Robert Siodmak directed the picture tensely. – *Film Daily*, November 22, 1943

But not everyone reacted to *Son of Dracula* favorably. The National Legion of Decency classed it as "unobjectionable for adults," which meant that it was in fact problematic for children. The Chicago Police Censor Board decreed that it was for adults only. And Ohio censors demanded several deletions, including "close up scenes of open coffins," Alucard putting Kay into a coffin, the bat biting Frank in his jail cell, Lazlo describing how vampires live off the blood of the living, and the entire scene with Tommy. Ohio also required the shots of Alucard choking Frank to be cut by half.

Such concerns had little to no effect on *Son of Dracula*'s success. *Variety* reported that the film was a "powerful puller" during its first few days at the Rialto: "should hit $16,000 or near." In Los Angeles, *Son of Dracula* and *The Mad Ghoul* opened at the Hawaii Theatre and generated record profits for the theater, including scoring a "new Sunday record." It remained strong in its second week at the Hawaii, its third being "fine" and its fourth week being "neat." On December 31, 1943, *Daily Variety* wrote:

> Universal horror team of *Mad Ghoul* and *Son of Dracula*, which recently closed five-week run at the Hawaii Theatre, grabbed close to $10,000 for the distributor on the sesh for average of $2000 a week or $5000 for first run booking of each picture. Figure is surprising, and indicator of strength of dual chiller bills with the paying customers. Bookings of the individual features with other shows as supporting attractions would have returned to U around half of amount obtained in the teamed dating.

Twice the horror meant twice the profits for a studio known as the home to monsters. For example, in St. Louis, the Missouri Theatre generated more than twice the previous week's profits, the dual bill becoming "its best record in a long time."

Reports from theater managers published in *Motion Picture Herald* varied from great to poor:

> This was the best horror show ever run in my theater. It has name draw, scenes that are unbelievable, a very good plot, and some honest to goodness horror scenes for those that scare easily. – State Theatre, Riverville, West Virginia

> Here is a good chiller-diller which pleased my patrons. We had better than average business for this type of show. – Paramount Theatre, Dewey, Oklahoma

> A little far-fetched and too eerie, but not a poor picture of its type. – Rand Theatre, Randolph, Nebraska

> Didn't do as well on this as we generally do on thriller features here. Business off about 20 percent. – Linder Theatre, Columbus, Ohio

> Here is another example of film waste. This was utterly incredible; even the children jeered. We did terrible business. – Winema Theatre, Scotia, California

With *Son of Dracula* following many of the plot beats of its progenitor, the 1931 *Dracula*, the stakes are high for Prof. Lazlo and Dr. Brewster, *Son*'s Van Helsing and Dr. Seward counterparts.

Such a range of response is not unexpected, even for a film as relatively successful as *Son of Dracula*, as disappointed exhibitors were often the most likely to report their news.

Dracula's Daughter-in-Law

At its core, *Son of Dracula* repeats the narrative of Browning's *Dracula*. A Dracula once again travels to another country in search of fresh blood (America, in this case, rather than England). A fatherly figure (Dr. Brewster, rather than Dr. Seward) tries to look after two different women. One of them, Kay, is, like Lucy in the 1931 film, predisposed to the nobleman's charms. That same fatherly figure relies on expertise from another country (Prof. Lazlo instead of Van Helsing). In these basic respects, the early sections of the film represent a loose remake of *Dracula*.

At times the similarities are striking. When Frank tells Kay, "We're not blind and we're not fools. We're just simple people that refuse to be fooled by a lot of superstitious nonsense," he sounds a good deal like the skeptical Jonathan Harker in the 1931 film. By contrast, Dr. Brewster seems somewhat open to suggestions of vampirism, more so than Dr. Seward is in the Browning's film. And, in a manner opposite of Browning, which leaves Lucy's story unfinished, the second half of *Son of Dracula* focuses on the Lucy character, to the extent that it becomes Kay's film.

Robert Paige and Frank Craven in the film's opening scene.

Shifting the locale to the Deep South from Transylvania and England introduces several new ideas, including subtle references to World War II and foreign invasion. Alucard tells Kate that Americans are a "young and vital race," just as he informs Lazlo, "I am here because this is a young and virile race, not dry and decadent like ours [in Hungary]." In another scene, Brewster realizes that Alucard has arrived in a "younger country, stronger and more virile" than his own. These references explicitly have to do with Alucard's need for blood, but in the context of the war – particularly given the film's repeated references to Hungary, then aligned with the Axis powers – they speak to real fears of attacks on American soil. To be sure, in November 1942, *Variety* spoke about the need for studios to shoot outdoor nighttime scenes in daylight (using special lenses), as "required by military dimout orders."

As for Dark Oaks, the plantation owned by Col. Caldwell (George Irving) and bequeathed to Kay in his will, and its surroundings, *Son of Dracula* presents some of the most impressive and atmospheric sets of any wartime horror movie. A key prop inside the mansion is a large painting of a burning ship at sea, tossed about in a tremendous storm. It's displayed prominently after the smoke appears on the terrace, the colonel's cigar having set the floor on fire after Alucard's attack. Later, the painting is clearly illuminated in the background of the otherwise dark house after Alucard carries Kay over the threshold. Alucard has (apparently) arrived by ship from Europe, then by train to the South, bringing with him storms both thematic and literal (as in the thunder and lightning outside the home of the justice of the peace, as the vampire and Kay prepare to tie the knot).

Of course Count Alucard is merely a pseudonym. As *The Hollywood Reporter* said in 1943, Alucard "is a name the audience is immediately invited to decipher as Dracula spelled backwards." For example, at the train station, Brewster sees the Alucard name on the count's luggage and reads in order the letters "D-R-A-C..." Queen Zimba informs Kay, "Alucard is not his name." Later, Brewster writes the letters of Alucard's name at an angle on a piece of paper, helping him to read it backwards. His phone call with Lazlo makes clear the name *is* Dracula, a point reiterated when Brewster is seen reading a page in a book titled *Dracula*, which features modified text from Stoker's novel (specifically Jonathan Harker's Journal of May 12), as well as two entirely new sentences.

Clarity that Alucard is *a* Dracula does not indicate whether he is *the* Dracula, of course. The film's title indicates that he is the son, and Lazlo speculates he is "probably a descendant of Count Dracula." Lazlo proceeds to mention that the last Dracula was destroyed in the nineteenth century, whereas Browning's *Dracula* is clearly staked in approximately 1930, given the automobiles seen in London. As Lyndon W. Joslin posits in his book *Count Dracula Goes to the Movies* (McFarland, 2017), Lazlo's commentary might "imply that there were at least two Count Draculas on the loose in Europe simultaneously, and apparently for some time. The mind boggles at the thought, which this film fortunately doesn't insist that we accept." Joslin makes an excellent point, as *Son of Dracula*'s vagueness on these matters overcomes the destruction of Dracula in Browning's *Dracula* and, for that matter, the need to reference *Dracula's Daughter*.

What is clear is that Chaney – the first actor to play Dracula in a Hollywood movie after Bela Lugosi and Carlos Villarías – appears quite differently than his predecessor, a point underscored not only by their inherently different looks, but also because Chaney has graying hair and wears a mustache. He dons a different style of black cape, one with a stiff collar that turns downward, one without a different colored lining, and one with a drawstring tied lower than his neck.

Chaney's vampire seems also more modern and less regal than Lugosi's, partially the result of an American actor who makes absolutely no effort to alter the accent of his voice. This new Dracula rides as a passenger in an automobile, literally sweats when panicked, and is notably more physical than Lugosi. Some film critics have given Christopher Lee credit for making his Dracula a much more physically powerful and active character than Lugosi's, but Chaney's version does so 15 years before Lee

1.

Count Alucard has an icon absent from all earlier vampire films: the raven, long believed to be a mediator between life and death, and one that feeds off carrion. The raven appears on Alucard's crest, as shown on his luggage (see photo 1). A raven (played by a raven, *not* by a crow, as online sites assert) appears in Queen Zimba's cabin, shortly before Alucard arrives in the form of a bat (see photo 2). And then there is the Dark Oaks guest house, where Alucard stores his luggage and supposedly stays. In the background, we can see two framed pictures of a raven, facing one another (photos 3 and 4).

2.

3.

4.

The raven is a "bird of ill omen…symbol of death," according to the 1935 Universal Horror *The Raven*. A raven brings even worse luck to the characters in *Son of Dracula*.

first portrayed the character on-screen.

For example, Chaney's vampire chokes Frank with his right hand, easily hurling him into the next room. He later chokes Brewster with his left hand, releasing him only when Lazlo produces a cross. He angrily throws down a spade when he sees Brewster entering the Dark Oaks mansion. Then, at the film's conclusion, he shoves Frank with great force, shakes him violently and chokes him with both hands. In a wild rage, he pulls a board off the wall and tries to extinguish a fire.

Though a physically larger and less talented actor than his father Lon Chaney, the younger Chaney's appearance in this film resembles some photographs of his father, resulting in an admittedly inexact but still fascinating hint of how the elder Chaney might have looked if costumed as Universal's Dracula. Nevertheless, the younger Chaney's suitability for the role, ranging from his acting ability to his physical size, have raised questions in recent decades.

Such was not necessarily the case in 1943. *Motion Picture Daily* opined that Chaney, Allbritton and Paige "deliver creditable performances which go a long way toward making the picture one of the best of its kind of late." In *Motion Picture Herald*: "Universal gives the exhibitor a treat presenting Lon Chaney in *Son of Dracula*." And from *The Hollywood Reporter*: "Chaney's Dracula is an outstanding job, accomplished without the gobs of makeup with which he is generally smeared. As a matter of fact, his performance takes on an almost romantic flavor."

What might best be said now? Many viewers (including myself) would have preferred to see Bela Lugosi or John Carradine play the role instead. That said, Chaney's limitations have been exaggerated. While it remains an improbable role for him, he does try to carry himself with some grace and gravitas, even shifting his manner of speaking from being demanding and angry in some scenes to being calmly duplicitous and at times genuinely sincere in others.

In any event, the film's standout role is Kay, so much so that a more apt title might have been *Dracula's Daughter-in-Law*. No previous female vampire or "vamp" (in the tradition of Philip Burnes-Jones, Rudyard Kipling and Theda Bara) was ever so devious. An occult enthusiast, Kay met Alucard in Budapest only to invite him to America in order to marry him (rather than just get bitten) so that she can then have her undead husband destroyed and transform her *true* love Frank into a vampire. As already noted, she does assume the Lucy character, but goes far beyond it due to her truly evil plans. (In fact, in a curious role reversal, it is not Kay who bites a child, as Lucy does in Browning's film, as if starting life as a vampire cautiously, but Alucard, who bites young Tommy.)

She is the screen's first female who *wants* to be a supernatural vampire, exuding great confidence about her plans and their temporary success. And *Son of Dracula* implies that she too has great physical strength, as the sheriff, Brewster and Lazlo discover that her coffin is missing from the morgue. Presumably without Alucard's assistance, she has moved it back to the Dark Oaks playroom.

Consider also the care Universal took with her appearance, including her black hair vs. the blonde hair of her morally upright sister Claire. The same is true of the costumes by Vera West. In her first scenes, including her visit to Queen Zimba, Kay wears a diaphanous gown, funereal in appearance, quite similar to those worn by Dracula's wives in the Browning film. Her second dress features artwork of leaves, symbols of Dark Oaks; she wears it at the reception for Alucard, as well as at the judge's office when it becomes clear she gives up considerable wealth in the colonel's will so that she alone will inherit the plantation. Her third outfit is mainly black, but with a white top that brings attention to the waistband she wears, one that appears similar to a bat. When Kay greets Alucard at the swamp and then gets married, she's robed in another funereal gown. Sitting in her bed, she wears – just as the shooting script specifies – ermine to greet Brewster, a fur long associated with heraldry and royalty, which as a countess she has just become. Thereafter, she wears the gown in which she was married.

In 1943, *The Hollywood Reporter* complained, "Louise Allbritton covers her sophisticated blonde charms with an unbecoming black wig and is wasted in a role any attractive ingenue could have done." Here again, initial response is at odds with later critiques: Allbritton's performance is unforgettable. With all of the women who played wonderful roles in classic horror films, not one is better at being bad than Allbritton, the most insidious of them all. Rightly remembered for this portrayal, Allbritton's legacy is secure.

Despite the differing merits of the actors who portrayed them, Alucard and Kay exist in a world of evolving vampire cinema. For example, like some of their forebears, they are able – thanks to John P. Fulton's uncredited special effects – to transform into bats. Kay's transformation is never depicted on-screen, but Alucard's is on four occasions. The first has him back up to fill most of the screen with the blackness of his cape; then a blurred bat fills most of the screen. It flies away from the camera, the initial lack of focus helping to create a fairly seamless transition. On three subsequent occasions, all featuring transformations from bat to human form, Fulton used animation. One might debate whether these special effects bested those created at MGM for *Mark of the Vampire*, but regardless, they remain effective. As the *Los Angeles Times* opined (November 19, 1943), the film's "really eerie touch is the manner in which Dracula changes, before your eyes, into a huge bat."

Where *Son of Dracula* makes important evolutionary strides is in the vampire's ability to appear as – in the words of Lazlo – "a small cloud of swirling vapor," which young Tommy describes as "fog." These smoke-like transitions were a new addition to vampire cinema, and they appear even more striking than the bat transformations. Alucard employs these powers on three occasions in the film; Kay does so twice.

As a result, *Son of Dracula* became an important marker, with Universal initiating what would become a pattern: The vampire's otherworldliness would increasingly be depicted not through an actor's portrayal, but instead through special effects. Even his death by sunlight provided the impetus for special effects, with his hand and wrist becoming skeletal right before audience members' eyes.

Narrative additions to vampirism in *Son of Dracula* come in the form of the count's ability to turn Kay into a vampire *after* her human death from gunshot wounds. How is this possible? Her "background was morbid," she was devoted to "black magic and the like," she became a vampire by choice, and Alucard put soil in her coffin.

Crosses continue to repel vampires in *Son of Dracula*, though for the first time on screen they appear in improvised form, with Brewster painting images of them on both of Tommy's neck wounds. And the ability to destroy vampires remains twofold, so Lazlo and Kay separately explain, meaning sunlight and/or a stake through the heart. But the film also provides a third possibility, with Lazlo suggesting the cremation of Kay's body would destroy her, a method employed by Frank at the conclusion.

And then there are brief and subtle suggestions of voodoo, a religion long associated with Louisiana where (according to page 2 of the script) the movie takes place. The use of chickens in voodoo ceremonies comes to mind in the script's desire for them to be mutilated. While only one reference to "dead chickens" remains in Frank's on-screen dialogue, Dr. Brewster does discover some live chickens caged in the mansion cellar, and feathers atop the soil in one of Alucard's chests. When he visits the cellar a second time, the chickens are missing, but their cage remains. Do these hold – even if largely unstated and unseen – importance for the story?

Vampires and implications of voodoo converge most clearly in one of the film's most memorable characters, Queen Zimba. Kay has brought her from Budapest. Frank specifically calls her a "Hungarian gypsy," one whose wisdom evokes comparison to Maleva (Maria Ouspenskaya) in *The Wolf Man*. She seems to possess telepathic abilities, as in mentally forcing Kay to visit her. And she seems psychic, prophesying that Kay will marry a corpse and live in a grave. At the same time, her title "queen" reminds us of the tradition of voodoo queens in Louisiana. Frank also calls her a "swamp cat," one who lives in a cabin brewing herbs and chanting unintelligible words. She is a Hungarian gypsy, but one who conjures visions of voodooism.

Endings

The question of where to end a story can be as difficult as where to begin it. To be sure, *Son of Dracula*'s

narrative conclusion is as clear as it is unique and poignant. The male hero cannot be reunited with the female victim, as Kay is no victim. She initiates all the evil that unfolds, which requires Frank to set her coffin ablaze, even though she is still "alive" in an undead state. She burns, but he is the martyr, one who must lose his true love and – once the closing credits have concluded – face further trials, personal and legal.

But of the film *Son of Dracula*, its ending is even more difficult to pinpoint. Should one cite the last screening of its original release, which continued well into 1944? Or its first reissue in 1948? Or its first appearance on television in 1957? Or when Universal renewed its copyright in 1970? Or the film's first appearance on VHS and Beta in 1988? Or the first time Chaney's vampire appeared on a magazine cover, as on *Mad Monsters* #8 in 1964? Or the first time Chaney's Dracula was merchandised as a toy, as in a 12" doll produced in 1998? These markers are all in addition to its title repurposed in everything from the 1974 film *Son of Dracula* to the 1975 *Son of Dracula* comic book (see illustration above).

But perhaps we should think of the conclusion to *Son of Dracula* purely in the future tense. The existence of this book, first published in the year 2019, suggests ongoing interest in the film. And it will likely continue for a number of decades, if not longer, in spite of – or even perhaps due to – its few faults, as much as for its many successes. We need not consult Queen Zimba to make this prophesy confidently, and – for such a truly remarkable film – happily.

> If we live long enough, it's possible, unless we can possibly avoid it, that we'll be seeing pictures entitled *Dracula's Great Granddaughter,* and *The Great Grandson of Dracula*. Universal Pictures will never let the Draculas die. – *New York Daily News,* November 6, 1943

SON OF DRACULA: THE RELEASE HISTORY

By Dr. Robert J. Kiss

There should be no doubt that Universal scored an appreciable wartime commercial success with *Son of Dracula*. In its November 11, 1944, edition, trade magazine *Boxoffice* tabulated the first-run performance of 336 features (excluding Westerns) released between fall 1943 and summer 1944, drawing on data from 22 major U.S. cities, as well as from mid-sized cities and small towns. With ticket sales that were 23 percent above average, *Son of Dracula* was pronounced a "hit" by the publication and moreover constituted Universal's best-performing horror or sci-fi movie during this timeframe, followed by *Jungle Woman* at 14 percent above average, *The Invisible Man's Revenge* at 13 percent above average, *The Mummy's Ghost* at five percent above average, and *The Mad Ghoul* at two percent *below* average. It likewise eclipsed all entries in the studio's horror-tinged Inner Sanctum and Sherlock Holmes series, with *Calling Dr. Death* chalking up a performance that was ten percent above average, *Weird Woman* and *The Scarlet Claw* both proving merely average, and *Sherlock Holmes Faces Death* coming in at two percent below average.

When compared with horror releases from all studios, *Son of Dracula* stood in joint third position behind 20th Century-Fox's *The Lodger* at 36 percent above average and Paramount's *The Uninvited* at 28 percent above average, while tying with RKO's *The Ghost Ship* at 23 percent above average. This still established *Son of Dracula* as the highest-placed "monster movie" in the line-up, just outperforming the other bloodsucker on the block, Columbia's *The Return of the Vampire* with Bela Lugosi, which nevertheless secured ticket sales that were an impressive 17 percent above average.

Son of Dracula and *Captive Wild Woman* reach Guadalajara, November 27, 1943.

The earliest regular openings: Mexico City and Manitoba

Despite achieving such domestic preeminence within its genre, *Son of Dracula* had been held back from release for around six months and actually premiered outside the United States. A possible reason for this can be located in the February 27, 1943, issue of *Motion Picture Herald*, which identified the film as one of a backlog of 162 features produced by Hollywood studios for which release dates had yet to be assigned. Some 34 of these features were war movies that typically needed to be accommodated into release schedules swiftly in order to retain their topicality, and the resultant constant shuffling and reworking of schedules following the United States' entry into World War Two was in part responsible for the backlog that had built up. At the same time, the pushing-back of domestic opening dates for non–war-themed (and therefore "non-urgent") features on occasion resulted in some international bookings taking place considerably closer to U.S. premiere dates than had been anticipated when they were arranged.

In the case of *Son of Dracula*, whose general release in the U.S. was ultimately announced for November 5, 1943, this meant that its earliest engagement in fact took the form of a long-booked two-week run at the Cine Olimpia in downtown Mexico City, beginning October 20, 1943. The Olimpia was a double-bill theater that had repeatedly been employed by Universal for the opening of its Spanish-dubbed new releases in Mexico, and on this occasion *El hijo de Drácula* – as the Siodmak/Chaney picture was now titled – topped the bill alongside *La mujer fiera*, more familiarly known as *Captive Wild Woman*. Since Mexican audiences had previously been exposed solely to Universal's Spanish-language *Drácula* starring Carlos Villarías, rather than to the English-language Lugosi version, *Son of Dracula* may arguably be considered to have premiered not as a second sequel to Tod Browning's movie, but to George Melford's. Villarías certainly remained synonymous with the role in the country, and continued to be billed as Carlos "Drácula" Villarías when making stage appearances there in 1943.

At least one long-standing booking in Canada also took place prior to the announced domestic release date. On November 1, 1943, *Son of Dracula* commenced a three-day run at the 598-seat Capitol Theatre in Brandon, Manitoba, with the hour-long Royal Air Force docudrama *Coastal Command* playing in support. Even from this very early juncture in its theatrical career, the "escapist" *Son of Dracula* does not seem quite so detached from the war when considered in the full context of the bill on which it played.

The November 5(ish) U.S. general release

Just as Alucard appeared on-screen as a small cloud of swirling vapor before manifesting fully, so *Son of Dracula* gradually came into view by way of screenings at a number of U.S. movie theaters during the six days *prior* to its announced November 5 domestic general release.

A gimmicky press preview in Hollywood on November 3 showcased it alongside *The Mad Ghoul*, which

Halloween engagement in Cedar City, October 30, 1943.

had likewise been assigned a November 5 release date as Universal's preferred co-feature for double-bill houses booking *Son of Dracula*. This facilitated the publication of advance reviews of both titles in *Motion Picture Daily* of November 4. Ed Raiden of *Showmen's Trade Review* offered the following insight into the press preview in his "Wandering Around Hollywood" column of November 6: "Universal decided to show the reviewers how the exhibitors should exploit *The Mad Ghoul* and *Son of Dracula* when they showed [them] to the trade boys, so, in the dark, just when one picture was finished, a couple of cuties came in dressed as nurses, jumped around taking care of those who 'fainted,' meanwhile slipping a piece of ice down a collar or two."

The two movies had actually already been "sneaked" individually as special "owl" and midnight attractions for Halloween at an extremely limited number of engagements in small towns and cities. As October 31

Alone With "The Son Of Dracula"

Lillian Brothers squares up to Alucard in Alabama, November 3, 1943.

fell on a Sunday – that is to say, right before a work or school day – these screenings were scheduled for the more audience-friendly night of Saturday, October 30. The 800-seat Tivoli Theatre in Maryville, Missouri, likely started its show earliest, at 11 p.m., with *Son of Dracula* accompanied by two "spooky" shorts in the guise of Universal's Walter Lantz-produced animated musical novelty *Boogie Woogie Man Will Get You If You Don't Watch Out* and the Three Stooges' *Spook Louder* – with the latter's plot firmly entrenched in wartime intelligence and espionage activities. At the 484-seat Parks Theatre in Cedar City, Utah, *Son of Dracula* constituted that night's screen component of Duke Montague's Midnight Spook Party, a spook show promoted with the tagline "Warning – the ghost may leave the stage and sit with you!!"

Over that same Halloween weekend, the Calhoun Theatre in Anniston, Alabama, ran a promotional competition to find a local woman who possessed "the nerve to sit alone with the lights out…while we put on a private screening of *Son of Dracula* at midnight, Tuesday, November 2nd." In marked contrast to the sham sisters of medicine at the Hollywood preview, the winning applicant was Mrs. Lillian Brothers of 1127 Leighton Avenue, a *bona fide* registered nurse with postgraduate qualifications. Following the screening (which technically took place on November 3), Brothers "told theater officials that she was too interested in the film itself to think about being afraid." She was rewarded with a "crisp new five dollar bill" and a pass that allowed her

to return to the theater with a friend to watch the movie again during regular hours. The 1091-seat Calhoun then opened *Son of Dracula* as a standalone attraction on November 4, still one day ahead of its announced general release. A small number of other venues around the nation also started the movie on this date, including the 678-seat Diana Theatre (now the Medina Theatre) in Medina, New York, which co-billed it with Hal Roach's barely-feature-length "Streamliner" comedy Western *Calaboose* starring Jimmy Rogers and Noah Beery Jr.

As far as the trade press was concerned, though, it was the standalone opening at the Rialto in New York City – nicknamed the "house of horrors" due to its lengthy association with Universal horror bills – on November 5 that constituted the effective premiere of *Son of Dracula*, even though the theater didn't bill the engagement as such. Generating a first-week gross of $11,000, the Rialto opening was certainly worth celebrating, with the movie's original two-week booking ultimately held over into a fourth week, causing the initial New York engagement of Laurel and Hardy's *The Dancing Masters* at the theater to be postponed twice, until December 1. (By December 10, the Rialto's bill had reverted to Universal horror with a two-week run of *The Mad Ghoul*, which grossed $9300 in its first week and $6000 in its second.)

A handful of other smaller movie houses, primarily in the south-east, also opened *Son of Dracula* on November 5. These included the State Theatre in Kingsport, Tennessee, and – by way of a special 11.30 p.m. screening – the Empire Theatre in Montgomery, Alabama.

A wartime theatrical first run

Following the initial smattering of Halloween and early engagements outlined above, *Son of Dracula* was rapidly rolled out to large towns and cities throughout the nation. In some metropolitan locations, it could already be found playing in second run as early as February 1944, and by mid-March it had effectively been seen in all major urban areas. However, it took considerably longer for the picture to penetrate small towns and rural communities, where the first run may accordingly be considered to have continued until mid-July,

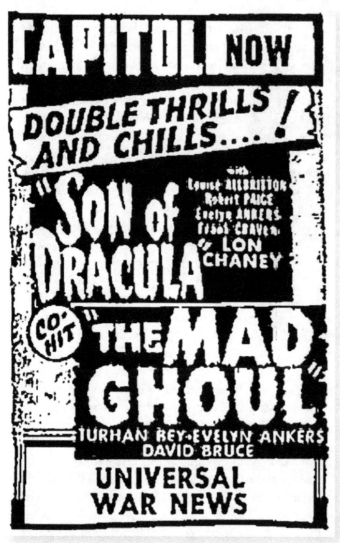

War footage as a standard fixture in Salt Lake City, January 6, 1944.

Bonds top the bill in Reno, Nevada, January 20, 1944.

concluding with a series of lumber town openings in the Black Hills of South Dakota.

Looking at a sample of 1500 theaters from coast to coast which played *Son of Dracula* in first run between Halloween 1943 and mid–July 1944 reveals that 36 percent of engagements took the form of a standalone presentation. The most common way to have first encountered the movie, however – at 38 percent of engagements within the sample – was on an all-horror double bill supported by Universal's preferred co-feature *The Mad Ghoul*. A further 25 percent of first-run screenings paired it with a different double-bill co-feature, with *Son of Dracula* topping such alternate bills roughly seven-eighths of the time. A final one percent of bookings offered audiences the altogether more unusual experience of seeing the movie on a bill with live entertainment.

Patrons' blood was not the only thing to run cold during the feature's considerable number of playdates

east of the Mississippi between mid-December 1943 and mid-January 1944, with the reviewer of the December 13 screening at the State Theatre in Schenectady, New York, already observing that the audience had "shivered" in equal measure at the movie's scares and the "auditorium temperature." The thermometer showed 15 degrees below when *Son of Dracula* reached Minneapolis, while the trade press ceaselessly alerted exhibitors to snowfall, blizzards and flu epidemics throughout the eastern half of the nation. However, none of these conditions really seems to have hampered hardy horror fans from getting to theaters. As for those who only got the chance to see *Son of Dracula* late in its first run, the situation had shifted to the opposite end of the meteorological spectrum, so that ads from as early as the May

31 opening at the Diana Theatre in Noblesville, Indiana, sought to lure potential patrons inside with images of icicles and promises of an auditorium that was "cool as an igloo."

One unavoidable constant throughout the first run was the presence of reminders of the ongoing war. Even though reviewers such as *Hartford Courant* columnist Marjorie Oakley Christoph sought to foreground the escapist potential of films like *Son of Dracula* and *The Mad Ghoul* – concluding her January 6, 1944, review of the double bill at the city's Regal Theatre with a cheery "You'll certainly forget the war" – others more soberly pointed out that these features were scarcely shown in isolation. A December 1, 1943, review of a standalone presentation of *Son of Dracula* at the Plaza Theatre in Asheville, North Carolina, instead concluded with the observation: "A sports reel, a news reel, and an animated cartoon follow to break the spell of the vampire." In fact, newsreels – in particular *Universal War News* and *The March of Time*, as well as government information reels – were often prominently billed outside theaters and in newspaper ads. On occasion the specific content of these accompanying shorts was highlighted, with publicity for the two-day opening of *Son of Dracula* and *The Mad Ghoul* at the Caldwell Theatre in St. Joseph, Michigan, on December 17, 1943, stressing the presence of footage of the capture of Tarawa by U.S. forces on the bill. More poignantly, the two-day run of *The Fallen Sparrow* and *Son of Dracula* at the New Calvin Theatre in Washington, Missouri, from January 25, 1944, promised "Pictures of Local Boys in the Service." Of course, it was not merely shorts that presented images and reminders of war, with *Son of Dracula* also playing on double bills alongside a range of explicitly war-themed co-features, from Howard Hawks' polished submarine drama *Corvette K-225* to Universal's sensationalist *The Strange Death of Adolf Hitler*.

Theaters furthermore dedicated considerable energy to urging patrons to buy war bonds. Some that screened *Son of Dracula* even arranged "free movie days" on which patrons who purchased a bond in any denomination at the box office would receive a free pass to see the movie. "Owl" and midnight screenings also started to take on special wartime significance, providing war workers with an opportunity to see movies that they otherwise would miss. A number of venues additionally arranged benefit performances; for example, the 1832-seat Broadway Theatre in Portland, Oregon, held a midnight screening of *Son of Dracula* and Universal's musical comedy *Top Man* during the night of December 18-19, 1943, for which attendees were each asked to cough up four packets of cigarettes in lieu of the admission price, so that these could then be shared out among sick and wounded servicemen spending Christmas at the nearby Barnes Army General Hospital in Vancouver, Washington.

Just as the war affected *when* home front and civilian workers were able to attend screenings of *Son of Dracula*, so it impacted heavily on *where* those who had been called up into the armed forces got the opportunity to see it. Prints were distributed to military bases at home and overseas from mid-November 1943, with the Hill Air Force Base in Utah showing the picture as a standalone as early as November 19. On that same date, the film premiered at the Capitol and Cameo Theatres in Sydney, Australia, with the next day's *Sydney Daily Telegraph* reporting not merely a "record crowd" at the Cameo that extended for half a block when the "house-full" signs went up, but also the presence of a group of young U.S. Navy servicemen in the line outside. The *Telegraph*'s journalist spoke to one of them, identified as Karl Davenport of West Virginia, who commented: "Me and my two buddies would rather see a horror film than any other, and that goes for Westerns, too. *Son of Dracula* on our first night's leave – that was too good. But 'Sold out' – that was too bad!" There was a certain poignancy also to the three-day engagement of *Son of Dracula* and *The Mad Ghoul* at the Parthenon Theatre in Hammond, Indiana, beginning February 7, 1944, which was announced in the local press as the last booking by the house's popular manager Harry Mintz prior to his departure for the army. Thankfully, after rising to the rank of sergeant, Mintz was able to return to his position at the Parthenon on September 28, 1945, following V-J Day.

Standalone presentation

The 36 percent of first-run venues that exhibited *Son of Dracula* as a standalone attraction supported by selected shorts represent a fairly typical statistic for the first half of the 1940s, indicating that many theater circuits and owners maintained their standard approach when booking the picture.

At premiere houses in major cities, week-long standalone engagements generated a box-office take that was very slightly better than usual. For example, *Son of Dracula* grossed $8500 at the Stanton in Philadelphia from December 16, when the average was $8000; $6500 at the Mayfair in Baltimore from December 23, when the average was $5900; and $4000 at the Gopher in Minneapolis from January 7, 1944, when the average was $3500.

Now with added fangs! Miami standalone opening,
November 13, 1943.

Though nothing to complain about, these figures are
markedly less impressive than what *Motion Picture Daily*
described as the "exceptional business" being done at premiere houses in other major cities which had elected to
show the movie on a double bill with *The Mad Ghoul*.

Outside of big cities, standalone bookings of *Son
of Dracula* generally lasted for two or three days only,
which was again absolutely typical for the period. In
other words, theater owners in such localities demonstrated their confidence in the movie's ability to attract
a crowd for a couple of days, but saw no reason to afford
it special treatment or to hold it over.

Co-billed with *The Mad Ghoul*

Following the Hollywood press preview on November 3, the first public pairing of *Son of Dracula* and *The
Mad Ghoul* took place at the 2400-seat Capitol Theatre in Binghamton, New York, from November 7. This
"double shock-and-shudder show," as it was widely referred to in publicity, of course also provided audiences

with a double dose of Evelyn Ankers (as had the earlier
Mexican presentation of the movie alongside *Captive
Wild Woman*). After the Binghamton opening, this
double bill remained commonplace in all parts of the
country, and in addition to constituting 38 percent of
first-run engagements, was thereafter widely attested at
second-run houses and discount theaters.

Single-venue openings of the bill at premiere houses in major cities brought some dazzling profits which
in several instances doubled average grosses. The Los
Angeles engagement at the Hawaii Theatre – another
venue that enjoyed a lengthy association with horror
movies – began on November 18 and during its first
week both broke the theater's Sunday record and generated a gross of $11,000, when the house average was
$5266. The bill grossed *another* $11,000 during its second week, and would ultimately be held over for five
weeks. A further November 18 opening, at the gargan-
tuan 3514-seat Missouri Theatre in St. Louis, yielded
a gross of $16,500, when the usual box-office take was
$8000. In Chicago, a two-week booking at the Woods
Theatre commencing on Thanksgiving weekend in turn
drew around $33,000, when the weekly average was be-
tween $7500 and $10,000. At the Esquire Theatre on
San Francisco's Market Street, the horror combo had its
initial seven-day run from December 14 extended twice,
causing the venue's next Universal double bill, comprising the musical comedies *Crazy House* and *Hi'ya, Sailor*,
to shift from being its intended pre–Christmas presentation to its New Year attraction. And as the mercury
plummeted in Indianapolis, one of the few things that
could still be described as "sizzling" by *Variety* was the
bill's $9500 gross at the 2000-seat Lyric Theatre for the
week beginning January 12, 1944, when the house average was $5000.

Multi-venue openings were altogether less common,
and proved considerably less successful. Despite an at-
tention-grabbing "Vampire vs. Ghoul" publicity campaign, a week-long three-theater engagement at Kan-
sas City's Esquire, Fairway and Uptown Theatres from
December 17 generated a collective gross of $12,450,
when the combined average weekly take at the three
houses was $12,800. With the benefit of hindsight and
on the basis of the bill's performance in other cities, it
seems likely that an exclusive single-venue opening
might well have grossed about the same amount; but
having to divide this gross three ways brought seasonal
joy to no one.

Outside of big cities, bookings once again most
commonly lasted for two or three days, in line with the
standard practices of the period. This is also how the

"Chiller-Dillers" invade St. Louis, November 18, 1943.

double bill was presented at three dozen Loew's circuit theaters across New York's five boroughs during January 1944. Meanwhile, the 800- seat Lyric Theatre in Lancaster, Ohio, merits singling-out on account of its bold – if not exactly truthful – promotional campaign for the opening of the double bill on December 17, 1943, which emphatically declared that the venue was screening "BANNED HORROR FILMS." According to the ad copy: "Both films are described as the most gruesome and frightening of horror films released to date and for this reason were banned in both New York and Chicago." At least there were some germs of truth underlying the bogus assertion: *The Mad Ghoul* had initially been rejected by the Chicago local censor board before a swift resubmission in early November led to its being passed for adult audiences only, while a lone New York radio station, WMCA, had declined to play a one-minute *radio teaser* for *Son of Dracula* on the grounds that it was "too gruesome."

Other double bills

Twenty-five percent of first-run houses elected to put together their own double bills, mostly with the objective of assembling a so-called "balanced program" comprising works of two distinct genres, which many in the trade believed held broader appeal than a single-genre pairing. At small town and rural theaters, *Son of Dracula* frequently topped the bill alongside a cheapie Western with a running time of around an hour. Elsewhere, a wide range of B-movie–length musicals, comedies, dramas and installments of mystery series were likewise deployed as

"balanced" supporting features. One highly uncommon "mother-and-son" twosome first attested at the Regent Theatre in Elmira, New York, on November 11, 1943, found *Son of Dracula* supported by the Republic drama *Someone to Remember*, and thus (no doubt unintentionally) constituted an all–"directed by Robert Siodmak" bill. The Valentine's Day 1944 line-up at the Beacon Theatre in Pittsburgh's Squirrel Hill neighborhood meanwhile amused *Pittsburgh Post-Gazette* columnist Charles F. Danvers on account of the marquee reading: "*The Son of Dracula – Nobody's Darling.*"

A limited number of theaters in towns where *The Mad Ghoul* had already played also chose to fashion their own "double horror programs" during early 1944, supporting *Son of Dracula* with the worthy first-run likes of *The Seventh Victim* or *The Ghost Ship*. Setting its sights at once higher and lower, the Ritz Theatre in Mansfield, Ohio, dressed its ushers as zombies for a three-day "chill a minute" show beginning March 22, 1944, at which the reissued Karloff vehicle *Doctor Maniac* served as the lower half of the bill.

Just about all of these alternate double bills were limited to local distribution circuits, with none finding widespread usage across the nation. However, roughly seven out of every eight engagements employed *Son of Dracula* as the top half of the bill, implying that it was regarded as the "better" or "more appealing" of the two features. All *70* lower-billed co-features within the sample of 1500 theaters nationwide are arranged alphabetically below; the month mentioned in each case is the earliest in which the pairing was attested. The 15 Universal titles on the list collectively represent barely 11 percent of bookings, indicating that the company made no particular effort to control these bills.

Mar. 1944 *Adventure in Iraq* (Warner Bros; John Loder)

Feb. 1944 *The Adventures of a Rookie* (RKO; Brown and Carney)

Feb. 1944 *Always a Bridesmaid* (Universal; The Andrews Sisters)

Non-standard all-horror bill in Eugene, Oregon, April 25, 1944.

Feb. 1944 *Arizona Trail* (Universal; Tex Ritter)

Jan. 1944 *Bar 20* (United Artists; William Boyd)

Mar. 1944 *Beyond the Last Frontier* (Republic; Eddie Dew)

Jan. 1944 *Black Market Rustlers* (Monogram; Range Busters)

Mar. 1944 *The Black Raven* (PRC; George Zucco)

Jun. 1944 *Boss of Boomtown* (Universal; Rod Cameron)

Nov. 1943 *Calaboose* (United Artists; Jimmy Rogers)

May 1944 *Calling Dr. Death* (Universal; Lon Chaney Jr.)

Feb. 1944 *Campus Rhythm* (Monogram; Johnny Downs)

Feb. 1944 *Canyon City* (Republic; Don "Red" Barry)

Mar. 1944 *Casanova in Burlesque* (Republic; Joe E. Brown)

Feb. 1944 *The Chance of a Lifetime* (Columbia; Chester Morris)

Feb. 1944 *Charlie Chan in the Secret Service* (Monogram; Sidney Toler)

Feb. 1944 *Coastal Command* (RKO; Royal Air Force)

Feb. 1944 *Colt Comrades* (United Artists; William Boyd)

Feb. 1944 *The Crime Doctor's Strangest Case* (Columbia; Warner Baxter)

Apr. 1944 *Death Valley Manhunt* (Republic; Wild Bill Elliott)

Mar. 1944 *Doctor Maniac* (independent reissue; Boris Karloff)

Feb. 1944 *The Falcon and the Co-eds* (RKO; Tom Conway)

Apr. 1944 *False Colors* (United Artists; William Boyd)

Feb. 1944 *Fighting Frontier* (RKO; Tim Holt)

Mar. 1944 *Fighting Valley* (PRC; Texas Rangers)

May 1944 *Footlight Glamour* (Columbia; Penny Singleton)

Apr. 1944 *The Ghost Ship* (RKO; Richard Dix)

Dec. 1943 *Gildersleeve on Broadway* (RKO; Harold Peary)

Feb. 1944 *Hail to the Rangers* (Columbia; Charles Starrett)

Mar. 1944 *Here Comes Kelly* (Monogram; Eddie Quillan)

Dec. 1943 *Hi'ya, Sailor* (Universal; Donald Woods)

Mar. 1944 *Hoosier Holiday* (Republic; Dale Evans)

Feb. 1944 *Hostages* (Paramount; Luise Rainer)

Feb. 1944 *King of the Cowboys* (Republic; Roy Rogers)

May 1944 *Klondike Kate* (Columbia; Ann Savage)

Mar. 1944 *Larceny with Music* (Universal; Allan Jones)

Feb. 1944 *Man from Music Mountain* (Republic; Roy Rogers)

Feb. 1944 *Mexicali Rose* (Republic reissue; Gene Autry)

Jan. 1944 *Never a Dull Moment* (Universal; Ritz Brothers)

Feb. 1944 *Nobody's Darling* (Republic; Mary Lee)

Feb. 1944 *O, My Darling Clementine* (Republic; Roy Acuff)

Jan. 1944 *Outlaws of Stampede Pass* (Monogram; Johnny Mack Brown)

Dec. 1943 *Petticoat Larceny* (RKO; Ruth Warrick)

Jan. 1944 *Pistol Packin' Mama* (Republic; Ruth Terry)

Jan. 1944 *Raiders of San Joaquin* (Universal; Johnny Mack Brown)

Feb. 1944 *Riders of the Deadline* (United Artists; William Boyd)

Mar. 1944 *Ridin' Down the Canyon* (Republic; Roy Rogers)

Jan. 1944 *Rookies in Burma* (RKO; Brown and Carney)

Apr. 1944 *Sagebrush Law* (RKO; Tim Holt)

Feb. 1944 *Sarong Girl* (Monogram; Ann Corio)

Jan. 1944 *The Seventh Victim* (RKO; Tom Conway)

Mar. 1944 *She's For Me* (Universal; David Bruce)

Feb. 1944 *Sing a Jingle* (Universal; Allan Jones)

Feb. 1944 *Smart Guy* (Monogram; Rick Vallin)

Feb. 1944 *So's Your Uncle* (Universal; Billie Burke)

Nov. 1943 *Someone to Remember* (Republic; Mabel Paige)

Mar. 1944 *Song of Texas* (Republic; Roy Rogers)

Jan. 1944 *Spotlight Scandals* (Monogram; Billy Gilbert)

Dec. 1943 *The Strange Death of Adolf Hitler* (Universal; Ludwig Donath)

Jan. 1944 *The Stranger from Pecos* (Monogram; Johnny Mack Brown)

Apr. 1944 *Sundown Valley* (Columbia; Charles Starrett)

Jun. 1944 *Swingtime Johnny* (Universal; The Andrews Sisters)

Jan. 1944 *Texas to Bataan* (Monogram; Range Busters)

Apr. 1944 *There's Something About a Soldier* (Columbia; Tom Neal)

Dec. 1943 *Thumbs Up* (Republic; Brenda Joyce)

Apr. 1944 *Timber Queen* (Paramount; Richard Arlen)

Dec. 1943 *Top Man* (Universal; Donald O'Connor)

Jan. 1944 *Wagon Tracks West* (Republic; Wild Bill Elliott)

Feb. 1944 *Whispering Footsteps* (Republic; John Hubbard)

Jan. 1944 *You're a Lucky Fellow, Mr. Smith* (Universal; Allan Jones)

As for the *13* top-billed co-features alongside which *Son of Dracula* played as the lower half of the bill within the sample of 1500 theaters, these are arranged alpha-betically below, with the month mentioned in each case again the earliest in which the pairing was attested. The titles on this list were either major studio A-pictures with a running time that exceeded that of *Son of Dracula*, or else comedies or installments in ongoing series that were being shown at houses where previous releases of their type had gone over especially strongly. All were exceptionally uncommon, with the use of Howard Hawks' Universal-released *Corvette K-225* restricted to a single major venue, the voluminous 3618-seat Loew's Metropolitan in Brooklyn, where *Son of Dracula* was essentially able to "ride on the coat tails" of the war-time epic, with the one-off double bill grossing a "great" $25,000 during a week-long stay that commenced on December 9, 1943. Meanwhile, the lavish 102-minute John Wayne Western *In Old Oklahoma* played top fiddle to *Son of Dracula* solely at Fanchon and Marco circuit houses in the city of St. Louis between January and early March 1944.

Feb. 1944 *Around the World* (RKO; Kay Kyser)

Dec. 1943 *Corvette K-225* (Universal; Randolph Scott)

Jan. 1944 *Crazy House* (Universal; Olsen and Johnson)

Feb. 1944 *The Dancing Masters* (20th Century-Fox; Laurel and Hardy)

Jan. 1944 *The Fallen Sparrow* (RKO; John Garfield)

Jan. 1944 *Government Girl* (RKO; Olivia de Havilland)

Feb. 1944 *Henry Aldrich, Boy Scout* (Paramount; Jimmy Lydon)

Jan. 1944 *In Old Oklahoma* (Republic; John Wayne)

Dec. 1943 *Is Everybody Happy?* (Columbia; Ted Lewis)

Mar. 1944 *Mexican Spitfire's Blessed Event* (RKO; Lupe Velez)

Mar. 1944 *True to Life* (Paramount; Mary Martin)

Dec. 1943 *The War Against Mrs. Hadley* (MGM; Edward Arnold)

Jan. 1944 *Whistling in Brooklyn* (MGM; Red Skelton)

With live stage accompaniment

The one percent of first-run bookings that paired *Son of Dracula* with a live entertainment performance fall broadly into two types. The first, in major cities, was readily comparable to the movie's Brooklyn opening alongside *Corvette K-225*, insofar as the horror film was effectively left to ride on the coat tails of the live attraction. Despite the prevailing subzero snap, Massachusettsans ventured out of their homes to see a bill of music, comedy and acrobatics headed by Glen Gray and his Casa Loma Orchestra at the RKO Boston Theatre in sufficient numbers for the bill to gross $25,000 in the course of a week-long engagement commencing January 6, 1944. Of the similarly high $23,000 gross at Cleveland's RKO Palace Theatre during the week of January 20, *Variety* wryly noted that "[b]lue chips are being raked into Palace by *Son of Dracula*, chiefly via heavy pull of Jan Savitt's band and Phil Regan." Contemporary reviews convey the impression that these events made for less-than-ideal environments for horror fans to secure their first glimpse of a new "classic monster" feature. *The Boston Globe* described the former engagement as being peppered with "girlish squeals" that led one to "[wonder] if Sinatra were in front of the mike," while *The Cleveland Plain Dealer* published its write-up of the latter show under the headline "Jitterbugs Spoil Good Palace Bill," with critic Glenn C. Pullen lamenting the "audience of noisy, unruly jitterbugs" who "shrieked and moaned in mock ecstasy" and "ran the gamut of childish exhibitionism in heckling the entertainers" to the extent that their "stomping and whistling" caused Phil Regan to break off his performance of "My Heart Tells Me" (from 20th

Part-live, part-undead show in Boston, January 6, 1944.

Century–Fox's *Sweet Rosie O'Grady*) and "rebuk[e] the exhibitionists."

The second type of bill, attested in small-to-medium-sized towns and cities, employed live entertainment of a strictly local character, and appears to have been at once less raucous, more ramshackle, and altogether less injurious to the possibility of enjoying the accompanying horror movie. While some of the live acts at such presentations were surely less than stellar – with news-

paper ads for a two-day opening at the Rivoli Theatre in La Crosse, Wisconsin, from January 28, 1944, for example merely promising an hour of unspecified variety numbers – others featured performers who enjoyed a significant regional following, such as singing cowboys Jim Hall and His Gang who headlined alongside *Son of Dracula* at the Pastime Theatre in Lumberton, North Carolina, for a two-day engagement commencing April 19, 1944.

The afterlife of a vampire: beyond the first run

Throughout the period from February to November 1944, plentiful second-run engagements of *Son of Dracula* took place in towns and cities of all sizes, at many of which the movie continued to be coupled with its original preferred co-feature *The Mad Ghoul*. A number of second-run theaters also seized the chance to pair it with Columbia's *The Return of the Vampire* starring Bela Lugosi, which had premiered a few days after *Son of Dracula* on November 11, 1943. In first run, the two pictures had occasionally opened at different venues within a single locality on the same day, as happened in Bonham, Texas, on December 9, 1943, but it was only at enterprising second-run theaters that the two started to be put together for one almighty double-bill vamp-off. In the 80,000-strong city of Lansing, Michigan, in particular, both movies had scored a phenomenal success (with their runs extended from four to seven days) when presented individually at the first-run Lansing Theatre in January 1944; and so it made sound business sense for the second-run Capitol Theatre to then book them *together* as an Easter weekend special that opened on April 7 (Good Friday), 1944. Lugosi also scored a peculiar (vam)pyrrhic victory of sorts over *Son of Dracula* in as much as he, rather than Lon Chaney Jr., was billed as the latter movie's star in ads for a number of theaters during all phases of its theatrical career, from first and second run through to repertory and reissue. Evidently Lugosi was so synonymous with the role of the Count that some theater owners, publicists and typesetters were simply unable to conceive of a Dracula movie not featuring him!

Bookings proved thin on the ground during 1945

Son of Dracula revived – with his dad! – in Philadelphia, November 7, 1946.

and much of 1946, until the Studio Theatre revival and exploitation house on Philadelphia's Market Street once again brought Lugosi back into the fold by screening *Son of Dracula* together with Universal's original 1931 *Dracula* for a week-long engagement beginning November 7, 1946. Promoted with simple-yet-eye-grabbing hand-drawn artwork, the so-called "double revival" more than earned its keep at the intimate 416-seat venue, and gave rise to a series of all-1940s-Universal-horror bills at metropolitan revival houses that variously paired *Son of Dracula* with *The Mummy's Tomb*, *House of Frankenstein* and *The Cat Creeps*. These revival showings may well have given impetus to Realart's October 1947 deal to reissue 24 Universal features at a rate of two per month.

Nominally identified in the trades as a January 1948 release, the earliest bookings of the Realart reissue of *Son of Dracula* took the form of week-long engagements at the Majestic (now the BAM Harvey Theater)

in Brooklyn, paired with *The Mummy's Tomb* from February 6, 1948, and then with its official Realart co-release, *The Ghost of Frankenstein*, at the Trans-Lux (later known as the State) in Boston from February 16. The *Son of Dracula-Ghost of Frankenstein* double bill additionally played for a week from May 27 at all five theaters of the Academy of Proven Hits revival house chain

Realart reissue bill in Boston, February 16, 1948.

in Los Angeles, which was operated by Paul Broder, the brother of Realart execs Jack and Al Broder. These Los Angeles screenings offered audiences the (slight) additional thrill of seeing "THE SON OF DRACULA *IN PERSON* ON STAGE" at all five venues – which was assuredly *not* a reference to Lon Chaney Jr. putting in a personal appearance! Engagements at revival and discount theaters remained steady throughout 1949 and 1950, with a lesser number of venues choosing to co-bill *Son of Dracula* with *The Invisible Man*, *Bride of Frankenstein*, *Frankenstein Meets the Wolf Man*, or – for the first time in its original English-language incarnation – *Captive Wild Woman*. Several prominent touring spook shows also made use of the Realart *Son of Dracula*, including magician and actor John Calvert's "Inner Sanctum Hour" from March 1948; Dr. Silkini's "Asylum of Horrors" featuring Jack Wyman on stage as the Frankenstein monster from June 1948; and Harry 'The Great' Valleau's "Hypnotic Thrill Show and Midnite Zombie's Jamboree" from October 1949.

Beginning in August 1951, *Son of Dracula* also formed part of Realart's "7 Days of Horror" package, which furnished theaters with 14 Universal reissues

John Calvert meets Realart in Tucson, March 13, 1948.

over the course of a week, making it possible to play a different double bill each day. The movie furthermore continued to play in support of newer genre works that included Realart's *Bride of the Gorilla* and Universal's *The Strange Door*, in addition to such sci-fi fare as *Invasion, U.S.A.* and even 2-D screenings of *Robot Monster*. As early as April 1951, Philadelphia's Girard Theatre had presented a double bill of Realart reissues of *Dracula's Daughter* and *Son of Dracula*, billed as "The Brother and Sister of Horror!"; and by July 1956, the Patio Theatre in Freeport, Illinois, could go one better by uniting the entire cape-loving family at a Friday the 13th midnight bill comprised of *Dracula*, *Dracula's Daughter* and *Son of Dracula*.

All three then made their way to television as part of Screen Gems' "Shock!" package of 52 pre–1948 Universal features that started to be rolled out from October 1957, giving rise almost overnight to the whole *Shock Theater*, Monster Kid and horror host phenomenon on a nationwide scale. *Son of Dracula* made its small-screen debut at 11.25 p.m. on November 11 (Veterans Day), 1957, on Channel 10 (WCAU) in Philadelphia, hosted by John Zacherle as Roland. Before the end of the year, the film had also aired on WGR in Buffalo, New York,

on KENS and KELP in San Antonio and El Paso, Texas, as well as on KTNT (now KSTW), covering the Tacoma-Seattle area of Washington. The first Los Angeles broadcast took place on Channel 5 (KTLA) at 9:30 p.m. on January 21, 1958, and the first New York City broadcast on Channel 7 (WABC) at 11 p.m. on April 10, 1958. By October 1958, *Son of Dracula* had played on stations from coast to coast, and on October 13 it experienced a return engagement on New York's WABC, hosted once more by John Zacherle during only his third week in his new guise as Zacherley. Having shifted allegiance from *The Mad Ghoul* to "The Cool Ghoul," the 1943 release would remain a staple of *Shock Theater* and *Nightmare Theater* programming, and was presented around the nation by a myriad of different hosts throughout the 1960s and 1970s.

Additional Reviews

Springfield (Massachusetts) *Republican*: Chaney's representation of the "undead" is a very corporeal one.

Pittsburgh Post-Gazette: [O]ur hero [Frank] … does away with both of them [Kay and Alucard]. Nothing personal, of course. Next week, *Dracula's Brother-in-Law*. …As Lew Lehr would say, things Draculian are getting screwier and screwier.

Cleveland Plain Dealer: *Son of Dracula* is, naturally, as bloodthirsty as Old Man Dracula of Bela Lugosi fame. It shoots the works in fantastic melodrama. One of its characters, a hayseed sheriff, goes around muttering, "This is incredible – just too incredible for me." His comment can be filed under the [heading] of understatements. …[Chaney] lays the weird blarney on so thickly that you will have a good laugh or two.

Motion Picture Exhibitor: This rates with the better shockers. The recent Paige-Allbritton buildup will also help the box office, but what is more this has the benefit of a stronger story than is usually seen in this type of thriller. … Production values are good, and the title, of course, is punch-packed. For houses that cater to the thrill trade, this is a natural.

The Princeton Bulletin: There are some good scary parts here and there and some good atmosphere, but we still expect Chaney to come out with a "which way'd he go, George" after *Of*

Ads for the film's WABC runs on April 10 and October 13, 1958.

Mice and Men.

Sydney (Australia) *Morning Herald*: [E]ven when a new and promising "terror" like Mr. Dracula's heir makes his debut in Universal's *Son of Dracula*, none laugh more heartily at him than the youngsters. …As the scowling Dracula junior, Lon Chaney is as terrifying as a grimacing child.

Schenectady (New York) *Gazette*: Before [Robert] Paige has destroyed Mr. and Mrs. Dracula Jr., there are enough horrible events to satisfy anyone who wants to see such things.

Asheville (North Carolina) *Citizen*: Son of Dracula…is not equal to the first Dracula film.

The Women's University Club: Although acting and direction are good, many people will hope that *Dracula* has no more progeny.

Minneapolis Sunday Tribune: The theme of the undead is a famous one in fiction, written or cinemized [sic]. In this instance, it gets standard, or A-1-A treatment, with cobwebs, low-key lighting, creaks and jittery incidental sound effects. …The bat which represents Mr. Chaney … is as clumsy as a wagtail pup, whereas Mr. Chaney as a wisp of smoke or as Mr. Chaney is possessed of some elegant grace.

The New York Times: Despite all the expected props, …this thriller is a pretty pallid offering. …The writers, it should be noted, show restraint in keeping the fatal casualties, including the count and his lady, down to four.

The Christian Century: A weird tale against everyday backgrounds, succeeds in producing dread, but certainly *not desirable* as film entertainment.

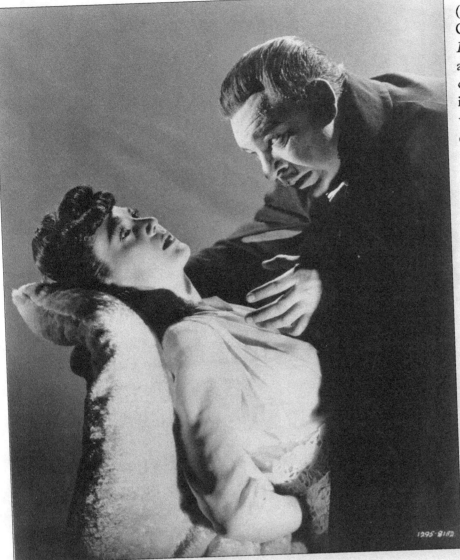

(Baltimore) *Evening Sun*: Comparison with the original *Dracula* of more than a decade ago is inevitable, and the son comes off second best. Perhaps it's because a wartime budget would not permit all of the elaborately macabre setting that enhanced the original….

(Montreal) *Gazette*: [Chaney's] opening metamorphosis from a bat won the applause of connoisseurs at the Princess yesterday but seems to have exhausted his acting powers. He chilled few. …[I]t was midnight so often in the picture that I went to sleep.

After Lon essayed Universal's flagship monsters Wolf Man, Frankenstein and Mummy, it occasioned little surprise when he next tackled the role of a Dracula. But nothing he does in the movie gives you the impression that Chaney has ever been anywhere east of Tuscaloosa, much less Transylvania.

WHEN LON DONNED THE DRACULA CAPE ... DID IT FIT?

By Rich Scrivani

First the Invisible Man came to America (*Invisible Agent*), then the Mummy (*The Mummy's Tomb*); next Dracula pulled up stakes and relocated here. Where's Homeland Security when you need 'em? (And by the way... what's with his feet in this photo?)

Ask most fans of Universal's Golden Age of Horror to name the best thing about of *Son of Dracula* and you might hear:

"It has a strong story by Eric Taylor and Curt Siodmak."

"It was well-directed by Robert Siodmak."

"George Robinson's atmospheric photography."

"There are a number of impressive visual sequences."

What you are likely *not* to hear: "Lon Chaney."

By 1943, Chaney was well-established as Universal's poster boy for screen horror. His Larry Talbot in *The Wolf Man* (1941) helped make the film a great success. He repeated the part in 1943's *Frankenstein Meets the Wolf Man* and in 1942 was cast as the Frankenstein Monster (*The Ghost of Frankenstein*) and Kharis the Mummy (*The Mummy's Tomb*). It was practically a foregone conclusion that he would don the vampire's cape in the upcoming *Son of Dracula*. But was his Midwestern American face and husky physical frame suitable for a character from whom viewers expected a measure of Continental charm?

David Pirie, author of *The Vampire Cinema*, took the position that it worked better "not having Chaney too sexually seductive"; Pirie felt that the actor "did his best in the part and the results were reasonable." In *A Quaint and Curious Volume of Forgotten Lore*, Frank Dello Stritto offered, "Chaney's best moments are by far without dialogue, for his stilted delivery simply does not work."

Chaney's Count Alucard was a vampire to be respected and feared, but was the actor portraying him properly cast? Could Chaney provide *any* of the nuances Bela Lugosi brought to the role of the Transylvanian nobleman in 1931? My answer to this question is unequivocally "no."

In the November 6, 1943, edition of the *New York Herald Tribune*, critic Otis L. Guernsey Jr. weighed in with: "Chaney is more wooden and less appealing than his ancestral vampire, Bela Lugosi, was in the original." Critic "G.K." was just a yak hair more flattering in November 19's *Los Angeles Times*: "Lon Chaney is fast catching up with his father in ability to project a horrific atmosphere."

One could go as far as to say that Chaney as Alucard was simply a case of miscasting. However, I have always been somewhat impressed by his performance. The question remains, then, did he have the talent to overcome these issues and somehow make the role his own? He may have fallen a bit short of that mark, but he did manage to create an arresting characterization using the abilities he had.

Chaney's best roles combined physical power with moments of vulnerability (Lennie in 1939's *Of Mice and Men*, "Dynamo" Dan in 1941's *Man Made Monster*, Larry Talbot). These qualities are most on display in *Son of Dracula*'s climax and help to make it one of the most vivid and exciting of Universal's 1940s horrors. Frank Stanley (Robert Paige) discovers Alucard's coffin in the drainage flume and sets it ablaze. Alucard appears on the scene, sees that Frank has torched his resting place and gives him the ragdoll treatment. Chaney, though, characteristically adds his touch of pathos with his desperate cries of "Put it out!"

Earlier in the story, Dr. Brewster's (Frank Craven) creepy encounter with Alucard in the Caldwell mansion basement is a chance for Chaney to deliver a quiet admonition nicely laced with menace:

> When I came to Dark Oaks, I was not graciously welcomed. Now the position is changed: *I* am master. Anyone who enters here without my permission will be considered a trespasser.

Though these words are uttered in a low voice, Chaney's delivery renders them a truly dire warning. If John Carradine had played this part, I'll risk the opinion that he would not have been as effective at that same speech; considering the Shakespeare in his background, I would imagine it coming across as more of a "grand announcement." And while I do feel that an

Blogger Keith Phipps wrote in 2018 that Chaney "tries to wrap his flat, American voice around purple lines that Lugosi would have turned into sonnets like, 'My land is dry and desolate. The soil is red with the blood of a hundred races. There is no life left there.'"

actor of Carradine's caliber might have made a more appropriate physical embodiment of Count Alucard, Chaney brought to the role a credible display of power that serves the film well.

In another scene where Chaney demonstrates brute strength, Alucard effortlessly hurls Frank from one room to another with just a single-handed shove. This striking moment foreshadows Dracula's (Christopher Lee) throttling of Van Helsing (Peter Cushing) at the conclusion of *Horror of Dracula* (1958). And one of *Son of Dracula*'s best visual effects is in the swamp scene where an Alucard baggage chest rises to the water's surface, and from it seeps vapor that transforms into the vampire's physical form. By the power of his will, he floats over the water's surface toward Kay on the bank. The sequence is hard to forget.

I must add that I will never forget a screening of *Son of Dracula* at film historian Tom Weaver's house. During the fiery final confrontation between the vampire and the leading man, Tom expressed his opinion in no uncertain terms:

"I like a Dracula who can kick ass!"

Fun Facts

By Tom Weaver

If vampires never age, how did the Son of Dracula ever get to be anything but a newborn baby?

Lon Chaney came *thisclose* to *not* getting the *Son of Dracula* title role: The Universal contractee was scheduled to go into the Army on December 21, 1942, which would have made *Frankenstein Meets the Wolf Man* his last picture for the duration of World War II. The 21st came and went and Lon remained in civvies, I don't know why. But Uncle Sam still wanted him. On February 7, 1943, gossip columnist Hedda Hopper ran this item: "Lon Chaney Jr.'s offering a bargain to someone. His station wagon, which is equipped with everything but a loudspeaker and set him back $3600 [over 52,500 in 2019 dollars], is up for sale. He's army bound."

In the early days of 1943, *Son of Dracula* was *not* the movie Chaney wanted to do next: For a year or more, he'd been counting on getting the top spot in Universal's remake of his dad's 1925 *The Phantom of the Opera*, and there had been times when, if gossip columns are to be believed, he *had* landed the macabre role (see the Hedda Hopper item above). But the Universal decision-makers went off the lot and signed Claude Rains for that Technicolor big-budgeter. Lon was "pretty bitter" about this turn of events, according to a January 1943 Hopper column. She continued, "When he first went into pictures, he declared he wouldn't do anything his father had, but when the *Phantom* came along, he was anxious to do it. Tells me he turned down a cook's job in the Coast Guard, expecting to get it."

If this new *Phantom* had been a close remake of the silent oldie, and the Phantom nothing more than the Paris Opera House's masked maniac in residence, Lon

THURSDAY, NOVEMBER 5, 1942

Hedda Hopper's HOLLYWOOD

"The Phantom of the Opera," which Universal has had on its schedule for lo these many months, will finally go before the Technicolor cameras in about three weeks, with none other than Lon Chaney Jr. in the role that his father created. George Waggner, who will produce it, and Lon have been haunting the Shrine Auditorium this week, where the San Francisco Opera is holding forth, to get atmosphere.

The femme lead is not set, but Gracie McDonald is being considered as the most like Mary Philbin, who did the role with Lon Sr.

Incidentally, the picture will be shot on the same stage that was built especially for the original version of the picture, and which has been called "The Phantom Stage" ever since.

The opening paragraph of a November 1942 Hedda Hopper column included good news for Lon Chaney fans. Unfortunately for Lon, it was *too* good to be true.

Jr. *might* have squeaked by. But in the opening scenes of Universal's 1943 re-imagining, we see the future Phantom as a milquetoast orchestra violinist. Assigning Lon Jr. that role would have been as fantastic a bit of casting as signing Rin Tin Tin to play a cow.

"Physical disabilities" got Lon nixed for military service, according to a February 1943 gossip column. It continued:

[A] few days before he left Talkie Town to go into the service, a bunch of pals got together and threw a soiree for Lon and gifted him with everything from pipe tobacco to silk striped undershorts. Now that he's been released from the army, Lon has returned all the presents the gals and guys gave him, and he's currently looking for a place to give them back the party they gave him originally.

French actress Michele Morgan was still a relative newcomer to the U.S. when she was interviewed by columnist Frederick C. Othman in April 1943. Morgan talked about doing *Joan of Paris* (1942), a tale of the French Resistance which antagonized the Nazis; she refused to do more movies like it because the Nazis now occupied France where her parents lived (and might pay a price). She told Othman that she turned down six such roles, and "then I had one other offer to play in a horror picture, about Dracula. I refused that on general principles." Given the timing, the picture must have been *Son of Dracula* and presumably the role of Kay.

Gossip queen Louella Parsons wrote in a January 1943 column that *Destiny* (*Son of Dracula*) "is a Universal drama that has been rumored for everybody from Dietrich to Gloria Jean."

From Hedda Hopper's January 17, 1943, column: "Alan Curtis has a romantic part in [*Son of Dracula*] he's not happy about. In *Flesh and Fantasy* he ran through a forest—the trees were trained to bash his head in. Now he has to dash through a swamp and be choked by Lon Chaney Jr. Says Alan, 'Trees are gentler.'"

As Gary Rhodes wrote in his production history above, Curtis sustained a knee injury on *Flesh and Fantasy* that kept him out of *Son of Dracula*. This was a break for Robert Paige, who inherited the part; for the most part, he'd hitherto been assigned to light comedy parts.

Dad's neck-biting inclinations have trickled down to his offspring but, apart from the standard-issue Vampire Uniform, Alucard doesn't remind you much of Lugosi's Dracula. This bloodsucker is physically imposing, boorish ("*Announce* me!"), mocking (his sweet smile as he tells the steaming-mad Frank, "I'm afraid I do not understand…"), patronizing (Alucard to Dr. Brewster, again with the taunting smile: "You see, *you* owe *me* an explanation") and bullying (stepping closer to the justice of the peace to spook him). No, he's not a bit like Bela; but he's an awful lot like Lon!

Robert Quarry to interviewer Don G. Smith, author of *Lon Chaney, Jr.—Horror Film Star, 1906-1973* (McFarland, 1996):

Two years before *Son of Dracula*, Robert Paige had a top role in *another* great unsung '40s horror flick, *The Monster and the Girl*. In this behind-the-scenes shot, Paige (behind star Ellen Drew) chats with director Stuart Heisler.

When [Lon Chaney] and I were both at Universal, Lon was having an affair with a young woman who booked films into the screening room. Sometimes after being with him, she would come to work wearing dark glasses to hide black eyes, or she would have bruises. One day I asked her, "Why do you put up with it?" She said, "He's very sweet when he's sober." Of course, that wasn't very often.

As Frank Stanley and Dr. Brewster wait on the train station platform for Count Alucard's arrival, there are wisps of steam in the air and we hear various train sound effects but we sure don't see a train, i.e., Universal didn't go to the expense of having a train, or any part thereof, on the set. It's kind of a Monogrammy way to shoot a meet-the-train scene, and no way to kick off the movie. (In an earlier shot when we saw a moving train through the depot windows, that was surely rear-projected train stock footage.)Fifteen years later, the indie *The Return of Dracula* featured a nearly identical scene and they too avoided

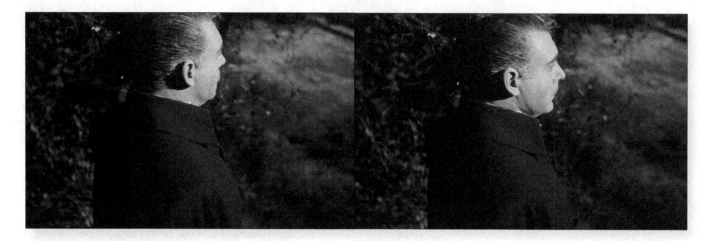

the expense of a train, this time by simply having the characters rush to meet the vampire's train but make a late arrival at the station!

One of *Son of Dracula*'s annoying shortcomings is that a few plot elements make no sense. At the train station, looking at Alucard's luggage and his coat of arms, Dr. Brewster notices that ALUCARD spelled backwards is DRACULA. But Dr. Brewster never heard of Dracula. Does he spell every new name backwards and then launch an investigation? It's as plausible as a *Return of the Vampire* character fixating on the fact that Tesla spelled backwards is Alset, a *Return of Dracula* character obsessing that Gordal spelled backwards is Ladrog, or an *Interview with the Vampire* character consumed by the knowledge that Lestat spelled backwards is Tatsel. It couldn't, wouldn't, shouldn't happen in any of these movies, *Son of Dracula* included.

Count Alucard wasn't the first vampire who liked to have fun with anagrams. Prof. Murray Leeder, the author of books about spiritualism and the cinema, points out that Alucard-Dracula could have been an idea with its roots in Sheridan Le Fanu's Gothic novella *Carmilla* (1871) and its bloodsucker Carmilla-Mircalla.

Perhaps the first (unintentional) laugh found in the script: Dr. Brewster's line to Frank, "The Count is coming for some duck hunting"!

Dark Oaks looks like a plantation that dates back to slave days, which isn't surprising: In real life, it's Universal's Shelby House, built for their *Uncle Tom's Cabin* (1927). And the plantation's name in *Son of Dracula*, Dark Oaks, calls to mind the Wilkes plantation *Twelve* Oaks in *Gone with the Wind* (1939). Then, too, there's Dark Oaks' assortment of black house servants and field hands. Between the black workers, a mule-drawn wagon, Frank Stanley coming and going on horseback, a house with no phone, etc., a sense of yesteryear permeates, and we get the impression that this little corner of the Land of Cotton has been mighty slow to make concessions to modern life.

The character is called Queen Zimba in the movie, Madame Zimba in the end credits and "Queen Zemba" on a music cue sheet. Frank Stanley has the best name for her: "that ol' swamp cat."

In the script, Kay is wearing riding togs when she goes sprinting over hill, dale and bullfrog to Queen Zimba's cabin. The movie improves on this by having her flit through the swamp blackness in a white gown reminiscent of the shrouds worn by lady vampires before her (Luna in *Mark of the Vampire*,

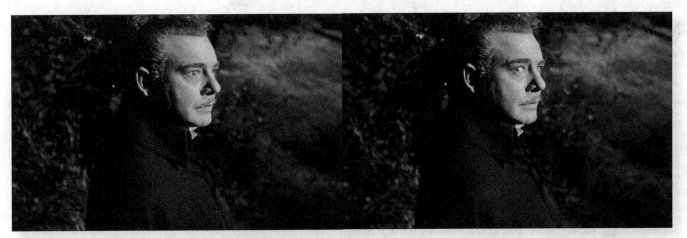

A great *Son of Dracula* moment: the start of the reception scene, as the camera (looking in the window) cranes back back back from the dancers until we see that Count Alucard is outside spying on the proceedings. It's as if he's become aware of our (viewers') presence as he slowly turns to give us a "You lookin' at *me?*" dirty look, before returning his attention to the activity inside. You don't often see "breaking the fourth wall" touches in horror oldies, but in a grotesque way, it works here.

1935) and after her (Jennie in *The Return of Dracula*). It's a great look for Kay, even if her dress' trailing train *is* picking up half the ticks in the bayou. The hiking-through-the-swamp scene, and other swamp scenes, were shot near Universal's Pollard Lake.

Queen Zimba looks like she's been living in that cabin since the Louisiana Purchase was still in the shopping cart, so it's a surprise to hear from Frank that Kay just now brought her over from Hungary. The ol' swamp cat certainly learned to speak English in a hurry, and her accent must have gotten lost in transit. When we see her dropping dried leaves(?) into her heated bowl of blood, she reminds us of Universal's favorite holy men, Kharis' various high priests, and their tana leaves rituals. The script specifies that the words of her incantation "are so indistinguishable as to be impossible to identify as voodoo or any other form of witchcraft that might get us in trouble."

Queen Zimba uses her bowl of blood like a crystal ball and sees Dark Oaks' future: "Weeds … vines growing over it … bats flying in and out the broken windows." The count should feel very much at-home there, as she's perfectly describing the cathedral-sized hall of Castle Dracula in the '31 *Dracula*.

In *Invisible Agent* (1942), Frank Griffin (Jon Hall), parachuting into Nazi Germany, becomes invisible as a four-note musical sequence repeatedly plays (A flat, D flat, G flat, D, for those of you with a keyboard at home). *Son of Dracula* made

The four-note Dracula theme heard in *Son of Dracula* and *House of Frankenstein*. (Courtesy Kathleen Mayne)

those four notes Dracula's theme. It's heard for the first time as the Dracula Bat, weirdly luminous, hovers in Queen Zimba's cabin doorway. The theme was reused in *House of Frankenstein* (1944) to mark the appearances of Universal's next Dracula, John Carradine.

The Dracula Bat invades Queen Zimba's cabin and never lays a talon on her, but it induces a heart attack in the old witch doctor. It's a nice grisly touch that as she slumps dead onto her table, her fingers are over her eyes, creating the impression that the bat snatched them out, even though it didn't.

The script in this book was Robert Siodmak's and it contains his scribblings throughout. Atop page 20, where Kay's retreat from the cabin is described, Siodmak hand-wrote "first app. [appearance] of Dracula against TREE." Apparently he was thinking of adding an exterior shot of the count lurking near the cabin, to make it clear to viewers that it was Alucard, in bat form, who "dood it."

For years, movie publicists writing about Samuel S. Hinds (*Son of Dracula*'s Judge Simmons) made mention of the unusual fact that he

Attention to Detail fans will appreciate this: According to musicologist Kathleen Mayne, when we see the musicians in the foreground during the reception scene, the bowing on the violin looks correct, as though the musician was actually playing the music. If one person was playing properly, probably they all were.

didn't become an actor until he was 53. Adeline De-Walt Reynolds, the wrinkle-faced five-footer who played Queen Zimba, makes Hinds' claim to fame less remarkable: *She* didn't begin her professional life as an actress until age *78.* "How old *was* she?": As a child, she watched Union soldiers pass her Iowa farm as they limped home after the Civil War. "My father believed in slavery, so he said, 'I don't want you feeding those damned Republicans.'"

"She has more energy and interest than most young-sters," director Robert Siodmak said of DeWalt Reynolds. "As a matter of fact, I've really had difficulty hold-ing her down in some scenes."

According to a 1945 article on "Addie," she "keeps in trim by fencing, swimming and tap-dancing. Now she's learning how to ride a horse...."

After playing Queen Zimba, the already el-derly DeWalt Reynolds lived another 18 years, about as long or much *longer* than the majority of the members of *Son of Dracula*'s screen-credited cast: By 1962, J. Edward Bromberg, Samuel S. Hinds, Pat-rick Moriarity, Etta McDaniel, George Irving and Frank Craven were all in their sarcophagi. Craven was the first to go, in 1945.

Son of Dracula is the first Dracula movie to show a vampire in the process of going from one form to an-other (man to bat and vice versa, vapor to man and vice versa). Honorable mention to *Mark of the Vampire*, which featured Luna as a woman-slash-bat in flight; *and,* in one of that movie's early script drafts, there was a flash-back scene in which the vampire, in the form of vapor, seeps into a room through the space under the bottom of a door.

On December 31, 1943, the reviewer for Louisville, Kentucky's *Cou-rier-Journal* newspaper reported that during a local theater's showing of the *Son of Drac-Mad Ghoul* double-bill, "the horror fans shouted, laughed and yelled by turns as one impossible situ-ation followed another. They even went so far as to ask young Count Dracula to 'do it again' when he dissolved into a vampire bat...."

The Universal Horrors didn't often provide work for black performers but *Son of Drac-ula* gave a passel of 'em a chance to put meat on the ta-ble. The only one to receive screen credit was Etta Mc-Daniel, who played Dr. Brewster's housekeeper Sarah. Etta's brother Sam plays the Caldwell house servant who answers the door and does a funny double-take at the sight of Alucard. Sam and their sister Hattie Mc-Daniel, an Oscar winner for playing Mammy in *Gone with the Wind* (1939), were known as the Dark Barry-mores. Although maybe jus' among theys selves.

Every time I watched *Son of Dracula* as a kid, I wondered how valet Steven got the wheelchair-bound Col. Caldwell from the ground floor to the second floor. The script contains the explanation: Steven carries Col. Caldwell upstairs, where a second wheelchair awaits.

Black actor Jess Lee Brooks, who plays Ste-ven, was stuck with servant and jungle native roles in Hollywood studio flicks but had more prominent parts in all-black indies. Apparently he was enough of a celebrity in *that* end of town that black papers occasionally splashed some gossip ink on his private life (see newspaper article above). He was born in Fort Benton, Montana, and died of a heart attack while driving to Paramount to continue playing his role as a hospital patient opposite Ray Milland in *The Lost Weekend* (1945).

To get a better look at Charles Moore, who plays servant Mathew, check out the slapstick "land yacht" scene in *Sullivan's Travels* (1941). When the land yacht (a giant trailer) goes off-road at high speed and starts hitting bumps, chef Moore is thrown around his kitchen in the back. After one bump, he hits the ceiling so hard that his head pops through the top of the trailer.

This ground was covered in *Scripts from the Crypt* #6, *Dracula's Daughter*, but it rates a second mention here: Universal never did get its act together when it came to vampires and mirrors. The rundown again: In *Dracula* (1931), Lugosi's Dracula has no reflection in a mirror. In *Son of Dracula*, Chaney's vampire *has* a reflection (in the hallway mirror outside Col. Caldwell's bedroom door). In *House of Dracula* (1945), John Carradine's Dracula and Onslow Stevens' Vampire Edlemann have no reflections. And in *Abbott and Costello Meet Frankenstein* (1948), Lugosi's Dracula *has* a reflection.

The shot of the three servants stomping out the fire in Col. Caldwell's bedroom always reminds me how much I enjoy Tip, Tap and Toe's *Pardon My Sarong* (1942) dance routine.

Son of Dracula exists "in a different universe" (as the kids say today) from the 1931 *Dracula* and the 1936 *Dracula's Daughter*: When Prof. Lazlo says that the vampire Dracula was destroyed in the 19th century, he makes us aware that the events in *Dracula* and *Dracula's Daughter* never took place in the universe of *Son of Dracula*. One of the pressbook articles actually refers to *Son*'s start-from-scratch approach: "Although *Son of Dracula* is not a 'continuation' of [the 1931 *Dracula*], it is based mainly on the same ghoulish legend of the vampire...."

The same tack was taken a year later by *The Invisible Man's Revenge*: All previous Invisible Man movies are kicked to the curb as a nutcase named Griffin (Jon Hall) becomes a guinea pig for a kooky recluse scientist (John Carradine) developing an invisibility formula. Coincidentally or maybe not, both of these out-with-the-old, let's-start-fresh series entries were Ford Beebe productions.

The script in this book opens with a scene not in the movie. In this scene, Dr. Brewster calls Dark Oaks "depressing" and "morbid," and says that Claire moved out because she could no longer stand it. In the movie itself, we learn that Dark Oaks has never had a phone, as though stuck in a past century; and when Kay says she wishes to continue to live there after her father's death, Dr. Brewster swears out an insanity complaint against her. Meanwhile, what do

Frank looks at Col. Caldwell's body and comments, "He looks as though he were literally frightened to death." But you see the colonel's face in the movie as well as you do in this still, and he doesn't look frightened at all.

Claire must be Kay's *younger* sister, because Judge Simmons mentions that Claire recently attained legal age. In real life, Evelyn Ankers (Claire) was then *older* than 22-year-old Louise Allbritton (Kay). Pictured: Samuel S. Hinds, Robert Paige, Allbritton, Ankers, Frank Craven.

viewers see of Dark Oaks? It's an immaculate place with a ballroom thronged with the pride and flower of the community, musicians playing, guests dancing, smiling servants eager to please, the swingin' times presided over by the gracious, good-humored Col. Caldwell and his two hostess-with-the-mostest pin-up–worthy young daughters. It's looks like the go-to spot for the bayou *beau monde*, not any kind of creep joint, and the Caldwells are a hit with everybody. So why all the negativity from Dr. Brewster?

Blooper: A bit after the movie's 20-minute mark, Frank leaves Dark Oaks and passes a window in which an off-camera boom microphone is clearly reflected.

Dr. Brewster tells Claire that he wants to have Kay declared insane and placed in an asylum. His evidence: Kay has an interest in the occult, like millions of other people; and (as mentioned above) she likes living at Dark Oaks, which looks like a *great* place to live. Any judge reading Dr. Brewster's insanity complaint would throw it out instantly, and then perhaps wonder how non compos *Dr. Brewster's* mentis is!

It's one of the great moments of '40s horror when Alucard's baggage box rises to the surface of the swamp water, vapor oozing out and coalescing into Alucard. In this same low-angle shot, we see him start to float toward the bank where Kay waits. Is it just Alucard, an Antichrist levitating across the water, or is the box beneath his feet like a slo-mo surfboard? The movie doesn't show us. I vote for the latter, perhaps because the scene makes me think of Charon ferrying newcomers to Hades across the River Styx. ...Okay, no it doesn't, but it *does* make me think of the ferry scenes in *Strangler of the Swamp*. The scene also makes me worry that the box might not be watertight.

In *Video Watchdog* magazine, Bill Cooke called the sequence "the stuff of Wagnerian opera." He goes on to say that *Son of Drac* is "arguably the most enjoyable Dracula film in the Universal canon."

Classic Horror Film Board stalwart and car enthusiast Hal Lane wants us to know that…

…Kay chauffeurs Alucard around in a somewhat ordinary 1939 six-cylinder Oldsmobile series 70 Club Coupe, while fiancé Frank follows in a much more cool upscale vehicle, appropriate for a guy who can afford a year-long honeymoon. It's a 1938 Packard 12-cylinder two-door convertible roadster, with two-piece raked windshield, center bar bumper guard, golf bag door and detachable "See-Rite" side mount notchstem mirrors, suitable for spotting vampires. Frank makes his courthouse break (after twice relating how his car was smashed by a tree) and speeds back to the swamp in a slightly older Packard with different details: lighter color, flat windscreen, suicide doors. Even if the movie tells us next to nothing else about him, we know that Frank's fleet is lousy with Packards.

Packard was one of the "Three P"s of American luxury vehicles: Packard of Detroit, Pierce Arrow of Buffalo and Peerless of Cleveland. And remember, PACKARD spelled backwards is DRAKCAP!

🦇 "Trailers from Hell"'s Joe Dante calls *Son of Dracula*'s script "occasionally faintly ludicrous, especially when the vampire has to take his inamorata to the justice of the peace before bedding her." Surely Alucard and Kay go to Justice of the Peace Kirby and marry because Universal knew it'd be risqué business to let them cohabitate unmarried under the Caldwell roof. You just *know* that it was Kay who popped the question, and I'd love to see the scene where she talked poor Alucard into it. Looks like she's already wearing the pants in the family. I'd also love to have been a fly on the wall for the presumably non-denominational ceremony, and to see if old Kirby got a tip.

Alucard and Kay in a love nest feathered without the blessings of a clergyman? Not in a 1943 movie, explaining their late-night visit to the justice of the peace.

🦇 The wind whistles and there's lightning and thunder as Alucard and Kay stand on the doorstep of the justice of the peace, as though Heaven is loudly protesting the union between the living and the undead. This is followed by a fade to black, but the script instead calls for a quick wipe to a "STOCK SHOT FROM MR. STALL'S PICTURE showing [Frank's] car driving to camera in a quick storm as a tree at the roadside crashes down in front of it, blocking the way." "MR. STALL" is director John M. Stahl and the movie is *When Tomorrow Comes* (Universal, 1939), which features a driver's point-of-view shot of a tree falling into the path of the car of stars Irene Dunne and Charles Boyer.

🦇 Alucard says he came to America because the pickens got mighty slim in his homeland, but 1943 audiences must have wondered if Nazis causing a führer in Europe mighta been another factor. For Dracula, keeping the local peasants off his grass was easy-peasy; dealing with a tank at his castle door, a regiment in his rec room and bombs over the Borgo Pass a whole 'nuther story.

Actually, a war-torn continent sounds like the *perfect* place for a vampire. Red, raging torrents of blood!

🦇 Dig the excited, pleased look on Kay's face as Alucard seizes Frank by the throat. As Alucard noisily shoves him through the double doors and onto the library floor, the stately Universal vampire briefly sinks (rises?) to the level of Universal's other Hall of Fame fiends (Frankenstein, the Wolf Man, Kharis, etc.), who went through every movie spoiling for fights. And Alucard does it without imitating a wild animal, as Count Christopher Lee of the later Hammer Draculas was wont to do when things got physical. It's

Don't pretend that you can see yourself in that mirror, Kay!

funny that there are fans who'll rag on Chaney for being stiff in *Son of Drac* but will happily praise Lee, who was always stiffer than a fold-out bed.

🦇 It's a good thing for Frank Stanley that Alucard *is* undead and impervious to his bullets. Try and picture Frank's murder trial, with Frank telling judge and jury, "I got in Alucard's face and antagonized and threatened him until he pushed me away, so I *had* to shoot him twice!" (Actually, he shoots Alucard four times: He pings two *more* bullets at him for good luck just before making his window getaway.)

🦇 Favorite moments from this scene: The Frank's-point-of-view shot of Alucard looking down at him on the library floor, gunsmoke (and silence) hanging in the air. Then, as Frank is edging back into the hall, the moving-camera Frank's-p.o.v. shot of Alucard as the vampire regards him quizzically and then lowers at him.

🦇 As mentioned earlier in this book, Curt Siodmak wrote in his autobiography *Wolf Man's Maker* that Bela Lugosi should have played the Son of Dracula. This strikes me as an absurd idea—the graying, puffy 1940s Lugosi as the *son* of the dark, sleek Lugosi from the 1931 movie. Yes, *Son of Dracula* exists in a "universe" where the 1931 *Dracula doesn't*, but try explaining that to 1943 viewers, who'd wonder why Dracula's son Lugosi looks older than his pop. As far as playing a member of a new, young, footloose generation of vampire, Lugosi's "use by" date had passed.

Siodmak went on: "Lon was on his worst behavior. His pet peeve was the then-reigning studio queen, Maria Montez. One night, Lon, in a drunken bout, threw feces at the bungalow shingle with Maria's name on it. In an alcoholic spell during shooting, he broke a vase over Robert's head. But Robert, always attracted to eccentric people, found Lon's behavior amusing. He was used to high-strung actors."

🦇 Curt Siodmak on *Son of Dracula* (*Starlog* magazine interview by Lee Server, 1990):

I had written one of my undying masterpieces, *Son of Dracula*, and I got Robert the job to direct. They gave him $125 [*sic*] a week. He came to me crying, "Look what they're paying me! It doesn't matter what the writer gets, but the

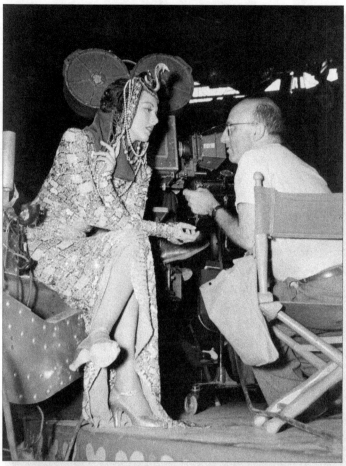

Maria Montez and director Robert Siodmak on the set of Universal's *Cobra Woman* (1944)—one of Chaney's next pictures after *Son of Dracula*.

director is so important." I said, "This is bullshit. Do it or not. I cannot get you any more money."

And then as soon as he began, I was off the job right away. He got another writer, Eric Taylor. He couldn't work with me. Who would be the boss? He couldn't push me around, I couldn't push him around. He only liked to work with new people.

…*Son of Dracula* became a kind of classic through Robert's handling of light and shadow. He was wonderful on mood, characterization, atmosphere, the psychology of it. He could make marvelous scenes. But he couldn't write. He had no construction. He would come and tell me his new ideas, and describe how he would do some scene—beautifully! But it didn't fit at all the story he was doing. It was just a scene. And Robert would try, psychologically, to destroy the writer and his work. He was best when he got a script he had to shoot in the next

Brawl in the Family: Kay's perfidious plan began with the killing of her own father. Her sister Claire (left) also needs to go.

Alucard, shoveling up soil for Kay's coffin with a sort of sacramental dignity, gets p.o.ed when unexpected company arrives. Alucard will be happier at Dark Oaks after he learns to lock the gate.

three days. Deadline. They call him, "You start in a week!" Then, he didn't have a chance of fooling around with the script and destroying it.

I liked director Reginald LeBorg (*The Mummy's Ghost* [1944], *The Black Sleep* [1956], *Voodoo Island* [1957], loads more), and when I interviewed him I got the impression that he was a straight shooter. But he told me this *Black Sleep* anecdote which I never found plausible:

There was—I won't say *hate*—but a rivalry going on between Chaney and Lugosi from the Universal days when they both played Dracula. You see, Lugosi was the great Dracula, but then something happened at Universal and they gave the part to Chaney [in *Son of Dracula*]. There was a terrible rivalry between them…and it came out on *The Black Sleep*. Chaney was sore at something Lugosi brought up and it nearly came to a fight. Chaney picked him up a little bit, but put him down—we stopped him. We kept them apart quite a bit.

Frank runs from the mansion until, gassed out, he collapses near a vault in a graveyard. The average viewer probably assumes he's ended up in a public graveyard. But later in the movie, when Alucard stashes Kay's body in the vault, we realize that this boneyard must be on the Caldwell property. According to the script, it's the *servants'* graveyard.

Speaking of the graveyard… In the Caldwell mansion, Frank shoots Alucard, plunges out the window and runs runs runs runs runs runs runs until the chopfallen fellow flops to the ground in the graveyard and passes out. But a little later, when Alucard (in the graveyard) watches Dr. Brewster arrive at the mansion, the graveyard is now a few steps from the driveway and front door! Did Frank run in a huge circle?

In the spring 2003 issue of *Monsters from the Vault* magazine, Bryan Senn covered *Son of Dracula* and wrote, "Actor Robert Paige told his cousin, James A. Healey, that [Robert] Siodmak wanted to shoot a real bat crawling on the actor's neck during one scene. Understandably, Paige refused, so the effects people dyed a mouse brown and attached plastic wings to create the nocturnal marauder."

Because Frank fell to the ground near a cross, Alucard can't get near him to finish him off. Wuss! In the same-year *The Return of the Vampire*,

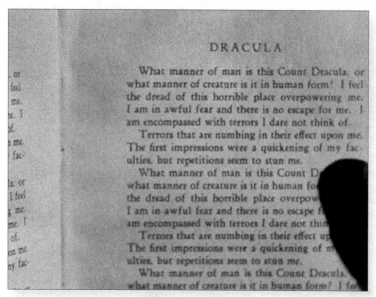

DRACULA

What manner of man is this Count Dracula, or what manner of creature is it in human form? I feel the dread of this horrible place overpowering me. I am in awful fear and there is no escape for me. I am encompassed with terrors I dare not think of.

Terrors that are numbing in their effect upon me. The first impressions were a quickening of my faculties, but repetitions seem to stun me.

What manner of man is this Count D... what manner of creature is it in human fo... the dread of this horrible place overpow... I am in awful fear and there is no escape f... am encompassed with terrors I dare not thin...

Terrors that are numbing in their effect up... The first impressions were a quickening of m... ulties, but repetitions seem to stun me.

What manner of man is this Count Dracula... what manner of creature is it in human form? I fe...

This insert shot is seen as Dr. Brewster reads the novel *Dracula*. On both of the pages seen, the same two paragraphs appear over and over and over.

bloodsucker Tesla (Bela Lugosi) makes a cemetery his home base and prowls around amidst a *forest* of crosses! P.S.: In the *Son of Drac* graveyard scene, the shot of the moon was the *first* shot in *Frankenstein Meets the Wolf Man*.

Perhaps partly because so many actors were off fighting the war, the early to mid–1940s was a high point in horror history for fans of female monsters, creeps and other oddities. Along with Louise Allbritton's vampiric Kay, the list includes Virginia Bruce (the title role in *The Invisible Woman*), Simone Simon (the cat-woman in *Cat People*), Jean Brooks (a devil worshipper in *The Seventh Victim*), Christine Gordon and Veda Ann Borg (zombies in *I Walked with a Zombie* and *Revenge of the Zombies*, respectively), Acquanetta (the Ape Woman in *Captive Wild Woman* and *Jungle Woman*), Vicky Lane (the Ape Woman in *The Jungle Captive*) and Nina Foch (a werewolf in *Cry of the Werewolf*).

Dr. Brewster learns during his phone conversation with Prof. Lazlo that Dracula was a Transylvanian nobleman of the Middle Ages, probably as unheard-of in Small Town 20th-century Louisiana as every *other* Transylvanian nobleman of the Middle Ages. But somehow Brewster very promptly lays hands on *Dracula*, a whole book about the guy. We see a page and, strangely, what should (in *this* "universe," in this free-standing sequel) be a biography of a medieval aristocrat is written in first-person in the breathless style of a vampire story.

Actually, the paragraphs we see in Dr. Brewster's copy of *Dracula* are from Stoker's *Dracula*. Kinda.

Brewster's copy: "What manner of man is this Count Dracula, or what manner of creature is it in human form? I feel the dread of this horrible place overpowering me. I am in awful fear and there is no escape. I am encompassed with terrors I dare not think of."

Stoker's *Dracula*: "What manner of man is this, or what manner of creature is it in the semblance of man? I feel the dread of this horrible place overpowering me; I am in fear—in awful fear—and there is no escape for me; I am encompassed about with terrors that I dare not think of…"

There's a neat transition when we go from a shot of Dr. Brewster putting Frank to bed (getting Frank to lie down on the office couch, covering him with a blanket) to a shot of Alucard doing the same for Kay (using a flat-headed shovel to spread a layer of soil at the bottom of her coffin).

As Alucard escorts Dr. Brewster into Kay's dusky bedroom, the background music fades and a mausoleum silence falls upon the soundtrack. And then the cold stare of George Robinson's camera captures the gripping m.o.s. shot of Kay (now a countess, after that quickie wedding) sitting up in bed. She looks waxen, her lips are fuller and darker, and her fur bed jacket covers her throat. Perhaps purposefully, the framing gives her too much headroom, adding to the sense of weirdness. To quote Lord Byron (the one in *Bride of Frankenstein* of course, not the real one), "*That* was a pretty chill!"

Alucard tells Dr. Brewster that he spends all his daylight hours "engaged in some scientific research." A Dracula played by Lon Chaney claiming to be a disciple of science? Now pull my *other* leg! It's easier to "buy" it when Dracula is John Carradine (in *House of Dracula*, turning to science for a cure) or Bela (in *A&C Meet Frankenstein*, going the Mad Scientist route himself). Lon eventually did play a scientist – ridiculously, hilariously – in the shoestring horror anthology *Dr. Terror's Gallery of Horror* (1967).

Dr. Peters, who talks about Frank's mental state in the sheriff's office, was played by

The newest initiate into the world of the hungry dead, Countess Dracula, *née* Katherine Caldwell.

London-born actor Cyril Delevanti, father-in-law of *Son of Drac* producer Ford Beebe. Beebe also found room for "Dad" in the casts of several other features and serials, most memorably giving him the role of the gnarled gatekeeper Torque in *Night Monster* (1942). The two probably had a bit more in common than most fathers-in-law–sons-in-law: They were born around the same time in the 1880s. In fact, Beebe may have been *older* than his father-in-law.

The script called for bloodstains on Kay's gown, but next to this paragraph, Robert Siodmak wrote **Hays**. And sure enough, there's no blood on her gown in the movie, perhaps due to Censorphobia. Siodmak wrote **Hays** near other script passages as well; see the illustration below.

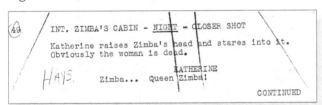

For a long uninterrupted stretch, over a third of the movie, Frank Craven is in every scene, usually the center of attention. Because film fans know Craven best as the wry, pipe-smoking on-camera narrator of *Our Town* (1940), and *Son* also has a small-town setting, his pipe-smoking presence in *Son*'s cast gives it a bit of an *Our Town* flavor. There are also whiffs of *Shadow of a Doubt* (1943), in which a serial murderer on the lam takes his place amongst the unsuspecting residents of a town similarly overstocked with wide-

eyed innocents and "Americana." Both *Our Town* and *Shadow of a Doubt* were written by Thornton Wilder.

Monster Kids debate whether Alucard is Count Dracula or the count's son. In the opening credits, the screen-filling "And LON CHANEY As COUNT DRACULA" confuses the issue right off the (pardon the pun) bat. But the title of the movie is ***Son of Dracula***, dagnabbit, and, in the long conversation between Dr. Brewster and Prof. Lazlo, the latter—an expert on Dracula—flat-out declares that the vampire Alucard is "probably a descendant of Count Dracula." Case closed as far as I'm concerned, Alucard is the son, and not the paterfamilias of the vampire tribe. But then, less than two minutes later in the same conversation, Brewster and Lazlo discuss the fact that Alucard died and was buried in Hungary, so now these two assholes have done a U-ey and are calling him the original Count Dracula!

You tell yourself that this was just a slip-up and that Alucard is the son. Then the movie proceeds to the jail cell scene and Kay tells Frank that Count Alucard's real name is Count Dracula:

Frank: You mean the Hungarian who's supposed to have become a—

Kay [*cutting him off*]: Don't use that word, Frank. We don't like it.

Kay never corrects Frank by adding, "No, Alucard is Count Dracula's son." After making Frank think that Alucard is the original Count Dracula, she leaves it there.

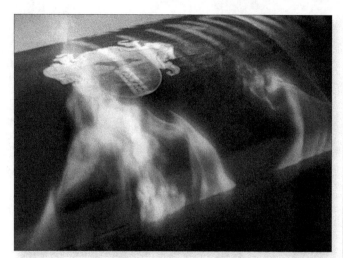

Vape escape! Shape-shifter Kay rises from her coffin the easy way (and then, off-camera, goes from vapor to bat).

I read scores of *Son* reviews from around the U.S. (and ones from Canada and Australia) and not a single critic thought Alucard was anything but a chip off the old bat.

🦇 The pressbook writers were also on the "Son side" of this hot-button issue. According to its synopsis, Dr. Brewster "suspects Alucard, whose name is 'Dracula' spelled backwards, of relationship to the infamous vampire," and one of the articles flat-out calls Alucard "a descendant of the 'vampire' man." A nearly full-page illustration has the big header **LIKE FATHER, LIKE $ON**. But the trailer seems to take the "Alucard *is* Dracula" side: It opens with the screen-filling words "THE HORROR THAT IS DRACULA returns…"

🦇 From William K. Everson's program notes for a 1983 *Son of Dracula* screening at Manhattan's New School: "*Son of Dracula* is actually a misnomer, since it appears that it's merely Dracula Sr. up to his old tricks again…." Well, Everson couldn't *always* be right.

🦇 More from Everson's program notes:

Son of Dracula was perhaps the last really good Universal horror film, before they turned the genre into as standardized a product as the B Western. …Despite its genre plot and trimmings, *Son of Dracula* is also very much of a film noir: a nightmarish story of entrapment, morbidly obsessed with death, and in which the nominal hero (Robert Paige) is quite as much of a "loser" as Mitchum or Lancaster in

A son of Hungary, J. Edward Bromberg plays Prof. Lazlo, who comes into the story as a laid-back character making light of his "vampire expert" rep. With the gray hair and glasses, he looks older than his real-life 39.

more traditional noirs. …[I]n the best German traditions of Lang, the color and glamor are all vested in the villain-vampires, and those pitted against them are a pretty drab, colorless lot. … Son of Dracula is a welcome reminder of the real care and craftsmanship that still went into relatively minor films in the '40s … especially when a director trying to establish a reputation for himself, was at the helm.

🦇 Prof. Lazlo is played by J. Edward Bromberg, bespectacled and made-up to look older and owlish when actually the actor was still on the sunny side of 40. Lazlo is this movie's Van Helsing surrogate, a character required by the rules of vampire film etiquette, but he's more like a Van Helsing in training: In his first scene, talking on the phone with Dr. Brewster, he says he neither believes nor disbelieves in vampires, and there's a touch of self-deprecation when he laughingly calls himself "somewhat of an authority on the subject." Hearing Frank's story nudges Lazlo over to the Believer side of the aisle, and he drives a stake into the movie's forward momentum by giving Dr.

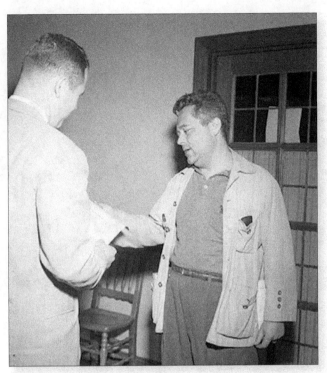

Serves him right?: In June 1951, J. Edward Bromberg – reputedly a Communist Party member – got a subpoena from a HUAC investigator (pictured) requiring him to testify. The actor was perspiring and pill-popping (he claimed to have a rheumatic heart) as he refused to answer the Committee's questions and accused them of witch-hunting. Before the year was out, stressed-out 47-year-old Bromberg was dead. Guess he wasn't kiddin' about that bad heart.
Actress Lee Grant had worked with Bromberg on stage. She claims in her autobiography that she was "young, basically uneducated and really ignorant," and didn't know from nuthin' about Communists, HUAC or anything else. Then, for being one of the speakers at his memorial service in New York City, she was blacklisted for 12 years.

Brewster a disquisition on vampires in a scene that's way too lengthy, and with too many close-ups.

But Prof. Lazlo's not quite ready to walk the Van Helsing walk: Monster Kids knew Van Helsing; and professor, you're no Van Helsing. When Alucard confronts Lazlo and Brewster, Lazlo is stunned into silence as the vampire does all the talking. (However, at the decisive moment, Lazlo does come up with a cross and saves the day.)

A friendly, good-humored guy, Lazlo is no doubt a hit around the Muirfield University water cooler, but when the going gets tough in the Alucard case, he never takes charge; he's just Dr. Brewster's easygoing tag-along pal. He's nothing at all like *Dracula* 1931's

Van Helsing (Edward Van Sloan), a monument to mirthlessness who swept into other people's homes and started giving orders like a military field officer.

The scene between Prof. Lazlo and Alucard coulda been a highlight, but the cat's got Lazlo's tongue, while Alucard makes a speech in which he mispronounces virile ("*vair*-al") and decadent ("duh-*kay*-dent"), so the opportunity is muffed. According to the reviewer for the *Rochester-Democrat* newspaper, "Chaney is an impressive evil figure when doing pantomime; when he speaks, his diction makes it hard to believe he is a Hungarian count, alive or undead."

Michael Brunas, co-author of *Universal Horrors*, also found Chaney to be miscast: "One gets the feeling that if Ward Bond, Broderick Crawford or Barton MacLane (all successful studio players in the same approximate range as Lon) were born with the name Chaney, Universal would be fitting them into a Dracula cape as well."

In 1949, Bromberg starred as Van Helsing in an Arden, Delaware, stage production of *Dracula*. Local newspapers, probably misinformed by the theater or maybe by Bromberg himself, wrongly reported that he was repeating the part he'd played in *Son of Dracula*.

Another difference between *Dracula* and *Son of Dracula*: In *Dracula*, the count is a fascinating, commanding character and he's all that the other characters talk about and, even though he's not on-camera a lot, his presence pervades every scene. In *Son of Dracula*, ol' Drac (well, Alucard) simply adds to his family's long résumé of mayhem in the conventional manner, while Kay is the offbeat, intriguing character. In fact, Alucard's destruction is just one step in the build-up to the point in the picture that viewers are probably more eager to reach, the final disposition of Kay.

Does *Son of Dracula* have *the* most powerful ending of all the Universal Horrors?: Frank standing mutely, perhaps in shock, as his former flame is reduced to ashes? (Notice that as the camera moves in for Frank's close-up, the actors behind him scoot out of the way so that he'll have the frame to himself at the fade.) If viewers think about the movie immediately after it ends, I bet they're thinking about Kay and Frank, not Alucard.

It was once pointed out to me that, in *Dracula's Daughter*, Gloria Holden, playing the title character, never blinks, at least not in close-ups or medium close-ups or anything close. And I've found that to be true. And it looks to me like Chaney never blinks in *Son of Dracula*—at least never in close-ups or medium close-ups. (Well, the brightness of the drainage tunnel fire makes him wince, but under those circumstances he probably couldn't help it.) And in Kay's first scene as a vampire, sitting in bed talking to Dr. Brewster, she doesn't blink either. I didn't check for this in her never-ending jail cell scene with Frank.

Maybe, like a lot of TV series, Universal's Dracula series had a "bible" full of dos and don'ts, and "Vampires don't blink" was one of them.

🦇 The script starts with a six-page scene between Frank and Dr. Brewster, during which little Tommy Land makes an appearance; he'd cut his hand and now it's bandaged. That scene is not in the movie. But notice that when vampire-bit Tommy is on Brewster's examining table, his hand is bandaged (see photo on page 26). Notice also that Tommy's bite marks are spaced far enough apart that it's obvious that the count went for the jugular in two-legged form, not bat form.

🦇 How long would Alucard's Southern-fried reign of terror have lasted? Probably not long. As soon as the count and countess began their series of vampire attacks, surely investigative lights would have begun shining on the newcomer who arrived in town waving his freak flag high. (I'm reminded of one character's reaction to caped weirdo Paul Wegener in 1926's *The Magician*: "He looks as if he had stepped out of a melodrama.") Heck, Alucard's very first victim Tommy Land survives and instantly pegs his attacker as "a foreign man" and got a good-enough look at him to make a police sketch artist's job a cinch. I'm picturing Alucard in a police lineup, sweatin' like a priest in a playground as little Tommy is gently escorted into the room.

🦇 The authorities place Kay's coffin in the county morgue. The only problem with *that* is, there have been no counties in Louisiana since around 1810. Monster Kid Scott Gallinghouse, who hails from the Creole State, tells me, "We are unique in the United States in having *parishes* instead of counties. We haven't had counties since we went the ecclesiastical route, so that reference to a county would be wholly erroneous!"

If we set aside *Abbott and Costello Meet Frankenstein* (entertainment perfection!), *Son of Dracula* is the last high-quality movie in the long line of thrillers featuring Universal's brotherhood of monster creations. Any arguments?

🦇 The blustery sheriff declares that Frank Stanley's money and position "don't rate him any better treatment than anyone else from me." It becomes obvious that Frank is receiving no special treatment when we see him in his jail cell wearing the same stained, grubby shirt from days earlier! By the end of this 80-minute movie, Frank has been wearing that shirt since the 27-minute mark.

🦇 From the 31-minute mark where we see Dr. Brewster reading *Dracula*, to the 57-minute mark, the movie turns into what could pass for the Halloween episode of the *Hangin' with Dr. Brewster* TV show, a real talkfest, and *this* leads into the interminable (14-minutes-plus) series of courthouse scenes that take us past the 72-minute mark. The script starts to drag and Robert Siodmak didn't do enough to take the curse off this arid stretch. And some critics noticed. Mildred Martin of *The Philadelphia Inquirer*: "It spends too much time listening in [on] long, presumably informative conversations between a distracted doctor and a Hungarian scientist who knows all about vampires. Horror exhibits shouldn't develop into conversation pieces. ...Frank Craven and J. Edward Bromberg are the garrulous old boys who'll talk your ear off if you let them."

🦇 As you'll see by the copy of the script in this book, Robert Siodmak did a lot of re-writing of the dialogue in the Frank-Kay jail cell scene, making it plainer that Kay is double-crossing Alucard for her benefit and Frank's. This plot twist—a duplicitous dame pretending to be in love with a man but only to help the guy who *really* lights her fire—must have appealed to Siodmak because we find it again in *The Killers* (1946), his film noir adaptation of Ernest Hemingway's short story. The *Killers* femme fatale is Kitty (Ava Gardner in her first major part), girlfriend of gangster Big Jim Colfax (Albert Dekker). Colfax plans a heist and brings in ex-pug "The Swede" (Burt Lancaster)—but Kitty pays the Swede a middle-of-the-night call to tell him that Colfax and the others plan to keep his share of the money. The Swede double-crosses the double-crossers, taking it all and running away with Kitty. But then *she* gloms onto the loot and runs out on *him*; Kitty *is* loyal to Colfax, and this was their way of getting it all for themselves. Kitty makes a chump out of the Swede exactly the way Kay made a chump out of the count.

The Classic Horror Film Board's Frederick Rappaport once pointed out this link between Siodmak's fright flick and his films noir, and concluded his post with, "I love the way *Son of Dracula* posits that even one as formidable as the Prince of Bloodsuckers can be played for a patsy by a two-timing dame."

🦇 *The Killers'* Ava Gardner is so good as the double-dealing Kitty that one wonders what this belle of the South (North Carolina) could have done with the role of Kay.

🦇 One more bit of proof that Alucard is *not* the original Dracula: Kay couldn't have played the real Dracula like a fiddle, the way she does Alucard.

🦇 In Frank's jail cell, Kay transforms into mist and seeps through the bars, en route to get the jailer's keys. In the script (see page 191 of this book), she becomes invisible and, in shots that would make viewers think of an Invisible Man movie, the jailer's desk is searched by unseen hands until a gun and the keys seem to float up out of the drawers and then float to Frank's cell.

🦇 Speaking of the plot twist of a woman pretending to be in love with a man but only to help the guy she actually loves: We find it again in the low-budget *Blonde Ice* (1948), with Leslie Brooks as the scheming

"The girl was morbid. That often means thanatophobia, fear of death." – Prof. Lazlo explains why Kay Caldwell (Louise Allbritton) went off the moral rails.

Son of Dracula ads called Louise Allbritton's ruthless Kay Caldwell "The Screen's New Temptress of Terror."

Unable to save the burning coffin, Alucard prepares to turn his fury *on* Frank. Lon Jr. never looked more than his dad than when he made his "Oooooh, now you're gonna *get* it!" face and did that claw-like thing with his hand.

female. Once more we flash back to *Son of Dracula* because the guy she *really* loves is again Robert Paige!

🦇*Son of Dracula* is set in a somnambulant Louisiana town but, except for the black players, *no one* tries for even a single syllable to sound like they live Down South. You'd think you were watching one of the Kharis pictures set in New England.

🦇Claire visits Frank in jail and, just before Frank's escape, as Brewster and Lazlo talk on the sidewalk in front of the courthouse, we hear passing cars and see a couple of pedestrians pass. The courthouse is open and the sheriff and his men are on duty. In 1943, was *every* Louisiana small town this wide-awake and active at what must be around five o'clock in the morning?

🦇In the drainage tunnel, Alucard uselessly swats at the burning crate with a wide plank, when there's a pool of water just a couple feet away. Watching this scene, all I can think is that on the night that the principles of firefighting were taught at Transylvania U, Alucard must have stepped out to get something to drink.

🦇As you'll see when you read the script, the plan for the Frank-Alucard tunnel encounter was for the scene to be a bit longer and the action to be even more hot'n'heavy, with Frank plinking more bullets into Alucard, Frank's clothes afire after Alucard hurls him toward the blazing coffin, and Alucard spouting more Bad Guy dialogue. At one point, Alucard

rages at Frank, "You would destroy a Dracula?"—another possible hint that Alucard is the Son. In your mind's ear, can you hear Bela Lugosi referring to himself as "*a* Dracula"?

In the interests of full disclosure, I also can't hear Bela telling the vampire bride who has presented him with a newborn son, "Let's name him *Anthony*," which according to the script is Count Alucard's first name.

🦇According to a news blurb that ran in 1945 newspapers, the same ornate gold and onyx Dracula ring was worn in 1930 by Lugosi in *Dracula* and in 1943 by Lon in *Son of Drac*, both times rented from H.B. Crouch, a Wilshire Boulevard jeweler. Universal was ready to rent it again for John Carradine in *House of Frankenstein* but it had been recently sold; "So the Crouch artisans produced a new Dracula-crested ring, which the studio purchased outright this time, just to be on the safe side." Does this *ring* true to you? I don't think there even *was* such a jeweler.

🦇We see Frank breathlessly running through the swamp to the drainage tunnel in a day-for-night shot. Four minutes later, after his battle with Alucard, we see the same Running Frank footage again, this time day-for-day, representing his flight *away* from the drainage tunnel. Did Frank just run in another big circle?

🦇Dramatically, visually and music-wise, *Son of Dracula*'s final shot is perfection, as the devastated Frank and the spellbound folks around him wordlessly stare into the raging playroom fire. Well,

In the jail cell, Kay stressed to Frank, "Be sure you don't get [to the drainage tunnel] until after the sun is up." Frank pays a price for not being a good listener. Notice that, in the first shot, Frank is unaccountably wearing a jacket.

The set of Universal's star-studded *Follow the Boys* (1944) would have been a good place to do *Son of Dracula* interviews. In the front row, right to left, having a mini–*Son* reunion, Evelyn Ankers, Robert Paige and Louise Allbritton. Skip past Andy Devine and Maria Montez and find Alan Curtis, the original choice for the role of Frank. Behind Devine, it's *Son*'s Samuel S. Hinds.

near-perfection: It always bugs me that not one of them—not even the sheriff or his deputy—has enough of a sense of civic responsibility to want to call the fire department. Maybe they know the mansion doesn't have a phone. Oh, well. Burn, baby, burn!

Son of Dracula was just one of several Universal features and shorts in which studio contractees Lon Chaney and Robert Paige both appeared. In this shot from 1943's *Frontier Badmen*, top-billed hero Paige mocks scarred baddie Lon.

🦇 In the latter part of *Son of Dracula* production, *Phantom of the Opera* got underway with Claude Rains in the title role that Lon Jr. had coveted. A biggie for Universal, *Phantom* was no doubt the talk of the lot the whole time it was shooting, so Lon might have been relieved that after *Son of Dracula*, he wasn't immediately placed in another picture. Bad enough to have been passed over for *Phantom*; but it might have been humiliating to have to work on the lot at the same time, playing (say) a supporting part in a crummy Western, or a Mummy movie, or a non-speaking part. Universal found more roles for Lon in the spring and summer: a supporting part in a crummy Western (*Frontier Badmen*), a Mummy movie (*The Mummy's Ghost*) and a non-speaking part (*Cobra Woman*).

🦇 According to Harrison Carroll's March 1, 1943, "Behind the Scenes in Hollywood" column, a few weeks after *Son of Dracula* finished up: "Husky-looking Lon Chaney, who never felt better, has been turned down by the Army—blood pressure too high and pulse too fast. Incidentally, Lon asks me to deny emphatically the reports of a rift in his marriage." From Ed Sullivan's "Little Old New York" column, March 3, 1943: "Young Chaney was sent home, 4-F, with a bad heart he never knew about."

🦇 *Son of Dracula* was one of five Universal Horrors featuring both Lon Chaney and Evelyn Ankers and the only one in which they're never seen together. This perhaps pleased Evelyn, who had little use for the Lonster. She tells why in "The 'B' and I," her introduction to Doug McClelland's 1978 book *The Golden Age of "B" Movies*. Her best zinger in that chapter was a throwaway line: "To get back to *The Mad Ghoul* (not Lon Chaney, but the movie of that title)…."

🦇 *Son of Dracula*'s main title music was heard again at the start of *The Spider Woman Strikes Back* (1946). In that movie, the opening credits were superimposed over a nighttime shot of Universal's Shelby House, i.e., *Son of Dracula*'s Caldwell mansion. The Shelby House behind the *Son of Drac* credits might have been a nice touch, rather than the solid black.

"Bela's Funeral," a portentous music cue from *The Wolf Man*, plays as Kay arrives at Queen Zimba's creepy cabin.

Universal may have skimped on the trimmings in a scene or two but production-wise *Son of Dracula* is still heads and shoulders above the usual run of the company's '40s fright flicks. (A prime example: *Son*'s co-feature, the dashed-off *The Mad Ghoul*.) And *Son* runs a "deluxe" 80 minutes, at a time when many other Universal Horrors barely cracked the hour mark. But when it came time to score the picture, the purse strings were suddenly drawn tight: Once you get past Hans J. Salter's main title cue, nearly all of *Son*'s music came from earlier pictures. Here's a rundown:

As Kay leaves the Caldwell mansion on foot for Queen Zimba's cabin, we hear the Charles Previn–composed cue "Wolf-Bane," originally heard in *The Wolf Man* during Larry Talbot, Gwen and Jenny's trip to the gypsy camp. Once Kay enters the cabin, it segues into a cue that the *Son of Dracula* cue sheets call "Queen Zemba" [*sic*] but it's actually more *Wolf Man* music: Frank Skinner's "Bela's Funeral." When the bat appears in the doorway, we get the abovementioned *Invisible Agent* cue, four notes of which serve in *Son of Dracula* as Dracula's theme (and Kay's theme, once she's vampirized).

We join the reception in progress as the on-camera musicians play Frank Skinner's waltz "When I Fall in Love" from the New Year's Eve party scene in *Back Street* (1941). When Alucard goes batty and invades the house, there's organ improvising mixed with the four-note Dracula theme. The *Son of Dracula* cue sheets indicate that the Jean Le Seyeux-Werner H. Heymann "Valse Coquines" and Frank Skinner's "Breakfast for Two" are the numbers played by the party musicians as Frank and Kay talk outside.

When Dr. Brewster and Claire snoop around in the Caldwell guest house, the Frank Skinner music cue "Limehouse" is from *Sherlock Holmes and the Voice of Terror* (1942)

Kay sets out in her car for a swamp rendezvous with Alucard as we hear Frank Skinner's *Saboteur* (1942) cue "Barry's Escape," written for the scene where Robert Cummings, under arrest, rides in the back of a police car. By the time Alucard's coffin breaks the water's surface and the materialized vampire starts floating toward Kay, that *Saboteur* cue has reached the point where Cummings makes his break, jumping out of the car and off the side of a bridge.

"The Meeting," the cue heard as Alucard joins Kay on the bank, was written for *The Invisible Woman* (1940) and heard in the scene where John Barrymore and the clothed-but-invisible Virginia Bruce arrive at the fishing lodge.

Alucard carries his new bride over the Caldwell threshold as we hear the Salter cue "Two Hours to Live" (raided from *The Invisible Man Returns*' [1940] opening scene where Radcliffe Manor residents fret over Sir Geoffrey's impending execution). There's more Skinner *Sherlock Holmes and the Voice of Terror* music as Alucard gets rough with Frank, and Salter's "Dr. Kettering's Death" (*Ghost of Frankenstein*) as Frank slinks out of the house past Alucard. When Frank is running outside, the Dracula Bat on his trail,

A cue very much like church music rings out just when it appears that Frank is going to get it in the neck—has he been spared thanks to divine intervention? (And what's with the see-through cross in this scene shot?)

Twice Dr. Brewster sleuths around amidst Alucard's effects in the Dark Oaks cellar and, quite appropriately, twice we hear Sherlock Holmes music on the track.

we hear the *Saboteur* cue played in that movie as Priscilla Lane, in one New York City taxi, is "On the Trail" of Norman Lloyd in another. That cue is replayed toward the end of *Son*, as jailbreaker Frank runs to the drainage tunnel. ("On the Trail"'s best-ever utilization: over Acquanetta's first woman-to-Ape Woman transformation in 1943's *Captive Wild Woman*.)

As moonlight makes a graveyard cross cast a luminous shadow, we hear the religioso cue "Little Cross," previously heard in an *Eagle Squadron*

(1942) scene in which Robert Stack and Diana Barrymore walk past a church. "Little Cross" gets a replay in the Dr. Brewster's Office scene where Prof. Lazlo gives Alucard a face-full of cross.

Alucard uses a shovel to spread a layer of soil at the bottom of Kay's coffin as the soundtrack dishes up Salter's "Graveyard" from *Frankenstein Meets the Wolf Man*'s opening-reel cemetery scene. It continues through Dr. Brewster's middle-of-the-night snoop-trip to the Caldwell mansion. When Brewster explores the cobwebby cellar, the music segues into *Sherlock Holmes and the Voice of Terror*'s "Christopher Docks" by Frank Skinner. (We hear "Christopher Docks" again later in the picture, during Brewster's second cellar descent.) Alucard lays down the new **NO VISITORS** law to Brewster to the accompaniment of more of *Frankenstein Meets the Wolf Man*'s "Graveyard."

In the graveyard, under the watchful eye of the sheriff and his deputies, Frank retraces his steps to music that the cue sheets call "Kay Discovered." Actually, it's just more recycled *Wolf Man* music. Unusual for a vintage Universal Horror: A loud, designed-to-startle musical stinger is incorporated as the sheriff opens the coffin and reveals Kay's body. When Frank weeps, there's another *Frankenstein Meets the Wolf Man* cue, Salter's "Second Transformation," the music heard just before Larry's change-overs into the Wolf Man.

In vapor form, Alucard slips under Dr. Brewster's office door and confronts the physician and Prof. Lazlo. The music in this scene was previously heard in *Invisible Agent*, after Peter Lorre knifes Cedric Hardwicke.

At the county morgue, Kay rises in vapor form from her coffin as we hear a cue from the *Ghost of Frankenstein* scene where Cedric Hardwicke, after filling a ward corridor with knock-out gas, uses suction to draw the gas back into the vent. I wonder what would happen to Vapor Kay if she got sucked into that vent. The four-note Dracula theme becomes Vampire Kay's theme when the shadow of the bat ... not the bat, but the *shadow* of the bat ... nibbles on the throat of sleeping jailbird Frank.

Throughout the endless jail cell palaver between Frank and Kay, Salter's "Baron Frankenstein's

Advice" (from *Ghost of Frankenstein*'s ghost scene) plays over and over. Frank's jailbreak is appropriately accompanied by Salter's "Roy's Escape," John Wayne's jailbreak music from the 1942 Western *The Spoilers*.

When Alucard backs Frank into the drainage tunnel, the accompanying version of the Dracula theme makes it suspenseful. In that cue's source, *Invisible Agent*, it's heard as invisible parachutist Griffin lands atop the barn. In the earlier movie, it's played much faster and sounds almost impish. Alucard's face is suddenly fire-lit as he sees that his coffin is ablaze, at which point the music switches to Frank Skinner's "Sabotage" from *Saboteur*'s opening-reel factory fire.

Alucard gives up trying to extinguish the coffin fire and turns his wrath on Frank as we listen to "Death of the Unholy Three," Salter's Monster-on-fire music from *Ghost of Frankenstein*. Frank Skinner's main title music for the Sherlock Holmes series rings out during Alucard's destruction scene, from the shot of the rising sun to the shot of Frank's horrorstruck reaction to the skeleton hand. The coda is slowed-down and punched-up to make it more dramatic.

Frank runs away from the tunnel to the accompaniment of Salter's cue "Troubled Dreams" (from the *Wolf Man* scene where Larry wakes up in bed the morning after killing the wolf). Once Frank gets to Dark Oaks to cremate Kay, we're treated to a lovely Salter-Skinner *Invisible Man Returns* cue (Sir Geoffrey restored to visibility) from that point all the way to the end title.

Fans of the music of Universal Horrors can really savor the abovementioned *Invisible Man Returns* cue because the last several minutes of the movie are enacted without a word of dialogue. (In the script, there's quite a bit of unnecessary chitchat in this final scene; making it dialogue-free was an inspired idea.)

Salter's End Cast music for *The Ghost of Frankenstein* is heard over *Son of Dracula*'s movie-ending castlist.

It's a nice romantic touch, in this dark mood drama of a movie, that Frank tenderly puts his engagement ring on Kay's wedding ring finger before setting the playroom alight. One of Hans J. Salter's most beautiful pieces enhances the moment.

Yes, we hear almost nothing but recycled music cues throughout *Son of Dracula*, *but*: According to musicologist John Morgan, 90-something percent of it was recorded anew for *Son*. "Most of this was done because of the different timings the two films needed for a scene," says Morgan. "Hans had Universal's bigger 'A' orchestra for *Son*. The Sherlock Holmes music [in the scene of Alucard's destruction] and other cues were goosed up orchestrationally for the bigger impact with the larger orchestra. To the *Invisible Man Returns* cue [heard when Frank returns to the Caldwell mansion and sets the playroom afire], Salter added a beautiful violin solo counterpoint to the original music for a more piquant ending."

The original plan for *Abbott and Costello Meet Frankenstein*, according to *Boxoffice* magazine, was for it to feature "Frankenstein, Dracula, **the son of Dracula**, the Wolf Man, the Mummy, etc." More evidence that Universal thought of Dracula and Alucard as two different characters.

When I interviewed Pat Fielder, screenwriter of *The Return of Dracula* (1958), she cheerfully volunteered that Hitchcock's *Shadow of a Doubt* was an influence on *Return*. It sure seems as though *Son of Dracula* must have been another: Leaving Europe behind, Count Dracula (Francis Lederer) arrives by train in Small Town U.S.A. to start a new chain

This still was sent to theaters playing *The Mad Ghoul* and exhibitors were encouraged to attract patrons with a contest, "HOW MANY OF THESE CHARACTERS CAN YOU NAME?" It probably led to a lot of confusion because whoever came up with the contest didn't know all the answers himself. The official answers: top row, left to right, Lon Chaney Sr. in *The Hunchback of Notre Dame*, Bela Lugosi in *Dracula* (no, that's Lon Chaney Jr. in *Son of Dracula*), Claude Rains in *The Invisible Man* (hard to tell!) and Boris Karloff in *The Mummy* (no, it's Lon Chaney Jr. in *The Mummy's Ghost*). Bottom row: Acquanetta as the gorilla girl in *Captive Wild Woman* (no, it's Ray Corrigan as the gorilla in that movie), Boris Karloff as the Monster in *Frankenstein* (no, *Son of Frankenstein*), Lon Chaney Jr. in *The Wolf Man* (no, *Frankenstein Meets the Wolf Man*), David Bruce in *The Mad Ghoul* and Chaney Sr. in *The Phantom of the Opera*.

of domination, using an alias (Bellac Gordal) in order to move in on the Mayberry family. A Van Helsing type, Merriman, and a Doubting Thomas reverend are soon on his trail, *à la* Prof. Lazlo and Dr. Brewster. Drac wants to make young Rachel Mayberry his vampire mate, holding out the promise of eternal life as the inducement as Alucard did for Kay: "The world shall spin and they all, all shall die—but not we." The finale takes place not in a tunnel but in a cave, with Rachel's boyfriend responsible for Dracula's destruction and the vampire reduced to a skeleton. Again like *Son of Dracula*, there's even a question as to whether Bellac is just a vampire or Count Dracula himself. Beyond the title, the movie itself never commits.

Despite its lulls in dramatic momentum, *Son of Dracula* turned out so well that it's a shame Robert Siodmak didn't do much more in the horror line. But he came close: In 1957, as the monsters started coming to TV via the *Shock* package and in new series of their own (Screen Gems' *Tales of Frankenstein*,

the English *The Invisible Man*), Robert was preparing to host and direct 39 episodes of *Robert Siodmak Presents Madame Tussaud*, to be shot in England and on the Continent. "Stories will concern those characters whose fame or infamy has earned them a place in the exhibition and in its chamber of horrors," *Variety* reported. "This is the first time in its 200-year history that the wax museum has lent its name and made its files available to an outside commercial venture."

John Carradine, the on-camera host of the abovementioned *Dr. Terror's Gallery of Horror*, introduces its fifth and final segment as "Count Alucard," but in the closing credits it's called "Count Dracula." And in the segment itself, no one calls the vampire anything other than "Count." ... Hammer's *Dracula A.D. 1972* (1972) featured Christopher Neame as hippie leader and Dracula devotee Johnny Alucard. ... And after teaming to produce the sex-horror bomb *Mary, Mary, Bloody Mary* (1975), Hollywood's Translor Films and Mexico's Proa Productions announced two more flicks, *Alucard* and *Alucard Returns from the Grave*, but neither was made.

The name "Alucard" has also popped up in more-recent movies and TV shows which you (not me) are more than welcome to catalogue.

On a mid–July 1973 episode of *CBS Evening News*, Roger Mudd (substituting for Walter Cronkite) announced Lon Chaney's death. The report that it took him 15 seconds to *read* probably took someone 15 seconds to *write*: It gave Lon's age at death at 58 (he was 67) and called him the star of such films as *The Mummy* and *Count Dracula*. This from the era *before* Fake News!

In the space of just four months, two actors gave the two most controversial performances in Universal Horrors history: Bela Lugosi as the Monster in *Frankenstein Meets the Wolf Man* and Lon Chaney as Alucard in *Son of Dracula*. Think how many thousands of hours (and pages) of debate the Monster Kid world would have been spared, if Lugosi and Chaney had simply switched.

My verdict: I'd be every bit as happy with *Frankenstein Meets the Wolf Man* if Chaney had played both monster roles, or even if Glenn Strange had begun wearing the electrodes one movie sooner. But *Son of Dracula* without Lon Chaney is a deal-killer. There are false notes aplenty in his performance, starting with the fact that Chaney does as fine a job of playing "foreign" as Iowa's own Adeline DeWalt Reynolds does as Queen Zimba. But a Dracula who's a bully, a lout and a hothead is fun and different, especially considering the polished, poised…and, frankly, occasionally verging-on-dull…Draculas who came before (Lugosi) and after (John Carradine). It adds to the tension knowing that Alucard, like Old Faithful, could blow up at any second. "Much like Daniel Craig's James Bond, Chaney makes a particularly potent working-class Dracula," Joe Dante opined in his "Trailers from Hell" tribute to *Son of Drac*.

🦇 Speaking of Dante, his *Matinee* (1993) famously features the film-within-a-film *Mant!*—and as its title *Mant!* appears on screen one letter (and the exclamation mark) at a time, we hear almost ten seconds of the *Son of Drac* main title cue.

🦇 Flashback to Transylvania: Picture an Average Night at Castle Dracula, with the three brides busy with woman's work and Dracula teaching his docile daughter Marya how to hypnotically bend mortals to her will. Meanwhile, dyslexic problem child Anthony stays in his room, taking some anger issues out on his punching bag and reading "See the U.S.A." travel brochures.

> Ned Comstock, Scott Gallinghouse and Dr. Robert J. Kiss were a huge help on this chapter. The lion's share of the info in the section on *Son of Dracula*'s music cues came from Rich Scrivani, John and Mike Brunas, John Morgan, David Schecter, Kathleen Mayne and Rich Bush.

When mysterious death comes (to Dark Oaks), the servants go. This short sequence, not in the movie, is described in the script; see page 104 of this book.

SON OF DRACULA
The Script

SON   OF   DRACULA

"DESTINY"

FADE IN:

1   INSERT - AN ENGRAVED INVITATION

reading:

>"Colonel and Miss Katherine Caldwell
request the honor of your presence
at a reception to be given Count
Anthony Alucard of Budapest.
>
>Dark Oaks,
Friday, October 13, 19--"

The card has been partially removed from its envelope
so that the last two numerals of the date are covered by
the edge of the envelope.

CAMERA PUSHES IN to BIG CLOSEUP of only the date line.

                     DISSOLVE TO:

2   INT. DR. HARRY BREWSTER'S OFFICE - <u>DAY</u> - CLOSEUP ON
CALENDAR

The calendar stands on the doctor's desk and is one
of that type with a separate sheet, which is torn off
daily, for each day of the year. The date showing now is:

               OCTOBER

               FRIDAY
                13

The VOICE of Dr. Brewster COMES OVER saying:

                   DR. BREWSTER'S VOICE
Kay sent the invitations out two
weeks ago... Why all the excitement
<u>now</u>?

CAMERA PULLS BACK TO:

al   2

3   INT. DR. BREWSTER'S OFFICE - <u>DAY</u> - MED. SHOT - DR. HARRY
     BREWSTER AND FRANK STANLEY

     The two are in the f.g. with DR. BREWSTER wearing a white
     physician's smock, busying himself with some casual office
     routine. FRANK STANLEY is facing him. The office is located
     in the old Brewster home in a small town in Louisiana and
     while it is equipped with modern medical furnishings and
     appliances, glimpses of an old-fashioned garden and oaks
     hung with Spanish moss seen through a large window in the
     b.g. will establish the locale.

     Frank is around thirty. The doctor is calm and smiling.
     Frank, who is big, amiable and serious, looks worried.

                         FRANK
               Read this letter I just got from
               Senator Manfield.

     He takes a letter out of his pocket, hands it to the
     doctor, who, after looking at him with a puzzled expression,
     opens it and reads aloud:

                         DR. BREWSTER
                       (reading)
               Dear Frank, I have not been very
               successful in prosecuting the
               inquiries you requested concerning
               Count Anthony Alucard. No one at
               the Hungarian Embassy knows of the
               family. At my request a cable
               was sent to Budapest. The reply
               states Count Alucard is unknown
               there.

     The doctor lowers the letter.

4   INT. DR. BREWSTER'S OFFICE - <u>DAY</u> - CLOSE TWO SHOT

     The doctor looks at Frank with an ironic smile
     and hands him back the letter.

                         DR. BREWSTER
               I hope Kay will appreciate what
               you've done.

                         FRANK
                       (warmly)
               If she doesn't, the Colonel will.
               He should never have let her go
               running all over Europe in the
               first place.

                                        CONTINUED

4   CONTINUED

Dr. Brewster smiles goodnaturedly.

                         DR. BREWSTER
               All right - all right! But don't
               you be the one to tell Kay her
               Count is an imposter.

                         FRANK
                    (defensively)
               Why not? You make it sound as if
               I'd done something wrong!

The doctor smiles wryly.

                         DR. BREWSTER
               It doesn't matter what I think.
               The question is: How will Kay
               take it?

                         FRANK
                    (resignedly)
               I suppose you're right.
                    (then more heatedly)
               She's got so everything around
               here is wrong and everything
               foreign is right!

They look off as a door is HEARD to open o.s.

5   INT. DR. BREWSTER'S OFFICE - DAY - MED. SHOT - AT DOOR TO
       SURGERY

CLAIRE CALDWELL, younger sister of Katherine, ENTERS with
Tommy Land, a boy of seven or eight, whose hand is freshly
bandaged. They cross toward the doctor and Frank.

6   INT. DR. BREWSTER'S OFFICE - DAY - MED. SHOT - GROUP

Claire and Tommy enter to the doctor and Frank.

                         TOMMY
               Hello, Mr. Stanley...
                    (then proudly)
               Look!

He holds up his bandaged hand for inspection.

                         FRANK
               What have you been doing, Tommy?

                                                 CONTINUED

al   4

6   CONTINUED

                              TOMMY
          I cut my hand - deep, too.

                              DR. BREWSTER
          He took it like a man, though,
          didn't he, Claire?

                              CLAIRE
          He certainly did.

                              DR. BREWSTER
          That's the stuff. Now you run along
          home and take good care of it. Tell
          your mother I want to dress it again
          Monday.

                              TOMMY
          All right, Dr. Harry. Goodbye...
          Goodbye, Miss Caldwell.

                              OTHERS
                         (ad libbing)
          Goodbye...

     Tommy crosses to the door, looks back to smile at them
     and EXITS. Claire turns to Frank, smiles and shakes hands.

                              CLAIRE
          Did I hear you two arguing while
          I was dressing Tommy's hand?

                              DR. BREWSTER
          We were trying to decide who'd
          drive you out to Dark Oaks tonight.

     Claire smiles at Frank.

                              CLAIRE
          I'll settle that... Neither of you
          will.
                         (turning to Dr. Brewster)
          I promised Sis I'd be there early
          and stay overnight. If you don't
          mind, I'd like to leave now.

                              DR. BREWSTER
          Go ahead.

     She smiles and nods to them both and EXITS, saying:

                              CLAIRE
          I'll see you both later.

                                        CONTINUED

al

6   CONTINUED - 2

        Frank looks after her, then turns to the doctor, who
        is removing his smock.

                        FRANK
                Then you're going... even though
                you know this Count is a fake?

                        DR. BREWSTER
                Of course I'm going... and so are
                you. In fact, we're both going to
                the train right now to meet him.

        He moves over closer to Frank, slaps his shoulder.

                        DR. BREWSTER
                Be sensible, Frank. The Count is
                coming for some duck hunting... In
                a couple of weeks he'll be gone
                and out of your life forever.

        He walks out of SCENE with the smock over his arm. Frank
        turns to look after him.

7   INT. DR. BREWSTER'S OFFICE - DAY - CLOSE SHOT - FRANK

                        FRANK
                I'd like to believe that... but
                Kay told me he proposed to her
                in Budapest. She invited him
                here to meet the Colonel...
                not to shoot ducks.

                        DR. BREWSTER (o.s.)
                Did Kay break your engagement?

                        FRANK
                No.

8   INT. DR. BREWSTER'S OFFICE - DAY - CLOSE SHOT - DR. BREWSTER

        He turns from a closet door with a coat. As he puts it on:

                        DR. BREWSTER
                Then, why don't you talk her into
                getting married right away?

        CAMERA PULLS BACK as he crosses to Frank.

9   INT. DR. BREWSTER'S OFFICE - DAY - MED. SHOT -
DR. BREWSTER AND FRANK

> FRANK
> She won't get married so
> long as the Colonel needs
> her. You know that.

> DR. BREWSTER
> (gravely)
> You ought to get her away from
> Dark Oaks. The place is depressing...
> Claire couldn't stand it. That's
> why she took up nursing. It was
> an escape.

> FRANK
> Kay's more conscientious than
> Claire.

> DR. BREWSTER
> Nonsense. She's just more introspective...
> too imaginative. The place is morbid,
> and I suspect she enjoys it. Get her
> out of there, Frank.

~~Before Frank can speak, the SOUND of a LOCOMOTIVE WHISTLE
COMES OVER from a distance.~~ *Frank looks at his watch — changes subject.*

> FRANK *Well*
> ~~There's the train~~ if you really
> want to meet him, *you'd better get started.*
> *The train's just about due.*

Dr. Brewster laughs.

> DR. BREWSTER
> I wouldn't miss it.

He takes Frank's arm and leads him toward the door.

> DISSOLVE TO:

10   EXT. RAILROAD STATION - DAY - LONG SHOT

The station is typical of a small and sleepy town in
the deep South. A few loafers, colored and white, loll
around. A negro is pulling a hand-drawn four-wheeled
station truck to the edge of the platform in readiness for
the train which can be HEARD approaching. Dr. Brewster and
Frank come out on the platform from the station building
and look off toward the train.

al

11   EXT. RAILROAD STATION - DAY - LONG SHOT - TRAIN

It comes up to the station and stops. It is a small local
train consisting of only a couple of day coaches and a
baggage car. The conductor and brakeman step down to the
platform.

12   EXT. RAILROAD STATION - DAY - MED. SHOT - AT CAR STEPS

The brakeman and conductor stand at the steps of the two
cars ready to assist the few passengers who alight. Dr.
Brewster and Frank ENTER to stand awaiting the appearance
of the Count. A woman with a girl of about fourteen get
off, then an older man who waves cheerfully at the two.

                         PASSENGER
              Hello, Harry... Frank....

They wave back and he hurries o.s. across the platform.
Two more women get off, then a man in hunting clothes,
who is carrying a pair of guns and a bag. He is obviously
an American. Apparently knowing no other passengers are
getting off, the conductor turns:

                         CONDUCTOR
                         (calling)
              'Board!.. All aboard!....

The doctor and Frank cross to him.

13   EXT. RAILROAD STATION - DAY - CLOSER SHOT - DOCTOR, FRANK
AND CONDUCTOR

                         CONDUCTOR
              Hello, Dr. Brewster... Mr. Stanley.

                         FRANK
              How are you, Charlie... Those all
              the passengers you have?

                         CONDUCTOR
              Just the four.

                         DR. BREWSTER
              You didn't put anyone off at the
              wrong station, did you? We came
              to meet a guest of the Caldwells -
              a Count Alucard.

                                             CONTINUED

bm   8

13   CONTINUED

                         CONDUCTOR
                      (shaking his head)
             There was no count on this train.
             All old customers.

He turns to help a woman passenger aboard, then says
over his shoulder.

                         CONDUCTOR (continued)
             There's a lot of stuff in the
             baggage car that might belong
             to your count.

                         DR. BREWSTER
             Thanks. We'll take a look at it.

As they start away, the conductor looks off and says:

                         CONDUCTOR
             The boy's unloaded it. There it
             goes on the truck.

The other two look off in the direction he points, and
Frank calls to someone o.s.

                         FRANK
                      (calling)
             Boy! Wait a minute!

They hurry out.

14   EXT. RAILROAD STATION - DAY - MED. FULL SHOT

      on a negro wearing a uniform cap as he pulls at a four-
      wheel baggage truck piled high with luggage. He hears
      Frank call and brings the truck to a stop. Frank and
      Dr. Brewster hurry in and pause beside the truck to examine
      the luggage.

15   EXT. STATION PLATFORM - DAY - MED. SHOT - AT BAGGAGE TRUCK

      Frank and Dr. Brewster enter to it. It is piled high
      with luggage. Among the pieces of baggage are several
      trunks and two large chests, all of which bear a crest
      and under it the neatly lettered name: ALUCARD. Instead
      of being printed in the normal way, however, the letters
      are placed one under the other beneath the crest thus:

                         A
                         L
                         U
                         C
                         A
                         R
                         D

                                              CONTINUED

15   CONTINUED

Frank and the doctor look casually at the mountain of
baggage, then glance at one another.

                    FRANK
          Does that look as if he means to
          stay just a couple of weeks?

                    DR. BREWSTER
                 (thoughtfully)
          No, it doesn't. I wonder what's
          happened to him.

                    FRANK
          Probably coming by auto. Don't
          worry -- he'll turn up.

He moves along the truck looking idly at the boxes and
trunks. Brewster is about to follow when something about
one of the boxes catches his eye and he turns back to it
curiously. This particular box has been placed on the
truck on its side so that the count's name runs horizontally,
the letters lying on their backs with the end of the name
at the left. Curiously Brewster reaches out a hand and
one by one touches the first three or four letters - D -
R - A - C -

16   INSERT: CLOSE ON NAME ON BOX

The letters, of course, are on their backs but read from
left to right, they spell: D-R-A-C-U-L-A. Brewster's hand
enters and touches the first three or four as OVER SCENE
COMES the SOUND of his VOICE musingly:

                    DR. BREWSTER'S VOICE

          D,r,a,c,u -

17   EXT. RAILROAD STATION - DAY - MED. CLOSE

on Frank and Brewster, the latter downstage looking at
the name on the box. Frank looks at him quizzically.

                    FRANK
          What are you mumbling about.

                                        CONTINUED

17   CONTINUED

Brewster snaps out of his preoccupation and dissembles,
not wanting to share his discovery with his friend.

            DR. BREWSTER
        Nothing - just a - a silly idea
        occurred to me, that's all.

            FRANK
        Well, I'd better get this stuff
        out to Dark Oaks, or Kay will be
        sore.

            DR. BREWSTER
        Go ahead - I'll run along back
        to the office.

As he starts out rather hurriedly,

                                    DISSOLVE TO:

18   INT. DR. BREWSTER'S OFFICE - DAY - CLOSE

on Dr. Brewster at his desk with the phone at his ear.

            DR. BREWSTER
            (into phone)
        I called Professor Lazlo at Muir-
        field University half an hour ago.
        Will you please check the call? ..
        ... Dr. Brewster, 228. Thank you.

He hangs up and lifting the corner of a sheet of paper
on the desk before him studies something printed on it
in pencil.

19   INT. DR. BREWSTER'S OFFICE - DAY - CLOSE

on sheet of paper held by Brewster's fingers. On it he has
printed the name Alucard as it appeared on the count's
baggage, one letter under another. In printing them, however, he has leaned each letter slightly to the left. The
name reads ALUCARD. Now his hand turns the paper so the
letters run from left to right. The tilted letters make
the name DRACULA very easy to read. Over the scene SOUNDS
the RINGING of the phone. The hand lays down thepaper
and reaches for the receiver.

20   INT. DR. BREWSTER'S OFFICE - DAY - CLOSE

on Brewster as he takes up the phone.

                                    CONTINUED

j

20   CONTINUED

                              DR. BREWSTER
                          (into phone)
                Hello... This is Harry Brewster
                speaking... Yes, fine, thanks.....

        He listens a moment, then:

                              DR. BREWSTER
                          (into phone, contd.)
                I called to ask if you know anything
                about a titled Hungarian family
                named Alucard, A-l-u-c-a-r-d.

21   INT. PROF. LAZLO'S STUDY - DAY - CLOSE SHOT - THE PROFESSOR

        He is a kindly-looking man of fifty or more. He speaks
        with a slight accent. At Brewster's query, he frowns
        thoughtfully.

                              PROF. LAZLO
                          (into phone)
                Alucard? No-o, I am sure there is
                no such family. The name is not
                Hungarian.

22   INT. DR. BREWSTER'S OFFICE - DAY - MED. CLOSE SHOT

                              DR. BREWSTER
                          (into phone)
                Well, can you tell me if there
                could be a Count Dracula still
                living?

23   INT. PROF. LAZLO'S STUDY - DAY - MED. CLOSE SHOT

        Lazlo reacts, startled at the question.

                              PROF. LAZLO
                          (into phone)
                Dracula! I am certain there is
                not! History says the last Count
                Dracula died in the Middle Ages!
                Why do you ask?

24   INT. DR. BREWSTER'S OFFICE - DAY - MED. CLOSE SHOT

                         DR. BREWSTER
                       (into phone)
              A Count Alucard is coming here to
              visit a friend of mine. I happened
              to notice that the name spelled
              backward is Dracula, and it made me
              curious.

25   INT. PROF. LAZLO'S STUDY - DAY - MED. CLOSE SHOT

      Lazlo is getting more and more interested and rather un-
      easy.

                         PROF. LAZLO
                       (into phone)
              That is strange. According to the
              legends of my people, the last Count
              Dracula became one of the un-dead --
              a vampire -- and was destroyed in the
              nineteenth century. I am something
              of an authority on the subject.

26   INT. DR. BREWSTER'S OFFICE - DAY - MED. CLOSE SHOT

                         DR. BREWSTER
                       (into phone)
              I know, Professor, that's why I
              called you. If this man is an
              imposter, why would he assume
              that name of all others?

27   INT. PROF. LAZLO'S STUDY - DAY - MED. CLOSE SHOT

                         PROF. LAZLO
                       (positively)
              He wouldn't ... not if he is sane!
              In Transylvania, the name is
              associated only with evil. I
              advise you to be very careful of
              that man!

28   INT. DR. BREWSTER'S OFFICE - DAY - MED. CLOSE SHOT

      Dr. Brewster hesitates a moment as if not sure he should
      ask the question in his mind.

                                          CONTINUED

j   13

28   CONTINUED

                          DR. BREWSTER
                         (into phone)
                From your tone, I gather you don't
                entirely disbelieve the legends
                about the former Dracula.

29   INT. PROF. LAZLO'S STUDY - DAY - MED. CLOSE SHOT

        Lazlo frowns uncomfortably.

                          PROF. LAZLO
                         (into phone)
                In my research, I have uncovered
                data I cannot refute. I wouldn't
                say I believe, but, in honesty,
                I cannot say I disbelieve. Let me
                repeat: Be very careful of the
                man, and if anything --- disturbing
                develops, please keep me advised.

30   INT. DR. BREWSTER'S OFFICE - DAY - MED. SHOT

                          DR. BREWSTER
                         (into phone)
                I shall, Professor, and thank you.
                Goodbye, sir.

        He hangs up the phone slowly, thoughtfully.

                                              FADE OUT.

        FADE IN:

31   EXT. DARK OAKS - NIGHT - FULL SHOT

        As SCENE FADES IN, the CAMERA IS TILTED UP to show an old
        rusty cut-out of the plantation's name positioned above
        the gateposts at the entrance of the drive that leads to
        the house. OVER the SCENE IS HEARD the SOUND of rusty
        hinges creaking dismally. CAMERA TILTS DOWN to show the
        gates themselves with the house at the far end of the
        drive, gloomy and rather forbidding in the night light.
        The branches of trees bordering it are festooned with
        Spanish moss. In the house itself, a window or two and
        a pair of French doors are lighted, seeming to make the
        old pile look more gloomy because of it. In the fore-
        ground, a negro has opened one of the two rusty iron
        gates of the drive and now swings the second gate open

                                              CONTINUED

j⁻   14

31   CONTINUED

          creakingly. Stepping to the head of his team, he takes
          them by the bits and starts along the drive with them,
          clucking to them.

                              MATHEW
          Come along, you Sam - Blackie!

          As the team move after him, he starts HUMMING a doleful
          negro plantation song.

32   EXT. DARK OAKS PORCH - NIGHT - MED. SHOT   Ext + Int.

          A lighted window in the building behind the porch. Kay
          is discovered standing downstage at the porch railing
          looking off past CAMERA toward the approaching team. She
          is dressed in riding togs. OVER the SCENE comes the
          SOUND of the driver's HUMMED SONG. The girl is beautiful,
          tall, statuesque and appears rather eager as she peers
          off into the darkness. After a moment, she calls off to
          the driver.

                              KATHERINE
                    Is that you, Mathew?

33   EXT. DARK OAKS - NIGHT - MED. PAN SHOT - ON MATHEW

          as he leads his weary team of mules along the drive. In
          response to the girl's query, he calls back respectfully.

                              MATHEW
                    Yas'm, Miss Kay. Dis is Mathew.

          He continues on his way leading the team.

34   EXT. PORCH - NIGHT - MED. SHOT - ON KAY

          standing as before looking off at the approaching wagon.
          Claire ENTERS SCENE from inside the house. Kay turns to
          her.

                              KATHERINE
                    Mathew's back from town. Now, Claire
                    we'll learn something.

                              but the can't did't come

                                        CONTINUED

rm

34   CONTINUED   *No - not yet*

                    CLAIRE
                 (good-naturedly)
          If you only had a phone, Frank
          would have called after the
          train arrived... Believe me, if
          I still lived here I'd have one,
          if I had to string the wires
          myself.

Katherine smiles without turning to the other girl.

                    KATHERINE
          There are other ways of
          communication.

Claire takes this lightly and slips a hand thru her
sister's arm.

                    CLAIRE
          Please, Kay - no lectures on
          metaphysics tonight.

Katherine turns to her still smiling knowingly.

                    KATHERINE
          You ought to give your mind a
          chance to explore the unknown,
          Claire... then you wouldn't
          laugh at telepathy. I know
          Count Alucard will be here
          tonight - without benefit of
          telephone.

35   EXT. DARK OAKS -NIGHT - MED. FULL SHOT

Both girls are on the porch watching as Mathew leads his
team in and stops near the porch.

                    MATHEW
          Ah got the boxes an' trunks,
          Miss Kay, but Mr. Frank say
          the Count didn't come on the
          train.

                    KATHERINE
          Very well, Mathew. Put them in
          the guest house where I told you.

                    MATHEW
          Yas'm, but Ah'll need he'p --
          they's most amazin' heavy.

                                        CONTINUED

35   CONTINUED

                              KATHERINE
            Get some of the other boys to
            help you.

                              MATHEW
            Yas, Miss Kay.

        As he finishes he starts off toward the rear of the house
        with the team.

36   EXT. DARK OAKS - NIGHT - MED. SHOT ON PORCH

        Katherine and Claire stand looking off after the retreat-
        ing wagon.

                              CLAIRE
            He probably missed the train
            and will come down tomorrow.

        She gives Katherine's hand a friendly little pat. Then
        she adds:

                              CLAIRE
            I must run in and see Dad a
            minute before I dress for
            our company.

        She finishes the line on her way inside. Katherine con-
        tinues to look after the wagon, then moves down off the
        porch and exits in the direction it took.

37   EXT. CALDWELL GUEST HOUSE - NIGHT - MED. FULL SHOT

        The wagon is being backed up to the porch of the guest
        house. Mathew and two other colored boys start unloading
        the heavy equipment. CAMERA PANS from them toward some
        gloomy looking shrubbery and shows Katherine approaching.
        She stops partly in the shadow of the shrubs.

38   EXT. DARK OAKS GROUNDS - NIGHT - MED. SHOT

        on Katherine watching the unloading of the luggage with
        interest, a slight smile of understanding on her lips.
        Now she glances off thru the trees, hesitates, then exits
        quickly in the direction she looked. CAMERA PANS her on
        her way and as she disappears among the shadows,

                                        DISSOLVE TO:

JC   17

39   EXT. SWAMP - NIGHT - LONG SHOT

        This is on a trail that only a native could follow, wind-
        ing as it does around the edges of black pools and vegeta-
        tion that looks solid but is actually growing out of the
        water. The growth is so rank that in places it completely
        covers the trail and has to be pushed aside to clear a
        passage. From time to time great and ominous SPLASHES will
        be HEARD that suggest alligators plunging into the water.
        The CROAKING of frogs, HOOTING of owls, and the SHRILL CRIES
        of other nocturnal birds and animals COME OVER. Once there
        is the DEATH SCREAM of some large animal as it falls victim
        to a larger or more savage creature. Along this trail comes
        Katherine. She walks toward CAMERA with sureness of foot
        and confidence, making good time but showing no effort to
        hurry. Her lack of fear and familiarity with her surround-
        ings suggest she has covered this ground frequently. She
        comes up to CAMERA and passes. CAMERA PANS TO:

40   EXT. SWAMP - NIGHT - LONG SHOT

        SHOOTING PAST Katherine to a tumbledown cabin in the bog.
        Light flickers in its only window and through the open door.
        The SOUNDS of the swamp continue to COME OVER. CAMERA
        HOLDS on Katherine as she approaches the cabin.

41   EXT. ZIMBA'S CABIN - NIGHT - MED. SHOT

        Katherine comes up to the door and stops. The SOUND of
        LOW CHANTING COMES OVER. Katherine looks inside.

42   INT. ZIMBA'S CABIN - NIGHT - FULL SHOT

        It is a shabby interior, the quarters of a female witch
        doctor, ZIMBA. She is an old wrinkled bag of a woman with
        straggling hair. She sits before a rude table decorated
        in keeping with the ceremony she is going thru. The room
        is lighted by a couple of tallow candles on the table.
        Lying on the table is the limp carcass of a dead but un-
        plucked rooster, the head lolling over the edge of the
        table, with the neck feathers ruffled and wet with what
        might be blood if the spectator's imagination takes him that
        far. A dark liquid (presumably but not specifically the
        rooster's blood) is in a shallow, cheap crockery dish which
        stands before Zimba who, with elbows on the table and boney
        fingers thrust thru her hair, is staring down into it, using
        it as a crystal ball. Also on the table are the usual weeds
        and herbs of the witch doctor, in addition to which, is a
        huge live toad which squats blinking stupidly. On Zimba's
        shoulder is perched a big black crow. Zimba is mumbling

                                                CONTINUED

JC   78

42   CONTINUED

      a sing-song chant, the words of which are so indistinguish-
      able as to be impossible to identify as voodoo or any other
      form of witchcraft that might get us in trouble. The only
      SOUNDS to be HEARD are the CROAKING of frogs outside and
      the occasional HOOT of an owl. The old woman is apparently
      in a state of self-induced hypnosis. Without looking up
      from the bowl, she beckons toward the door with one hand.
      Katherine appears in the doorway, pauses briefly, then
      moves downstage to the table, her movements a bit uncertain
      - appearing rather puzzled. As she approaches the table,
      the old woman speaks, but without lifting her eyes from
      the bowl.

43   INT. ZIMBA'S CABIN - NIGHT - MED. CLOSE SHOT

                          ZIMBA
                     (in a monotone)
                 You do not know why you came here
                 tonight. It was because I wished
                 you here.

                          KATHERINE
                     (uneasily)
                 Why? Isn't Count Alucard going to--

      Zimba stops her with a limp upraised hand.

                          ZIMBA
                 I wished you here to warn you.
                 The Angel of Death hovers over a
                 great house --
                 I see the house in ruins -- weeds
                 and vines growing over it -- bats
                 flying in and out the broken windows.

44   INT. ZIMBA'S CABIN - NIGHT - CLOSE SHOT

      on Katherine. What the witch has said is of less importance
      to her than other things she has on her mind. Ignoring the
      words she speaks:

                          KATHERINE
                 What of Count Alucard?
                 coming? ... Can you hear me,
                 Queen Zimba?

45   INT. ZIMBA'S CABIN - NIGHT - CLOSE SHOT

      on Zimba. Without looking up she replies:

                                                  CONTINUED

45 · CONTINUED

                          ZIMBA
          Alucard is not his name. You must
          stop him before it is too late.
          Stop him before Death comes to Dark
          Oaks.

46   INT. ZIMBA'S CABIN - NIGHT - MED. SHOT

      on Katherine and Zimba.

                          KATHERINE
          Tell me if he is coming tonight.
          I know what I am doing.

                          ZIMBA
          You cannot know what you are doing.
          It is unholy. I see you marrying a
          corpse and living in a grave... I
          see....

CEILING

47   INT. ZIMBA'S CABIN - NIGHT - MED. SHOT

      on open doorway. A huge bat flutters into the doorway
      from outside, remains poised with wings flapping for a
      moment, then flashes out swiftly toward Katherine and
      Zimba o.s.

48   INT. ZIMBA'S CABIN - NIGHT - MED. FULL SHOT

      For the first time, Zimba's eyes lift from the bowl before
      her as if she is wrenched from her state of hypnosis.
      She stares off toward the bat in the doorway. Katherine
      whirls and follows the look with her own eyes. She starts
      back and Zimba rises as the bat flies in, heading straight
      at the old woman's head. It circles round her. The
      crow flaps off her shoulder, and Zimba shrieks and pitches
      forward across the table. The bat flutters on off stage.
      Katherine recovers her wits and quickly moves to raise
      the old woman's head.

49   INT. ZIMBA'S CABIN - NIGHT - CLOSER SHOT

      Katherine raises Zimba's head and stares into it.
      Obviously the woman is dead.

                          KATHERINE
          Zimba... Queen Zimba!

HAYS.

                                          CONTINUED

1g   20

49   CONTINUED

There is no response. Wide-eyed, Katherine lowers the
head slowly to the table and backs away, the CAMERA
PANNING her to the door through which she disappears
quickly into the night.

                                          DISSOLVE TO:

50   INT. CALDWELL MANSION - NIGHT - FULL SHOT - BALLROOM

The room is large and ornately decorated in the French
manner with crystal chandeliers, etc. Along one end of
the room are tables with punch and the food for buffet
supper, with a couple of white-jacketed colored servants
in attendance. A colored orchestra of about seven pieces
provides the music to which the company, in evening
clothes, is dancing. The musicians are in their "Sunday
best", not evening clothes, but dark suits of various
styles and stiff collars. The company is comprised of
mostly young people, with a few older folks around.
Among those dancing are Katherine, Claire, Dr. Brewster
and Frank, also in formal dress. Surrounded by a few
older men, Colonel Caldwell is in a wheel chair with a
large and powerful colored servant to move him around.
He is slender, delicate looking and old. A blanket covers
him up to the waist.

51   INT. BALLROOM - NIGHT - MED. SHOT - COLONEL AND GROUP

                        COLONEL
          This excitement over Kay's count
          has worn me out. If you all will
          excuse me, I'll let Steven take me
          upstairs.

                        FRIENDS
                      (ad libbing)
          Suppose you'll have this all to do
          over again when he does arrive...
          Goodnight, Will....
          Don't let us keep you up, Colonel....

The Colonel lifts his hand in a little goodnight gesture
and is wheeled away by the servant, CAMERA PANNING with
them to a wide doorway with the Colonel continuing to
wave goodnight to other friends and the dancers who pass.

                                          WIPE TO:

52   INT. SECOND FLOOR LANDING - <u>NIGHT</u> - MED. SHOT

Colonel Caldwell's servant is carrying the Colonel up the
last couple of steps to the landing. A second wheel chair
stands before an open window through which a light breeze
is blowing on the filmy curtains. The colored servant
places the Colonel gently in the wheel chair and wheels him
out of SCENE along the o.s. hallway. As he disappears, a
large bat flutters into the opening between the curtains of
the window, where it hovers with flapping wings for a moment.

53   INT. SECOND FLOOR HALL - <u>NIGHT</u> - LONG SHOT

SHOOTING along the hall from the head of the stairs o.s.
At the extreme end of the hall, the end is partially cur-
tained off by heavy drapes drawn back with tie cords. The
portion of the hall beyond the drapes is dimly lighted. A
window at the far end shows black against the night outside.
The servant is wheeling Colonel Caldwell upstage toward his
room on the downstage side of the drapes. The servant
pauses, opens the door and, as he starts to push the wheel
chair into the bedroom, the big bat flies in from CAMERA
and flaps lazily upstage, passing the Colonel's door just
after the servant and Colonel have left set. As the blackness of the bat is lost against the darkened window at the
end of the hall, it disappears (by a HOLD-CUT) and standing
in the shadows, framed by the portieres, is Count Alucard
in Inverness worn over a dress suit. He looks after the
Colonel and moves back into partial concealment behind one
of the portieres.

54   INT. COLONEL'S BEDROOM - <u>NIGHT</u> - FULL SHOT

It is a richly furnished, typically masculine room, with
bed, comfortable chairs, a large smoking stand with a box
of cigars, etc. The servant wheels the Colonel over toward
the bed.

                    COLONEL
          Just leave me by the window, Steven.
          I'll smoke a cigar before going to bed.

                    SERVANT
          Yes, suh.

He wheels the chair over near the window, moves the drapes
a little, then places the smoking stand within reach of
the Colonel and opens the cigar box. The Colonel takes a
cigar which the servant lights for him.

                    COLONEL
          That'll be all for now, Steven.

                    SERVANT
          Thank you, suh.

He turns and starts toward the door.

J   22

55   INT. SECOND FLOOR HALL - NIGHT - MED. SHOT

        The door of the Colonel's room opens. The servant appears,
        closes the door and EXITS PAST CAMERA. The Count steps
        out from behind the portiere, looks after him, then opens
        the door and EXITS inside.

                                                DISSOLVE TO:

56   EXT. PORCH - NIGHT - MED. SHOT - KATHERINE AND FRANK

        (The MUSIC of the orchestra indoors comes OVER SOFTLY.)
        They come from the French doors in the b.g. and cross to
        the porch rail. Katherine, looking pale and tense, stares
        out across the grounds. Frank is awkwardly silent for a
        moment, then:

                        FRANK
                You're worried tonight, Kay. I
                wish you'd tell me what it is.

        Katherine turns to face him in a way that suggests she had
        forgotten he was there.

                        KATHERINE
                Wouldn't you be upset if you
                gave a reception, and your guest
                of honor didn't appear?

        CAMERA ADVANCES TO:

57   EXT. PORCH - NIGHT - CLOSE SHOT - KATHERINE AND FRANK

        He looks at her with a troubled expression, but she turns
        her face away abstractedly.

                        FRANK
                That's not all that's troubling
                you.

        Katherine looks around at him thoughtfully. Frank takes
        her hands.

                        FRANK
                Isn't there something I can do to
                help?

        Katherine at first looks as if she is going to pull her
        hands free; then she softens and smiles a little.

                        KATHERINE
                        (smiling)
                Thanks.... I don't need anyone's
                help.

                                                CONTINUED

57   CONTINUED

                    FRANK
        Sure?

                    KATHERINE
                  (lightly)
        Positive.

Frank watches for a reaction to his next remark.

                    FRANK
        How are you going to explain the
        death of that stupid old gypsy
        you brought here from Hungary?

Katherine turns quickly on him, her smile fading.

                    KATHERINE
        Queen Zimba?

                    FRANK
                  (grinning)
        Was she a queen? That old swamp
        cat with the cabin full of toads
        and stuffed lizards and dead
        chickens? Good riddance, if you
        ask me.

Katherine has been watching him narrowly.

                    KATHERINE
        How did you know she was dead?

                    FRANK
        Such news travels fast... One of
        the field hands told me - He also
        said you were there when she was
        killed.

                    KATHERINE
                  (rather defiantly)
        What if I was?

                    FRANK
                  (gravely)
        It may be embarrassing for you
        at the inquest.

                                        CONTINUED

57   CONTINUED -2:

                           KATHERINE
              You mean they'll think I killed
              her?

                            FRANK
              Of course not, but they'll ask
              you what did kill her.

Katherine turns her eyes away from Frank and speaks with
infinite scorn in her voice.

                           KATHERINE
              And if I tell the truth, no one
              will believe me - the blind fools!

                            FRANK
                           (quietly)
              You're wrong, Kay. We're not blind,
              and we're not fools. We're plain,
              sensible people who won't be fooled
              by a lot of supernatural twaddle
              and....

                           KATHERINE
                         (interrupting)
              Twaddle!

                            FRANK
              Exactly! There's no magic in toads
              and dried lizards and dead chickens!

During the speech Katherine has turned irritably away from
him. He takes her by the shoulders and turns her back so
she must look into his face.

                            FRANK
              Let me take you away from all this
              morbid mess, Kay. A six months'
              honeymoon abroad... or a year! We
              won't come back till you've forgotten
              it and become the girl I used to know
              and fell in love with!

Katherine lowers her eyes and shakes her head. When she
speaks, her voice lends sincerity to her words.

                           KATHERINE
              I'm sorry, Frank.

                            FRANK
              Claire and a nurse can take care
              of your father, if that's what's
              stopping you.

                                        CONTINUED

57   CONTINUED - 3:

                          KATHERINE
                    No; it isn't that.

Frank's hands slowly relax.

                          FRANK
                    Does that mean you're breaking
                    our engagement, Kay?

It is now Katherine's turn to show concern. She looks up
at him quickly as she replies.

                          KAY
                    Oh, no, I'll never do that.
                    It's just that I... Oh, I can't
                    explain it to you now! Some day
                    I shall, and you'll see it's best
                    for us both! I know what I'm
                    doing, Frank; really I do! You've
                    got to believe me!

Frank doesn't reply for a moment, then:

                          FRANK
                    Has it anything to do with
                    Count Alucard?

Katherine does not answer, but as she turns her face away
it is obvious that the answer is yes.

                          FRANK
                         (without rancor)
                    I see. Then I'm afraid I must
                    tell you, Kathy... your count
                    is an imposter... a fake.

                          KATHERINE
                         (turning on him)
                    How can you say such a thing?

                          FRANK
                    I wrote Senator Manfield. There
                    is no Count Alucard known to the
                    Hungarian embassy, nor in Budapest.

Katherine glares at him furiously.

                          KATHERINE
                    You must feel proud of yourself
                    for that bit of snooping!

                                        CONTINUED

57   CONTINUED -4

                              FRANK
                          (defensively)
                    I only did what any man would
                    to protect the girl he intends
                    to....

          He is stopped by o.s. VOICES calling. Both turn and
          look toward the house.

                              STEVEN'S VOICE
                    Dr. Brewster! Miss Kay! Miss
                    Claire, come quick!

          They look about. Frank sees and points off and up.

58   EXT. COLONEL'S BEDROOM WINDOW - NIGHT - MED. FULL SHOT

          SHOOTING UP. Smoke is rolling from the window and inside
          may be seen a suggestion of flames licking up the edge
          of a portier. A huge bat flies out the window and on
          OUT OF SCENE.

59   EXT. PORCH - NIGHT - MED. SHOT

              on Frank and Katherine looking up. With one accord they
              rush to the french doors and enter thru them.

60   INT. RECEPTION HALL - NIGHT - MED. FULL SHOT

          Guests are moving curiously into scene to the foot of
          the stairs. Some start up. Frank and Katherine hurry in
          and Frank rushes up the stairs, passing guests and
          leaving Katherine to follow.

61   INT. UPPER HALL - NIGHT - FULL SHOT

          The door of the Colonel's room is open. Some smoke but
          no fire is drifting thru it into the hall. Now Brewster
          ENTERS thru the smoke carrying the body of Colonel
          Caldwell in his arms in a way that keeps the latter's
          face hidden from CAMERA. Midway to CAMERA, Frank
          hurries in from o.s. Without stopping, Brewster speaks.

                              DR. BREWSTER
                    Hold the guests, Frank, till I
                    see how serious it is.

                              FRANK
          Of course.

                                              CONTINUED

61   CONTINUED

Dr. Brewster goes on into Katherine's room (or merely
EXITS PAST CAMERA along the hall), as Katherine ENTERS
to join Frank.

62   INT. COLONEL'S BEDROOM - NIGHT - FULL SHOT

A couple of male guests and servants are beating out
the fire which by now is more smoke than blaze. The
portiers and the blanket spread over the seat of the
wheelchair show evidence of the fire and are still
smoldering as is the carpet before the window.

                    MR. THOMPSON *FRANK*
            Better throw the portiers out the
            window and rip up the carpet to be
            sure the floor isn't smoldering.

                    STEVEN
        Yes, suh.

All start to obey. Steven bends to the carpet near
the wheel chair.

63   INT. COLONEL'S BEDROOM - NIGHT - MED. SHOT

on group as they pull down portiers and otherwise busy
themselves. Steven, who has been bending to rip up the
carpet, rises with a partly smoked cigar between his
fingers.

                FRANK STEVEN
            Mr. Thompson, suh, it looks like
            the Colonel fell asleep an' dropped
            his cigar, an' it set fire to the
            curtain.
                        FRANK
                    MR. THOMPSON
                (examining the cigar)
            Seems a reasonable explanation.

The servants continue the work of cleaning up the ruined
portiers, et cetera.

64   INT. KATHERINE'S ROOM - NIGHT - MED. SHOT

on Dr. Brewster, Frank, Katherine and Claire grouped about
the bed on which the Colonel has been placed. Dr.
Brewster is drawing a coverlet up over the form. He
stands looking down thoughtfully.

                                        CONTINUED

bm

64   CONTINUED

                              DR. BREWSTER
                    There are no indications of
                    asphixiation. I believe his heart
                    failed before the fire. He may
                    have even died in his sleep.

                              FRANK
                    But he looks as if he were literally
                    frightened to death!

Brewster turns quickly to him, evidently anxious to change
the subject.

                              DR. BREWSTER
                    Purely a reflex of facial muscles.
                    It would be a good idea to ask
                    the company to leave.

                              FRANK
                         (still staring down
                          at Caldwell)
                    But what are those two little scars
                    on his throat? They don't look
                    like burns.

Brewster reacts uncomfortably but before he can speak,
Katherine cuts in, obviously not wanting any further
investigation of the scars.

                              KATHERINE
                    Dr. Brewster is right, Frank. The
                    guests should be asked to leave.

                              FRANK
                    Certainly, Kay.

CAMERA PANS him to the door and out. Katherine is
obviously relieved by his going but not too sure how
much Brewster may know or suspect.

65   INT. COLONEL'S ROOM - NIGHT - MED. SHOT

on Steven and other servant as they are finishing cleaning
up the results of the fire. Andy looks toward o.s. door
to be sure they are alone; then he speaks quietly to
Steven.

                              ANDY
                    I boun' they's somethin' mighty
                    funny 'bout this. First Queen
                    Zimba drop daid, nen ol' Colonel
                    get himse'f burnt to death.

                                        CONTINUED

65   CONTINUED

                              STEVEN
              Ol' colonel didn't git burnt. The
              look on his face say he was scairt
              to death.

                              ANDY
              A ha'nt, you reckon?

                              STEVEN
              I don' reckon nothin'. I jest
              wonderin' who'll be next.

                              ANDY
              That's what they askin' out in
              the servant quarters. Come mornin'
              they won't be ary one on the place.

                                        WIPE TO:

66   EXT. SERVANT'S CABINS - <u>NIGHT</u> - FULL SHOT

SHOOTING ALONG a row of several cabins of cheap construction. There are lights on inside the cabins, and from the
flitting of shadows across the windows there is considerable
activity within as well as without. There is no sound. On
the little "stoops" before the cabins, odds and ends of
small household goods and hastily tied bundles are stacked.
A couple of one-mule wagons with wheels mostly Jack-deuce
stand before the buildings, one of them well downstage,
headed away FROM CAMERA. One of the servants stands on a
wheel stowing away bundles in the rickety wagon. Another
is handing up other equipment. From cabins along the
line servants and field hands are carrying their belong-
ings to the other wagon or are hoisting bundles on their
shoulders to start off. Suddenly, a huge bat like the one
seen at Queen Zimba's cabin flies into scene from CAMERA
and circles with flapping wings about the two men, chatter-
ing at them. Both men duck and strain to watch its movements. It persists in fluttering around them. One takes
a swing at it with a broom but misses.

                              SERVANT
              Ne'mind the rest. Le's git!

As he speaks he is scrambling to the seat. As the other
swings aboard over the end gate, the first one smacks the
mule with a buggy whip, and the vehicle rattles upstage
along the little street.

67   INT. CALDWELL RECEPTION HALL - MED. - <u>NIGHT</u>

    at door, camera SHOOTING OUT through it to show the porch
beyond. The Colonel's manservant stands in the open doorway watching as a car pulls away from the porch. The
sound of other cars is heard. There is no one on the
porch. The old servant closes the door and turns to
EXIT past camera. He has taken but one step when there
is heard a LOUD KNOCK on the door. Since there was no
one outside when he closed the door, the servant reacts
in surprise to the knock. He turns back and opens the
door, then steps back with a show of slight alarm at the
figure of Count Alucard just outside the threshold
staring fixedly at him.

                      COUND ALUCARD
          Kindly announce Count Alucard.
          Explain that I came by motor
          and was delayed by mishap.

68   INT. CALDWELL RECEPTION HALL - CLOSE - <u>NIGHT</u>

    on the servant. He is looking off at Alucard with an
unnamed fear in his eyes.

                      SERVANT
          Ah'm sorry, but they's been a
          death in the house, suh. Every-
          body's gone but the family, suh.

69   INT. CALDWELL RECEPTION HALL - <u>NIGHT</u> - MED. CLOSE

    on Alucard, shooting over the servant's shoulder.
Alucard's eyes harden and with the air of one not used
to being balked he rasps:

                      ALUCARD
        Announce me!

                      SERVANT
              (bowing and backing away)
        Yes, suh.

    Alucard enters slowly and passes close to camera as he
EXITS. As the door closes.

                        FADE OUT.

FADE IN:

70   EXT. DARK OAKS MANSION - <u>DAY</u> - FULL

Two cars are parked at the porch steps, one a weather-
beaten sedan, the other a nice looking medium priced
coupe. Nearby is tied a saddle horse.

                        DISSOLVE TO:

71   INSERT - CLOSE

on back of document in man's hands. It is plainly
labeled: "Last Will and Testament of William Geddes
Caldwell." As the hands start to open the document,
the Judge's VOICE is heard o.s.

                    JUDGE SIMMONS' VOICE
        You will find this will a comparatively
        simple document ---

As he is reading the line,

                        DISSOLVE TO:

72   INT. LIBRARY - <u>DAY</u> - MED. FULL

The Judge sits back of the library table, briefcase,
etc. before him. Grouped about him informally are
Kay, Claire, Frank and Brewster. The Judge continues
his speech.

                    JUDGE SIMMONS
        -- chiefly because you two girls
        are the only living kin of Colonel
        Caldwell. In essence it divides the
        entire estate, cash, securities and
        all equally between ----

                    KATHERINE
              (interrupting)
        Pardon me, Judge Simmons. May I
        ask the date of that will?

The Judge examines the paper with a slight show of
surprise.

                    JUDGE SIMMONS
        August twenty-fourth. It was made on
        the occasion of Miss Claire's attain-
        ing legal age and responsibility.

                    KATHERINE
              (pleasantly)
        Then there is a will of later date.
                    CONTINUED

72   CONTINUED

All react in surprise. Kay rises and crossing to a panel
or wall safe, opens it and from several papers removes
a long envelope. She takes it to the Judge who opens it
with a puzzled look as she returns to her seat. As
Kay returns she smiles at Claire and says casually:

                    KATHERINE
          There's no important difference
          between them.

                    JUDGE
                (looking up)
          There's a mighty important difference
          to you, Kay. According to this you
          get nothing but the plantation.
          Claire gets all cash and securities.

He runs his eyes over the document thoughtfully and
continues.

                    JUDGE
          It's properly witnessed and can't
          be disputed – but I can't imagine
          what your father was thinking of.

                    KATHERINE
          It's the way I wanted it. To divide
          the estate otherwise would have
          meant selling the plantation. I
          love Dark Oaks and hope to live
          here – always.

                    JUDGE SIMMONS
          But my dear child, it takes real
          capital to run a plantation of
          this size.

                    FRANK
                (smiling)
          Don't let that worry you, Judge.
          I think Colonel Caldwell knew what
          he was doing.

He turns toward Katherine with a little smile. She
returns the look a bit less warmly. The Judge looks
from one to the other and realizes the full significance
of Frank's meaning.

                    JUDGE SIMMONS
          Oh, I see. I'd offer congratulations,
          but this hardly seems the proper
          time.

                              CONTINUED

72   CONTINUED - 2

He rises and starts putting away his papers speaking
as he does so.

                    JUDGE
          That seems to end the matter. I'll
          start the legal machinery in motion
          at once.

Tucking his briefcase under his arm he takes up his hat
preparatory to leaving.

                    JUDGE SIMMONS
          I may start things today, if the
          clerk's office is still open. Good
          bye.

Then as Claire starts to rise to accompany him to the
door, he stops her gently with:

                    JUDGE SIMMONS
          Don't bother, Claire. I can find
          my way out.

——— He smiles in friendly fashion at the others and EXITS. ———

73   INT. LIBRARY - DAY - MED. SHOT

on Katherine, Brewster, Frank and Claire as they look
after the Judge. Brewster now turns to Katherine.

                    DR. BREWSTER
          Kay, do you mind if I try to
          talk Claire into coming back to
          work?

Katherine gives him a friendly smile.

                    KATHERINE
          Of course not. Just because I
          prefer to live at Dark Oaks is
          no reason she should.

                    DR. BREWSTER
          I don't quite see how you manage
          without servants. I take it they
          haven't returned since that night.

                    KATHERINE
                    (easily)
          No, but I'll arrange for others
          shortly - if I feel I need them.

                                        CONTINUED

73   CONTINUED

                    DR. BREWSTER
                  (resignedly)
          I guess you know what you want,
          Kay. Come along, Claire. Let's
          leave these two alone for a moment.

He leads her to the door where he turns and continues.

                    DR. BREWSTER
          I'll see you again before I leave.

He opens the door and he and Claire EXIT into the reception hall.

74   INT. RECEPTION HALL - DAY - MED.

Claire and Brewster come in from the library. As the
doctor closes the door, Claire shakes her head with a
little expression of worry.

                    CLAIRE
                  (softly)
          I feel terribly sorry for Frank.
          I'm afraid he's living in a fool's
          paradise.

They have turned away from the library door and the
CAMERA DOLLIES WITH THEM as they cross to the exterior
door. They continue talking as they walk.

                    DR. BREWSTER
                  (surprised)
          A fool's paradise?

                    CLAIRE
          Yes. I'm positive Kay doesn't in-
          tend to marry him.

                    DR. BREWSTER
          What's the trouble - Count Alucard?

By now they have reached the outer door. Brewster opens
it and Claire precedes him through it.

75   EXT. PORCH - DAY - MED. PAN

as Claire and Brewster walk to the edge of the porch
talking.

                                        CONTINUED

75   CONTINUED

> CLAIRE
> She couldn't marry <u>him</u>! There's
> something -- well, repulsive
> about him -- the way he came in
> the night father died and -- oh,
> I don't know.

She ends with a little shiver. As they stop at the edge
of the porch Brewster speaks.

> DR. BREWSTER
> I understand he left almost im-
> mediately. At least that was
> decent of him.

> CLAIRE
> Yes, but --

She hesitates, Brewster watching her narrowly. After a
moment she turns to him as if she feels she must confide
in someone.

> CLAIRE
> I'm positive Kay's seeing him
> more or less secretly.

Brewster is obviously becoming more interested.

> DR. BREWSTER
> Why do you say that?

> CLAIRE
> A couple of nights ago after I'd
> gone to bed, I heard them talking
> in the hall downstairs. Somehow I-
> I didn't like it and I went to
> the head of the stairs to make sure.

She stops. Brewster prompts her quietly.

> DR. BREWSTER
> And?

> CLAIRE
> Kay was alone in the lower hall,
> but she was looking up at me as
> if she'd been caught at something
> she - well, something she wasn't
> very proud of.

> DR. BREWSTER
> I see. Did you mention it to her?

CONTINUED

75   CONTINUED - 2

                    CLAIRE
          Yes, but she pooh-poohed the idea -
          said I probably was dreaming. I
          let it go at that, but I wasn't
          dreaming. I hadn't been asleep.

                    DR. BREWSTER
                  (musingly)
          That does sound strange.

He hesitates and looks off toward the guest cottage.

                    DR. BREWSTER
          Have you been in the guest house
          since the night your father died?

                    CLAIRE
                  (quickly)
          No, but surely you don't think
          Count Alucard is ---

                    DR. BREWSTER
          I don't know what to think. He
          couldn't be staying in town with-
          out my knowing it.

He thinks briefly, reaches a decision and looks
quizzically at the girl, continues.

                    DR. BREWSTER
          I'd like to look over his belong-
          ings - unless he's taken them away.

                    CLAIRE
          He couldn't have done that alone.
          They were too heavy.

Together they EXIT toward the o.s. guest house.

                                        WIPE TO:

76   INT. GUEST HOUSE LIVING ROOM - DAY - MED. FULL

It is a comparatively small room but nicely appointed -
a divan, coffee table, a few comfortable chairs, etc.
There is a small fireplace. Standing against one
wall are the Count's two trunks. The chests are missing,
Brewster and Claire are crossing to them.

77   INT. GUEST HOUSE LIVING ROOM - <u>DAY</u> - CLOSE SHOT - THE
      TWO TRUNKS

      Dr. Brewster looks at them for a moment, shifts one a
      little as if to test its weight.

                          DR. BREWSTER
                  Two big chests as well as the
                  trunks came on the train.

                          CLAIRE
                  I don't know what's become of
                  them, but they were put in here.

      CAMERA PANS with Dr. Brewster as he crosses to the bedroom
      door and looks in. He returns to Claire, CAMERA PULLING
      BACK with him. He looks at Claire apologetically.

                          DR. BREWSTER
                  It may not be ethical, but there
                  are reasons why we ought to find
                  out more about the Count.

      Claire nods in agreement and the doctor takes up a poker
      from the fireplace, inserts it under the lock hasp very
      quickly as if afraid Claire will change her mind and stop
      him. The hasp flies back under the pressure and the
      doctor opens the trunk. They both look into it.

78   INSERT - THE EMPTY TRUNK

      There is nothing in it except four iron bars wedged along
      its sides to give it weight.

79   INT. GUEST HOUSE LIVING ROOM - <u>DAY</u> - CLOSE SHOT -
      DR. BREWSTER AND CLAIRE

      They stand beside the trunk looking at each other.

                          CLAIRE
                  That's strange! He didn't
                  have any handbags. He can't
                  be traveling around with only the
                  clothes he has on.

      Brewster stands looking thoughtfully at the trunk. The
      SOUND of a slamming door o.s. at a distance causes them
      to turn and look out a window toward the mansion.

pg   38

80   EXT. DARK OAKS HOUSE - DAY - LONG SHOT

          on Frank as he comes out, slams the door and crosses
          angrily to his horse. Jerking the rein loose, he throws
          an angry look back toward the house, then makes a fast
          mount and spurs on his way - obviously in something of a
          temper.

81   INT. GUEST HOUSE LIVING ROOM - DAY - MED.   FRONT PORCH?

          on Claire and Brewster looking thru window at preceding
          scene. The girl turns to Brewster.

                              CLAIRE
                    You see what I meant? ---
                    About Kay and Frank?

          Brewster nods his head slowly and his eyes turn again to
          the trunk with its strange equipment.

                              DR. BREWSTER
                    I don't like it, Claire - don't
                    like it at all.

          He tosses the poker down on top of the trunk, then
          reaching a decision, turns to the girl.

                              DR. BREWSTER
                    You've got to leave here ---
                    get back to town, and the sooner
                    the better.

                              CLAIRE
                            (in surprise)
                    You sound as if I'm in some
                    kind of danger.

                              DR. BREWSTER
                    I'd rather not go into that. But
                    I insist you go back to town.
                    You can go in with me and send back
                    for your things later.

                              CLAIRE
                    'I can hardly leave Kay here alone.
                    If I'm in danger, she must be too.

                              DR. BREWSTER
                    I'm going to make a last attempt
                    to persuade her to leave. If she
                    won't ---

                                        CONTINUED

81   CONTINUED

He stops abruptly as if what he has to say is a difficult
task, then as if it is something that must be done,
he hurries on:

> DR. BREWSTER
> --- if she won't, I want you
> to join me in swearing out an
> insanity complaint against her!

> CLAIRE
> (gasping)
> An insanity complaint. Are you
> serious?

> DR. BREWSTER
> (earnestly)
> Never more so. Believe me,
> Claire, everyone's in danger
> here, Kay more than the others.
> If she won't leave voluntarily,
> we've got to force the issue.

As he finishes speaking, he leads the way out
determinedly.

                                            FADE OUT

FADE IN:

82   EXT. CALDWELL MANSION - NIGHT - FULL

The house is in darkness save for the reception hall.
The remainder of the house seen thru the trees appears
gloomy - forbidding. The door opens and Kay enters
scene quickly. She hurries to her car which is waiting
at the steps.

83   EXT. CALDWELL MANSION - NIGHT - MED.

at Kay's car. She enters it quickly, starts it and
drives out toward the gates. THE CAMERA PANS with the
car and comes to rest on a thick growth of trees and
shrubs an appreciable distance from the house. A figure
in gray emerges from the shadows and stops in a spot of
moonlight, looking after the car.

84   EXT. DARK OAKS GROUNDS - NIGHT - MED.

        on Frank standing in the spot of moonlight looking after
        the o.s. car, the sound of whose motor is dimming rapidly.
        Now he turns and runs off in a different direction from
        that taken by the car. CAMERA PANS him a short way thru
        the shrubbery, then loses him.

85   EXT. DARK OAKS GATES - NIGHT - MED. FULL PAN

        on Katherine's car as it moves along the drive and
        disappears thru the gates.

                                                   DISSOLVE TO

86   EXT. SWAMP - NIGHT - MED. FULL

        CAMERA is shooting from a point beside the road to show
        an expanse of treacherous-looking swamp. Over the scene
        may be heard the sound of frogs croaking and bats
        chittering and in the distance a heron's eerie cry.
        Above this comes the sound of an approaching auto.
        CAMERA PANS from the swamp to the road which runs beside
        it past a ghostly cane-brake. Kay's car is seen
        approaching along the dirt road. As it nears camera,
        the girl leans slightly from the window looking ahead to
        establish the identity of the driver.

87   EXT. SWAMP ROAD - NIGHT - FULL

        CAMERA is on a low set-up showing the top of the bank
        at the road's edge in f.g. Kay's car is approaching
        camera and slowing down. As it nears camera, most of
        the car disappears leaving us a view of only the wheels.
        The front wheels stop at the edge of the bank in f.g.
        and a portion of the loose earth, clods and small boulders
        are dislodged so they roll down hill past camera.

88   EXT. SWAMP - NIGHT - MED. SHOT

shooting down thru interlaced branches to show ugly water
at the swamp's edge. Some of the clods and small stones
from preceding scene roll down into scene and as they
reach the bottom of the incline where they clatter on
a surface which gives forth a hollow sound. After a
moment, the surface starts to lift, bringing with it a
certain amount of loose soil, twigs, etc. The surface is
oblong in shape and develops into the cover of one of
Count Alucard's chests which has been buried at the very
water's edge. As the lid lifts, a hand appears at its
upper edge, pushing it up and up.

89   EXT. SWAMP - NIGHT - CLOSE

on the edge of the chest lid as it rises. The fingers
of the hand folding over the edge show the ring which
Count Alucard wears on an index finger.

90   EXT. SWAMP ROAD - NIGHT - MED. SHOT

on Katherine's car standing waiting. The girl at the wheel
looks about casually, then glancing down toward the swamp,
she smiles.

91   EXT. SWAMP   NIGHT MED. SHOT

on the chest beside the water, showing all but a small
portion of the lid. The lid now lowers. As it fits home,
CAMERA PANS from the chest and shows Count Alucard standing at the end of the chest with the swamp behind him.
He is evidently the one who just lowered the lid. He
smiles grotesquely up at Kay and exits in her direction.

92   EXT. SWAMP ROAD - NIGHT - MED. FULL SHOT

A car appears around an upstage bend in the road and drives
toward camera, slowing down as it comes. It stops in
f.g. and the driver leans out the window to peer ahead
curiously. It is Frank.

93   EXT. SWAMP ROAD - NIGHT - MED. SHOT

at Katherine's car as Count Alucard opens the door and
steps inside to take his seat beside Katherine. The car
drives out. CAMERA PANS it on its way.

                                                    DISSOLVE TO:

ml   "DESTINY" - Changes 1/2/43   *Company*
                                                      To Robt. Siodmak 42

94   EXT. JONATHAN KIRBY'S HOME: NIGHT: FULL SHOT

This is a small, unpretentious brick house on a middle class
residential street. A sign on a post above the picket fence
shows the legend:

                    JONATHAN KIRBY
                    JUSTICE OF THE PEACE.

Katherine's car comes into scene and stops before the gate.
Alucard alights from the car and helps her out. Together
they start up the walk to the front porch.

95   EXT. KIRBY HOME: NIGHT: MED. SHOT

on the porch. Alucard and Katherine enter, step to the
door and the count raps with the knocker. After a moment
the door opens and Kirby appears, a typical small town
justice in smoking jacket, slippers, and glasses and
smoking an old curved stem pipe. In one hand he has a newspaper which he has been reading. As he opens the door he
happens to be looking more directly at Katherine than at
the count.

                    KIRBY
          Yes? What is it?

As he speaks, his eyes turn naturally to Alucard and something in the count's appearance causes him to draw back
slightly - seemingly a natural reaction in all who see him
for the first time. Katherine steps quickly into the breech.

                    KATHERINE
          Don't you remember me, Mr. Kirby?

Kirby turns quickly to her, but still with his mind more on
Alucard as he replies:
                    KIRBY
          Oh, yes -- of course. You're
          Colonel Caldwell's daughter. Sorry
          to hear about your father.

                    KATHERINE
          Thank you.....

Then as Kirby continues to wait, she continues:

                    KATHERINE
          May we come in? We're here to be
          married.
                    KIRBY
              (eyes widening)
          Married?

                                        CONTINUED

ml   "DESTINY" - Changes 1/2/43   43 & 44

95   CONTINUED

There is so much surprise in his voice as he again looks
at the count that he realizes it is not very complimentary
and covers by quickly assuming a more cordial tone.

                   KIRBY
        By all means -- come right in.

Then without waiting he turns and as he starts off into the
house calls to someone o.s.

                   KIRBY
        Oh, ma! Cecily.

96   EXT. KIRBY PORCH: NIGHT: CLOSER SHOT

on Katherine and Alucard before the open door. The count
bows low to Katherine and says softly:

               COUNT ALUCARD
       In a few moments, my dear, you
       will be the Countess Alucard!

As he speaks they turn to the open door and on the end of
his line there comes a terrific flash of lightning and crash
of thunder, presumably engendered by the very idea of the
unholy alliance.

                       QUICK WIPE TO:

97   STOCK SHOT FROM MR. STALL'S PICTURE

showing a car driving to camera in a quick storm as a tree
at the roadside crashes down in front of it, blocking its
way.

98   INT. FRANK'S CAR: NIGHT: CLOSE SHOT

on Frank for a reaction to the narrow escape. He is effectively blocked from driving farther.

                     DISSOLVE TO:

99   OMIT

100   OMIT

101   OMIT

102   INT. DARK OAKS RECEPTION HALL: NIGHT: MED. SHOT

The door opens and Alucard appears framed in the doorway
carrying Katherine lightly. He crosses the threshold and
sets her down lightly.

(This eliminates page 44 of previous continuity. F.B.)

AMENDED DIALOGUE - "<u>DESTINY</u>" - Sc. 102 - 1/14/43

102   CONTINUED

                              KATHERINE
                    Everything has worked out as we
                    planned, Anthony. This house is
                    old, but it is <u>ours</u>... no one
                    else has any claim on it.

Alucard looks about and smiles faintly.

                              ALUCARD
                    I like old houses... and I like
                    your countryside and the swamp
                    land.

Katherine links her arm thru his and they move down the
hall.

103   INT. RECEPTION HALL - NIGHT - CLOSE TRUCKING SHOT

                              KATHERINE
                    It's very different from your
                    own homeland.

                              ALUCARD
                    That is why I like it. My land
                    is dry and empty. The soil is
                    red with the blood of a hundred
                    races... but there is no life
                    left there.

They pause at the library door. Alucard smiles signifi-
cantly as he continues:

                              ALUCARD
                    Here you have a race that is young
                    and vital.

Katherine opens the library door and they move thru.

104   CONTINUED

They come to the center of the room. He moves in closer, his eyes burning into hers hypnotically. Katherine returns the look as if fascinated.

                    KATHERINE
                    (softly)
          You have hinted at much about your
          people but have told me very little
          about them - their legends - their
          mystery - their gifts.

105   INT. LIBRARY: NIGHT: CLOSE SHOT

on Katherine and Alucard.

                    COUNT ALUCARD
          Perhaps some day we may return
          there.

He laughs softly and continues:

                    COUNT ALUCARD
          As I have told you, ours will be
          a different life -- without
          material needs - a life that will
          last through eternity.

As he speaks he takes her in his arms and as he finishes he lifts her scarf and starts to bend forward as if to kiss her on the throat only to be interrupted by a knock on the door. The count straightens angrily. Katherine readjusts the scarf about her throat.

                    KATHERINE
          I'll see who it is.

Alucard stands rigid looking after Katherine as she exits toward the door.

106   INT. RECEPTION HALL: NIGHT: MED. SHOT

at the door. Over it sounds another knock. Katherine enters and opens the door disclosing Frank standing outside. Frank starts to speak but Katherine stops him short by speaking.

                    KATHERINE
                    (coldly)
          I told you before you are not to come
          here any more. I'm sorry.

ml   "DESTINY" - Changes 1/2/43   47

106   CONTINUED

      She starts to close the door, but Frank stops its swing
      with a hand and steps impetuously across the threshold,
      speaking as he enters - less angry than pleading, his con-
      cern more for the girl than for himself.

                         FRANK
                       (entering)
              I've got to talk to you, Kay. I
              know you're meeting Alucard secretly.
              I saw you with him tonight. I don't
              know where you went because I lost
              you, but --

                         KATHERINE
                      (interrupting)
              We went to Mr. Kirby's and were
              married.

      Frank stares at her nonplussed.

                         FRANK
              Married!

      Then he continues almost in a whisper:

                         FRANK (cont.)
              Oh, no - you couldn't have!

      His attention is attracted to something o.s. It is Alucard
      who steps into the open doorway to the library. Frank pushes
      past Katherine toward him, furious. Katherine follows.

107   INT. RECEPTION HALL - NIGHT - MED. SHOT

      on library doorway as Alucard appears in it and stands
      looking off at Frank coldly. (This intercuts with previous.)

108   INT. RECEPTION HALL. NIGHT. MED. SHOT

      Frank enters determinedly to Alucard and stops facing him.
      Katherine follows and lays a detaining hand on his arm. Ig-
      noring this Frank addresses Alucard.

                         FRANK
              You'll save us all a lot of unpleasant-
              ness by going back to town with me
              tonight and taking the first train out
              in the morning.

                         ALUCARD
                     (smiling coldly)
              I am afraid I do not understand.

                                             CONTINUED

108   CONTINUED

FRANK
Then I'll make it clear....

The Count's eyes blaze and he looks at Frank murderously.

FRANK (continuing)
I'm taking you into town... In
the morning you'll leave on the
first train. Kay will have the
marriage annulled, and if you
try to stop her, or show up in
this part of the country again,
you'll be jailed.

The Count's hand strikes at Frank's throat, seizes it and
squeezes, while Frank's arms thrash around helplessly.

109   INT. RECEPTION HALL - NIGHT - CLOSE SHOT - KATHERINE

She stands motionless, her eyes shining excitedly and
her mouth hard, cruel.

110   INT. RECEPTION HALL - NIGHT-CLOSE SHOT - FRANK AND
        COUNT ALUCARD

The Count's fingers are fastened into Frank's throat like
steel talons. Frank's arms are motionless, his legs are
limp, and he appears to be held upright only by the strength
in the Count's arm. The Count suddenly relaxes his grip,
flinging Frank past him into the library o.s. Katherine
comes in to the Count. The Count moves a couple of steps
into the library, leaving Katherine standing behind him.

111   INT. LIBRARY - NIGHT - MED. SHOT - FRANK, COUNT ALUCARD
        AND KATHERINE

Frank lies on the floor, breathing with an effort, and
resting on one arm, as if he has tried to rise, but is
unable to make it. His throat is black from the grip of
the Count's fingers and thumb. The Count watches him
from near the door as if waiting to finish him. Katherine,
just behind the Count, is watching coldly.

112   INT. LIBRARY - NIGHT - CLOSE SHOT - ANGLING DOWN ON FRANK

He moves a little, shifts his hand and brings it up with
gun. He looks completely insane as he levels it at the
Count o.s.

bm

113   INT. LIBRARY - NIGHT - MED. CLOSE SHOT - COUNT ALUCARD
       AND KATHERINE

       The Count is watching Frank o.s. exactly as he was, with
       apparently no concern for the gun. Katherine looks on
       as if hypnotized.

114   INT. LIBRARY - NIGHT - MED. SHOT - THE THREE

       As Frank fires twice, Katherine, directly behind the Count,
       screams and falls. The Count remains motionless; yet the
       bullets must have passed through him to hit Katherine. A
       look of wild incredulity is on Frank's face. As he struggles
       to his feet he fires two more shots at the Count who remains
       motionless. Wildly, Frank turns and runs to the doors and
       out.

115   EXT. CALDWELL HOME - NIGHT - MED. SHOT

       at door. Frank runs into scene thru the doors, gun in hand.
       CAMERA PANS him to the drive along which he runs panting
       and half-sobbing toward his car which is parked upstage in
       the direction of the gates at some distance from the house.

116   EXT. CALDWELL DRIVE - NIGHT - MED. SHOT (SPECIAL EFFECT)

       on Frank's car. The form of a huge wolf-dog with frothing
       jaws dissolves in in front of the car, legs braced and
       evidently there to prevent Frank from getting into the
       car. Frank runs in from CAMERA but stops at sight of the
       dog barring his way. He levels the gun at the dog.

117   EXT. CALDWELL DRIVE - NIGHT - MED. SHOT

       on Frank as he levels the gun at the dog o.s., and fires
       twice, then a third time. The third time the hammer falls
       on an empty chamber. Dropping the gun he turns and runs
       crazily off toward the brush and trees.

118   EXT. CALDWELL'S DRIVE - NIGHT - MED. SHOT (SPECIAL EFFECTS)

       The dog stands in front of the car snarling at Frank o.s.
       OVER SCENE COMES the SOUND of the two o.s. SHOTS. They do
       not affect the dog. (This for INTERCUTTING with previous
       scene.) Now the dog DISSOLVES OUT of scene and from the
       deep shadows under the car where he stood flies the enormous
       bat we first saw at Queen Zimba's cabin. It flies out in
       the direction taken by Frank.

bm

119   EXT. SERVANTS' CABINS - NIGHT - FULL SHOT

The cabins are deserted and lifeless. Frank runs in from
CAMERA in a sobbing panic, stumbling, catching himself and
running on. As he disappears in the runway between two of
the cabins, the huge bat flies in FROM CAMERA and follows
after him.

120   SHOT OF NIGHT SKY

as the moon goes behind a bank of scattering clouds dimming
the light.

121   EXT. GRAVEYARD (SERVANTS') - NIGHT - FULL SHOT

as Frank runs in. The scene is flat lighted and gloomy
without highlights and shadows. He stumbles and falls
across a grave presumably having passed out from the
fright of the past few minutes. The bat flutters in and
swoops down on him. A cross stands leaning on the grave.
But it casts no shadow.

122   EXT. SERVANTS' GRAVEYARD - NIGHT - MED. CLOSE SHOT

on Frank lying on the grave. The bat settles on his
shoulder near his neck and inches its way into position
so he can reach the carotid artery from which he presumably
will suck blood. As he reaches this position;

                                                    CUT TO:

123   SHOT OF NIGHT SKY

as the moon starts to emerge from behind fleecy clouds.

124   EXT. SERVANTS' GRAVEYARD - NIGHT - MED. CLOSE SHOT

on Frank with bat at his throat as the o.s. moon comes out
from behind the cloud, and striking the cross, casts its
shadow directly across Frank. As the shadow of the cross
grows sharp, the bat leaves its position, flutters back
a bit away from it, then flapping its wings flies up and
out of the scene.

125   EXT. SERVANTS' GRAVEYARD - NIGHT - MED. FULL SHOT

SHOOTING AWAY FROM the grave and toward trees and shrubs

                                                    CONTINUED

125   CONTINUED

upstage.   The big bat flies in FROM CAMERA and heads for
the shadows of the trees.   By HOLD-CUT, the bat disappears
and in its place we see the Count backing away from CAMERA,
his hands held before his eyes to shut out the sight of
the cross.

126   EXT. SERVANTS' GRAVEYARD - NIGHT - CLOSE SHOT - ANGLING
DOWN ON FRANK

He lies motionless, the shadow of the cross still over his
body.

                                              FADE OUT:

FADE IN:

127   INSERT - AN OPEN BOOK

At the top of the page to which it is opened is the title
DRACULA.   Below this title is the following text for as
much of it as can be read in a moment:

          "What manner of man is this Count
          Dracula, or what manner of creature
          is it in human form?   I feel the
          dread of this horrible place over-
          powering me.   I am in awful fear
          and there is no escape for me.   I
          am encompassed with terrors I dare
          not think of."

128   INT. DR. BREWSTER'S OFFICE - NIGHT - MED. CLOSE SHOT -
DR. BREWSTER

He is wearing a robe over trousers and shirt.   The room
is lighted with only a table lamp by which the doctor
reads and beyond the narrow sphere of its light the room
is dark, shadowy.   There are a number of books on the desk
before the doctor in addition to the copy of "Dracula".
He holds a pencil in his hand, and nearby is a pad of note
paper.   The doctor turns pages to another part of the book,
apparently scanning through it and makeing notes.   He starts
to read a passage that attracts him when a KNOCK COMES OVER
from the front door.   The doctor puts down the pencil and
looks up.   The KNOCKING CONTINUES.   The doctor rises and
crosses to the door, CAMERA PULLING BACK with him.

129   INT. DR. BREWSTER'S HALL - <u>NIGHT</u> - MED. SHOT -
        DR. BREWSTER

        He comes from the office and crosses to the front door.
        CAMERA ADVANCES TO:

130   INT. DR. BREWSTER'S HALL - <u>NIGHT</u> - CLOSE SHOT -
        DR. BREWSTER AND FRANK

        As the Doctor opens the door, Frank appears in it. His
        clothing is torn, his hair matted, and his eyes are wild,
        insane. The black bruise of the Count's fingers shows
        through his open shirt. He is so exhausted that only the
        Doctor's quickly given support prevents him falling into
        the hall. He stares at the Doctor without recognition.
        CAMERA PULLS BACK as the Doctor leads Frank across the
        hall and into the office.

131   INT. DR. BREWSTER'S OFFICE - <u>NIGHT</u> - MED. SHOT -
        DR. BREWSTER AND FRANK

        The Doctor places Frank on the couch, where there is a
        folded blanket, then crosses to a cabinet, CAMERA
        PANNING with him.

132   INT. DR. BREWSTER'S OFFICE - <u>NIGHT</u> - CLOSE SHOT - DR.
        BREWSTER AT CABINET

        He is about to take out a bottle of brandy when a call
        from Frank o.s. stops him.

                            FRANK
                        (calling o.s.)
                Harry!...

        The Doctor turns quickly. CAMERA PULLS BACK with him as
        he crosses to Frank.

133   INT. DR. BREWSTER'S OFFICE - <u>NIGHT</u> - MED. CLOSE SHOT
        DR. BREWSTER AND FRANK

        Frank is sitting upright on the divan, his face haggard
        with worry.

                            FRANK
                How did I get here?... Did
                you bring me from Dark Oaks?

                            DR. BREWSTER
                No; you came alone... a minute or
                two ago. What's happened, Frank?

                                                    CONTINUED

Frank, choked to death's door by Alucard and rocked by the knowledge that he shot Kay, is almost catatonic by the time he arrives at Dr. Brewster's.

133   CONTINUED

> FRANK
>
> I have killed Kay.

He rubs a hand over his eyes and continues:

> FRANK (continuing)
>
> It's all mixed up, but I know
> I shot her - twice.

He lurches to his feet, grabs the doctor's shoulders.

> FRANK
>
> Am I insane, Harry? Could I have
> shot right through Alucard and
> killed Kay without hurting him?

He laughs insanely and the doctor reacts with a start of
fear.

> DR. BREWSTER
>
> Sit down, Frank.

He forces Frank down on the divan, sits beside him.

> DR. BREWSTER
>
> (gently)
> Tell me exactly what happened.

Frank looks at him angrily.

134   INT. DR. BREWSTER'S OFFICE - NIGHT - CLOSE SHOT - FRANK

> FRANK
>
> You're trying to humor me...
> You think I am crazy.

> DR. BREWSTER
>
> No, Frank, I don't.

Frank laughs hysterically.

> FRANK
>
> But I shot right through him. Kay
> screamed and fell, and he stood
> there staring at me. You don't
> believe that... Nobody will.

135   INT. DR. BREWSTER'S OFFICE - NIGHT - CLOSE TWO SHOT

The doctor nods slowly, yes. Looking at Frank
sympathetically, he says quietly:

> CONTINUED

135   CONTINUED

                        DR. BREWSTER
          I believe you.

Frank gives him a quick suspicious glance, but before he
can speak, the doctor continues:

                        DR. BREWSTER
          Have you got your revolver?

Frank looks puzzled, as if searching through obscure
memories for one elusive fact. His face brightens.

                        FRANK
          No; I dropped it in the drive.

                        DR. BREWSTER
          But you haven't told me. Just
          what happened?

Frank looks embarrassed, then blurts out:

                        FRANK
                     (defiantly)
          Kay and Alucard were married tonight!
          I know, because I'd gone to the Oaks
          to spy, and I followed them!

The doctor gives a little start.

                        DR. BREWSTER
          Didn't you try to stop the
          wedding?

Frank shakes his head.

                        FRANK
          I didn't know what to do...
          I couldn't think.

The doctor nods understandingly.

                        FRANK (continuing)
          But I followed them back to
          Dark Oaks, and I got into a
          fight with him.

Frank grabs the doctor suddenly.

                                        CONTINUED

135   CONTINUED - 2

                                FRANK
                    He got me by the throat. It
                    was like one of those crazy
                    nightmares where you can't move
                    or struggle. I had no more
                    strength against him than a
                    baby. At last he threw me off.
                    That's when I fired at him. The
                    bullets passed through him without
                    hurting him and killed Kay!

                                DR. BREWSTER
                    Can you remember what you did
                    then?

        An involuntary shudder crosses Frank's face. He shakes
        his head in bewilderment.

                                FRANK
                    I seemed to be running and falling.
                    But it's all mixed up with a wolf
                    and a bat... I don't remember much
                    of anything else until I found myself
                    here.

        CAMERA ADVANCES TO:

136   INT. DR. BREWSTER'S OFFICE - <u>NIGHT</u> - CLOSEUP - FRANK

        The bruises on his throat stand out clearly as he moves
        his head to look off at the Doctor with a searching,
        pleading expression.

                                FRANK
                    I don't know if any of it's real...
                    Maybe it's all a nightmare.... or....

        He stops as if afraid to continue.

137   INT. DR. BREWSTER'S OFFICE - <u>NIGHT</u> - CLOSE TWO SHOT

        The Doctor is looking fixedly at the bruises on Frank's
        throat.

                                DR. BREWSTER
                    Rest for a minute, Frank.... We'll
                    find out how much of it happened.

        He turns away and CAMERA PANS with him as he crosses to a
        water cooler, draws off some water into a paper cup and
        then goes to a medicine cabinet.

138   INT. DR. BREWSTER'S OFFICE - NIGHT - CLOSE SHOT - THE
        DOCTOR

        He shakes a few tablets out of a bottle and drops them
        into the water cup, stirs it for a moment, then starts
        toward Frank o.s.

139   INT. DR. BREWSTER'S OFFICE - NIGHT - MED. CLOSE SHOT -
        FRANK

        as the doctor comes in with the water.

                        DR. BREWSTER
                Take this, Frank.

        Frank takes it automatically, but lifting it to his mouth,
        hesitates. The doctor smiles reassuringly. Frank drains
        the cup, gives it to the doctor.

                        DR. BREWSTER
                Lie down while I get ready.

        Frank relaxes back on the couch. The doctor turns away,
        CAMERA PANNING with him as he crosses to the desk.

140   INT. DR. BREWSTER'S OFFICE - NIGHT - CLOSE SHOT - THE
        DOCTOR

        He closes the open book on the desk, then slips off his
        robe, throwing it on the chair. CAMERA PANS him to a
        closet. He reaches into it and brings out a coat. As
        he puts it on, he looks off at Frank.

141   INT. DR. BREWSTER'S OFFICE - NIGHT - MED. SHOT - FRANK

        He is lying down almost asleep as the doctor comes in and
        stands looking down at him. One of his arms falls
        heavily over the side of the couch. He is sound asleep
        now. The doctor bends over, lifts Frank's arm and puts
        a pillow under his head. Frank's breathing becomes
        deeper. The doctor watches him for a moment, unfolds the
        blanket and spreads it over him, then walks quietly to
        the door, CAMERA PANNING with him. As he EXITS,

                                        DISSOLVE TO

142   EXT. DARK OAKS GRAVEYARD - NIGHT - FULL

        Under the fitful moon the graveyard spreads out eerily,
        the smaller graves making a proper setting for the family
        vault which stands some distance from camera. The figure
        of a man in black may be seen near the vault working with
        a shovel, although at this distance the nature of his
        work may not be so well defined.

143   EXT. GRAVEYARD - NIGHT - MED.

on Count Alucard. He has a long-handled shovel with which
he lifts a clump of earth from a hole of fair size from
which he has apparently taken other earth. CAMERA PANS
him to the door of the vault which stands open. He enters
with the shovelful of earth.

144   INT. VAULT - NIGHT - FULL

It is a fair-sized family vault with a dozen or more
compartments for the remains of those who have died,
most of them with plaques establishing their identity.
One of them is open. The body of Katherine lies stretched
out on its back, hands folded conventionally across the
breast. Alucard enters with his shovelful of earth and
scatters it in the open compartment.

145   INT. VAULT - INSERT

close on open vault compartment. It already has a slight
sprinkling of earth on the bottom. Alucard's shovel
enters scene and scatters its load over the bottom of the
compartment.

146   INT. VAULT - NIGHT - MED. FULL

Alucard leaves the compartment and walks to the door with
the shovel.

147   EXT. VAULT - NIGHT - MED.

Alucard comes from the open door of the vault with the
shovel and CAMERA PANS him to the place where he has been
digging. He starts to shovel up more earth when the sound
of a motor attracts his attention. He pauses and looks
off. A look of rage comes to his eyes as he sees:

148   EXT. DARK OAKS - NIGHT - FULL

from Alucard's viewpoint as Brewster's car drives in and
disappears around the house.

149   EXT. GRAVEYARD - NIGHT - MED. CLOSE

on Alucard. He is staring off at Brewster's car. Now he
starts as if to go to investigate. He stops as he realizes
he must not leave Katherine and the vault this way. He
hesitates, then taking up another shovelful of earth, he
heads once more for the vault, CAMERA PANNING him to show
him enter presumably to repeat what we have already seen
him do.

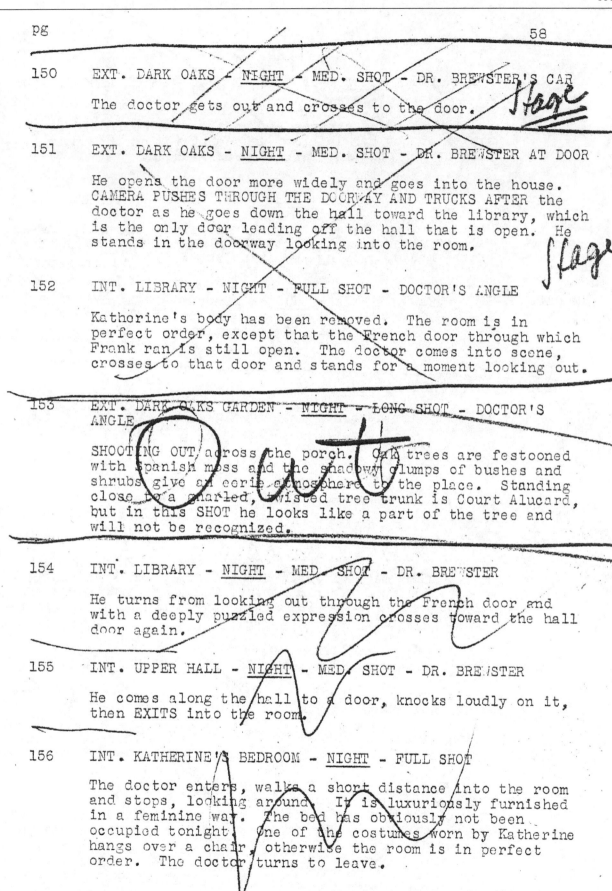

150   EXT. DARK OAKS - NIGHT - MED. SHOT - DR. BREWSTER'S CAR
       The doctor gets out and crosses to the door.   *Stage*

151   EXT. DARK OAKS - NIGHT - MED. SHOT - DR. BREWSTER AT DOOR

       He opens the door more widely and goes into the house.
       CAMERA PUSHES THROUGH THE DOORWAY AND TRUCKS AFTER the
       doctor as he goes down the hall toward the library, which
       is the only door leading off the hall that is open. He
       stands in the doorway looking into the room.

                                                        Stage

152   INT. LIBRARY - NIGHT - FULL SHOT - DOCTOR'S ANGLE

       Kathorine's body has been removed. The room is in
       perfect order, except that the French door through which
       Frank ran is still open. The doctor comes into scene,
       crosses to that door and stands for a moment looking out.

153   EXT. DARK OAKS GARDEN - NIGHT - LONG SHOT - DOCTOR'S
       ANGLE

       SHOOTING OUT across the porch. Oak trees are festooned
       with Spanish moss and the shadowy clumps of bushes and
       shrubs give an eerie atmosphere to the place. Standing
       close to a gnarled, twisted tree trunk is Court Alucard,
       but in this SHOT he looks like a part of the tree and
       will not be recognized.   *Out*

154   INT. LIBRARY - NIGHT - MED. SHOT - DR. BREWSTER

       He turns from looking out through the French door and
       with a deeply puzzled expression crosses toward the hall
       door again.

155   INT. UPPER HALL - NIGHT - MED. SHOT - DR. BREWSTER

       He comes along the hall to a door, knocks loudly on it,
       then EXITS into the room.

156   INT. KATHERINE'S BEDROOM - NIGHT - FULL SHOT

       The doctor enters, walks a short distance into the room
       and stops, looking around. It is luxuriously furnished
       in a feminine way. The bed has obviously not been
       occupied tonight. One of the costumes worn by Katherine
       hangs over a chair, otherwise the room is in perfect
       order. The doctor turns to leave.

134

157   INT. VAULT - NIGHT - MED. CLOSE SHOT - COUNT ALUCARD AND
       KATHERINE

       He lifts her and carries her to the open space and as he
       starts to put her into it, we see stains on the upper
       part of her costume where she was wounded.

158   INT. RECEPTION HALL - NIGHT - MED. SHOT - DR. BREWSTER

       He comes down the stairs and turns along the hall, CAMERA
       PANNING with him. He continues along it toward the back
       of the house, passing the open library door.

159   INT. RECEPTION HALL - NIGHT - MED. SHOT - DR. BREWSTER

       He comes in and opens a door that leads to the cellar
       stairs and EXITS through it.

160   INT. CELLAR - NIGHT - MED. SHOT - AT STAIRS

       Dr. Brewster descends into SCENE, comes all the way down
       the stairs and walks a short distance into the cellar,
       then stops to look around. It is unlighted except for
       the light that comes from above, and that from the out-
       doors which comes through the small windows set high in
       the walls.

161   INT. CELLAR - NIGHT - PANNING SHOT

       OVER THE CELLAR FROM THE DOCTOR'S ANGLE. There is the
       usual assortment of discarded articles, old furniture,
       etc. found in a big old house. There are trunks new and
       old, packing cases, presumably empty, and near them a
       crate containing live chickens.

162   INT. CELLAR - NIGHT - MED. SHOT - AT CHICKEN CRATE

       The doctor comes into it, stands looking at the few live
       chickens. He walks past it to look behind the packing
       cases.

163   INT. CELLAR - NIGHT - MED. SHOT

       SHOOTING PAST THE DOCTOR to a space about two feet wide
       between the packing cases and the wall. In this space is
       one of the Count's chests bearing his coat of arms and
       name on the end. The doctor steps in close to the case,
       raises its top. He looks in.

164   INT. CELLAR - <u>NIGHT</u> - CLOSE SHOT - DOWN ANGLE

SHOOTING INTO THE CHEST. It is empty except for an inch
or two of earth on the bottom and carcasses of a number
of chickens, still feathered but mutilated.

165   INT. CELLAR - <u>NIGHT</u> - MED. SHOT - DR. BREWSTER

With an expression of revulsion he lets the cover fall
back on the chest with a REVERBERATING THUD and walks away.

166   INT. CELLAR - <u>NIGHT</u> - MED. SHOT - DR. BREWSTER

He comes in quickly to the foot of the stairs, looks up
and stops.

167   INT. CELLAR - <u>NIGHT</u> - MED. SHOT - COUNT ALUCARD ON STAIRS
SHOOTING UP FROM DOCTOR'S ANGLE

He is about half way up the stairs, looking down and
blocking the doctor's way.

168   INT. CELLAR - <u>NIGHT</u> - CLOSE SHOT - DR. BREWSTER

He looks up at the Count o.s. with a tense expression.
The Count's VOICE COMES OVER, asking:

                         COUNT ALUCARD
               May I inquire what you are doing
               here?

The doctor smiles.

                         DR. BREWSTER
               I was about to ask you the same
               question.

CAMERA PANS with him as he goes up the stairs to face
Count Alucard.

                         COUNT ALUCARD
               I married Miss Caldwell tonight.
               I am now the head of this house.
               You see, <u>you</u> owe <u>me</u> the explanation.

The doctor forces a smile, shrugs.

                                        CONTINUED

168   CONTINUED

> DR. BREWSTER
> I came to see Katherine. The door
> was open. She didn't answer my calls
> and I thought I heard someone in the
> cellar.

The Count gives him a fixed look.

> COUNT ALUCARD
> I, too, thought I heard someone in
> the cellar....Come.

He gestures with his hand, urging the doctor to precede
him. The doctor goes on with the Count following.

169   INT. RECEPTION HALL - NIGHT - MED. SHOT - DR. BREWSTER
        AND COUNT ALUCARD

They enter from the cellar door. The doctor turns to face
the Count. CAMERA MOVES IN CLOSER.

> COUNT ALUCARD
> I realize you are an old friend of
> the family, but isn't it a bit absurd
> to ask the Countess to receive you
> at this hour?

The doctor looks the Count in the eyes with a stubbornly
determined expression.

> DR. BREWSTER
> Give her my apologies and explain
> that it's a matter of importance.
> You might add that I won't leave
> without seeing her...even if I
> have to remain here until morning.

Hate flashes on the Count's face, then he puts on a smooth
front, bowing quietly and saying:

> COUNT ALUCARD
> The Countess has retired, but I'll
> convey your message. Will you kindly
> wait in her sitting room?

He gestures toward the door o.s. The doctor gives him a
curt nod and walks down the hall.

> DISSOLVE TO:

gs   62

170   INT. KATHERINE'S SITTING ROOM - <u>NIGHT</u> - CLOSE SHOT -
       THE DOCTOR

       He is sitting back in a deep chair with feet propped up
       on another. Beside him is an ash tray with six or eight
       half-smoked cigarettes in it. He crushes out the cigarette
       he is smoking as a door o.s. is heard to open. CAMERA
       PANS TO:

171   INT. KATHERINE'S SITTING ROOM - <u>NIGHT</u> - MED. SHOT - COUNT
       ALUCARD

       He comes from the door, CAMERA PULLING BACK with him as
       he crosses to the doctor, who rises. The Count stops,
       makes an imperative, beckoning gesture.

                              COUNT ALUCARD
             Come.

       The doctor looks dubious, but after a moment's hesitation
       follows the Count to the door. They EXIT.

                                             WIPE TO:

172   INT. UPPER HALL - <u>NIGHT</u> - MED. SHOT - AT DOOR TO
       KATHERINE'S ROOM

       The Count and doctor come in to it. The Count knocks
       politely, then without waiting for a response opens the
       door, motioning to the doctor to enter.

173   INT. KATHERINE'S BEDROOM - <u>NIGHT</u> - FULL SHOT

       The room is brightly lighted now and is as we saw it last
       except that the mirrors have been removed from dressers,
       etc. Katherine is sitting up in the bed with a pillow
       propping her. She is wearing an ermine-trimmed bed-
       jacket or negligee, presumably over a nightgown. It
       fastens high around the throat, the soft fur coming almost
       to her chin. Her eyes appear wide and staring; her lips
       are fuller, more voluptuous than previously. The doctor
       and Count enter from the hall and cross to the bedside
       as CAMERA ADVANCES TO:

174   INT. KATHERINE'S BEDROOM - <u>NIGHT</u> - MED. CLOSE SHOT -
       THE THREE - FAVORING KATHERINE

       She looks at the doctor and smiles. There is a strange-
       ness to her smile now; it is cruel, crafty, but her voice
       is perfectly normal as she speaks.

                                             CONTINUED

174   CONTINUED

                           KATHERINE
          Dr. Brewster! What on earth brings
          you here at this time of the night?

She looks more serious and continues:

                           KATHERINE (continuing)
                    (anxiously)
          I hope nothing's happened to Claire.

The doctor shakes his head, smiles.

                           DR. BREWSTER
          No; she was worried that something
          had happened to you.

Katherine tries to look concerned, but the result is
insincere.

                           KATHERINE
          I'm sorry.

She closes her hand quickly over the doctor's and he reacts with an involuntary start. Seeing this, Katherine's
eyes blaze with hate for an instant, then she smiles
coquettishly.

                           KATHERINE
          Count Alucard and I were married
          tonight.

                           DR. BREWSTER
          The Count has already told me.

                           KATHERINE
          It was the way we wanted it...quiet
          and alone. That's the way we're
          going to live, Harry.

                           COUNT ALUCARD
          I am engaged in certain research work
          that occupies all my days.

                           KATHERINE
          And we'll have no time for social
          life.

                           COUNT ALUCARD
          We'd like you to explain this to
          Claire.

Katherine looks sincerely concerned for a moment.

                                        CONTINUED

gs   64

174   CONTINUED - 2

                              KATHERINE
                    And to Frank...I'm fond of
                    Frank...
                              (smiles reminiscently)
                    ...but of course, he must never
                    come here again.

          She looks at the Count curiously. He nods, as if encour-
          aging her in the recitation of some lesson she has learned.

                              KATHERINE
                    I should like you to tell all our
                    friends not to come. If Judge
                    Simmons has papers for us to sign,
                    ask him to bring them in the evening.

          The doctor looks at her searchingly.

                              COUNT ALUCARD
                    Katherine is going to devote her
                    days to assisting me in my work.

                              DR. BREWSTER
                    I see.

          He rises.

                              DR. BREWSTER (continuing)
                    As long as I'm here on a pointless
                    errand, I may as well leave. Good-
                    night, Kay.

          She gives him a smile that is meant to be warm, but is
          cruel, frightening.

                              KATHERINE
                    Goodbye, Doctor....And say goodbye
                    to Frank.

          The doctor gives her a little nod, turns to go. The Count
          falls in with him, CAMERA PANNING them to the door.

175   INT. UPPER HALL - NIGHT - MED. SHOT - DOCTOR AND COUNT
        ALUCARD

          They come from the room and start down the hall, CAMERA
          TRUCKING with them.

                              COUNT ALUCARD
                    Perhaps I should emphasize certain
                    wishes Katherine expressed.

                                                  CONTINUED

175   CONTINUED:

The doctor looks at him questioningly.

> COUNT ALUCARD
> When I arrived here I was not
> graciously welcomed... Now my
> position is changed.

They reach the head of the stairs and stop. The Count
turns to the doctor with angry, blazing eyes.

> COUNT ALUCARD
> I am the master of Dark Oaks. No
> one may enter here. All who do
> so will be treated as trespassers.

He gives the doctor a curt nod of dismissal, gestures to
the stairs and turns away, EXITING from SCENE along the
hall. The doctor starts down the stairs with an engrossed,
worried expression.

> FADE OUT:

FADE IN:

176   INSERT - A METAL PLAQUE (RAIN IS FALLING PAST IT) - DAY

It reads:

> HARRY BREWSTER, M.D.
> Physician and Surgeon

> DISSOLVE TO:

177   INT. DR. BREWSTER'S DINING ROOM - DAY - (RAIN) - FULL SHOT

Rain is falling past the window. Dr. Brewster's colored
housekeeper, SARAH, is carrying a coffee pot to the table,
which is set for one, as the doctor enters from the hall.

> DR. BREWSTER
> Good morning, Sarah. Will you set
> another place? Mr. Stanley slept
> on the couch in the office last
> night.

Sarah looks a little surprised.

> CONTINUED

177   CONTINUED

                            SARAH
            There ain't nobody there now, suh.
            There's a blanket on the couch,
            but no sign of Mr. Frank. Why
            didn't you put him in a spare
            bedroom? No wonder he never
            stayed for breakfast.

The doctor comes in to the table, sits down. He looks
tired.

                            DR. BREWSTER
            Just give me coffee this morning,
            Sarah.

178   INT. DR. BREWSTER'S DINING ROOM - DAY - MED. CLOSE SHOT
        AT TABLE

Dr. Brewster sits down. Sarah looks at him curiously,
appears about to voice an objection to his having only
coffee, then closes her lips in a determined way and pours
a cup. Before the cup is filled a DOORBELL RINGS. Sarah
puts the pot down and EXITS to the hall. The Doctor stirs
the coffee to cool it, then takes a sip or two and puts it
down. Sarah's VOICE COMES OVER from the hall:

                            SARAH (o.s.)
                            (Calling)
            Here's Judge Simmons, Doctor.

The doctor pushes back his chair, gets up and crosses to
the door, CAMERA PANNING with him.

179   INT. DR. BREWSTER'S DINING ROOM - DAY - MED. SHOT - DOCTOR,
        JUDGE AND SARAH

As the latter two enter from the hall, the Judge stops to
hand Sarah his hat and umbrella.

                            DR. BREWSTER
            Give Sarah your coat and join me
            in a cup of coffee, Judge.

                            JUDGE
            I'll keep my coat on... I can
            only stay a minute.

CAMERA PULLS BACK AS THE Doctor and Judge cross to the
table and sit down.

180   INT. DR. BREWSTER'S DINING ROOM - DAY - MED. CLOSE SHOT
        DR. BREWSTER AND JUDGE

        The Judge wipes his face with a handkerchief.

                         DR. BREWSTER
                      (making conversation)
                Quite a rain we had

        The Judge nods, pockets his handkerchief, saying:

                         JUDGE
                It started about four o'clock
                and has been pouring ever since.

        Sarah comes in with a cup, fills it with coffee for the
        Judge.

                         JUDGE
                Claire isn't here yet?

        Sarah places the cup before the Judge, puts sugar and
        cream in reach and EXITS.

                         DR. BREWSTER
                No, but I expect her any minute.

                         JUDGE
                I was up most of the night studying
                the insanity complaint you drew
                up against Katherine.

        He puts sugar and cream in his coffee.

                         DR. BREWSTER
                What did you decide?

                         JUDGE
                If I didn't know you and Claire, I'd
                be suspicious of your motives. You've
                got no evidence of insanity, Harry.
                The fact that she wants to live alone
                at Dark Oaks may be eccentric, but it's
                nothing more. Her infatuation with
                this Count, even if he is an imposter,
                may be bad judgment but cannot be
                construed as insane.

        The Doctor nods, drinks a litte of his coffee and the Judge
        sips his.

                         DR. BREWSTER
                They were married last night by
                Kirby.

                                        CONTINUED

180   CONTINUED

       The Judge puts down his cup with a small clatter.

                         JUDGE
               I'm sorry... Katherine's like
               a niece to me.

       He looks down at his cup with a somber expression. The
       RINGING of a PHONE in another room COMES OVER quietly.

                         JUDGE
               You can still have a court
               insanity hearing, but I advise
               strongly against it.

       The Doctor nods.

                         DR. BREWSTER
                       (abstractedly)
               I'm afraid it's too late to do
               anything now.

       The Judge looks at him curiously as if not quite following
       his meaning. Before he can speak Sarah comes in to them.
       They both look up at her.

                         SARAH
               You're wanted on the phone, Judge
               Simmons. It's Missus Simmons, sir...
               She says it's important.

                         DR. BREWSTER
               Take it in the office, Judge.

       The Doctor rises to take the Judge to the phone. CAMERA
       PANNING them to the door.

181   INT. DR. BREWSTER'S HALL - DAY - MED. SHOT - DR. BREWSTER
       AND JUDGE

       They come up to the office door where the doctor stops,
       opens the door and the two EXIT into the office.

182   INT. DR. BREWSTER'S OFFICE - DAY - MED. SHOT - DR. BREWSTER
       AND JUDGE

       Rain is beating against the window in the b.g. The Doctor
       leads the Judge to the desk, picks up the phone and hands
       it to him.

                                             CONTINUED

182   CONTINUED

                              JUDGE
                          (into phone)
                    Yes, dear....... What?!

The Doctor starts to walk back toward the door, but the
Judge commands him to stay with quick, imperious gesture
of his hand. The Doctor pauses, comes back to the desk.

183   INT. DR. BREWSTER'S OFFICE - DAY - CLOSE SHOT - THE TWO

The Doctor watches the Judge's serious face uneasily as
the Judge, on the phone, listens intently.

                              JUDGE
                          (into phone)
                    I'll go right over to the Court
                    House... Goodbye.

He hangs up, turns to the Doctor with a grim expression.

                              JUDGE
                    Frank Stanley surrendered to the
                    sheriff a while ago. He tells
                    some story about killing Katherine
                    ~~Cordell~~.

There is a moment of tense silence, then the Doctor says
quietly:

                              DR. BREWSTER
                    I'm afraid Frank is not entirely
                    responsible. He came here in the
                    middle of the night in a delirious
                    condition and told me the same
                    thing. He was obviously suffering
                    from shock.

                              JUDGE
                          (stunned)
                    And you did nothing about it?

                              DR. BREWSTER
                    I gave him a sedative and drove
                    out to Dark Oaks. I talked to
                    Katherine. It was long after
                    Frank said he'd killed her.

The Judge shakes his head soberly.

                              JUDGE
                    You'd better come over to the
                    Courthouse with me.

Dr. Brewster nods.   CONTINUED

bm   70

183   CONTINUED

                         DR. BREWSTER
            Certainly.

184   INT. DR. BREWSTER'S OFFICE - DAY - MED. SHOT - DR. BREWSTER
       AND JUDGE

       They cross to the hall door and EXIT through it.

185   INT. DR. BREWSTER'S HALL - DAY - MED. SHOT - DR. BREWSTER
       AND JUDGE

       The Judge stands waiting while the Doctor crosses to a
       closet. As he opens its door, he calls:

                         DR. BREWSTER
                          (calling)
            Sarah!

       He reaches into the closet for a raincoat and hat. As
       he is getting into them, Sarah comes hurrying with the
       Judge's hat and umbrella, which she gives to him.

                         DR. BREWSTER
            Sarah, Professor Lazlo is arriving
            from Memphis on the morning train...
            He'll be staying here for a few days.
            Make him comfortable, will you?

                         SARAH
            Yes, Doctor.

       He turns and walks to the front door with the Judge.

                                             DISSOLVE TO:

186   INT. COURT HOUSE CORRIDOR - DAY - MED. SHOT

       The corridor is barren, drab. At the moment there is
       considerable activity in it, rain-coated men hurrying along
       it, entering and leaving various offices. The Doctor and
       Judge Simmons come into scene and cross quickly to a door
       marked: SHERIFF. The Judge opens the door and they EXIT
       into it.

187   INT. SHERIFF'S OFFICE - DAY - FULL SHOT

       The Sheriff, MORLEY DAWES: a deputy, SAM ARNOLD; and the
                                             CONTINUED

187   CONTINUED

coroner, DOC PETERS, all in rain-coats or slickers, are
in the large, cold, crudely furnished room as the Doctor
and Judge Simmons ENTER. The Sheriff is a tight-lipped,
hard-eyed man of indefinite age. He is of the eye-for-
an-eye type of law officer. He wouldn't be unfair
according to his lights, but he would be merciless. The
Deputy is a doggedly faithful but not overly-bright
assistant to him. Doc Peters, in the mid-fifties, is
the typical politico doctor, lazy and old-fashioned. The
Sheriff is standing behind the big, crude desk, the Deputy
is just behind him, and Doc Peters is seated with his
medical bag at his feet. The three nod in greeting to
Dr. Brewster and ad-lib goodmornings to the Judge.

                    THE THREE
                   (ad-libbing)
          Howdy, Judge...
          Good morning, Judge... etc.

                    THE JUDGE
          Good morning, gentlemen...

He looks directly at the Sheriff, then to ask:

                    JUDGE
          Where's Frank, Sheriff?

CAMERA ADVANCES TO:

188   INT. SHERIFF'S OFFICE - DAY - MED. SHOT - GROUP

                    SHERIFF
          A deputy's fetching him. We're
          all going out to Dark Oaks.

                    JUDGE
          I don't think that will be necessary.
          Dr. Brewster says Frank's insane.

The Sheriff looks at the Judge and Dr. Brewster questioningly.

                    DR. BREWSTER
          I talked to Katherine and her
          husband after Frank was supposed
          to have killed her.

The Sheriff frowns, looks thoughtful for a moment, then:

                    SHERIFF
          So? Well, I'd better go out to
          Dark Oaks anyway and talk to them
          myself.

                                        CONTINUED

188   CONTINUED

Dr. Brewster looks disappointed, then tries to appear
casual as he says:

                    DR. BREWSTER
          No use going before evening.
          Katherine and her husband will
          be away all day.

The Sheriff looks surpised.

                    SHERIFF
          Yeah..... where'll they be?

                    DR. BREWSTER
          I don't know. But they said to
          tell Claire they wouldn't be at
          home.

The Sheriff considers this for a moment.

                    SHERIFF
          I'm going to take Frank out there
          anyway - maybe he'll come to his
          senses if we make him go over the
          ground like he covered it in his
          confession.

                    DR. BREWSTER
          I wish you wouldn't, Sheriff.
          Frank is suffering from shock...
          he needs complete relaxation.

189   INT. SHERIFF'S OFFICE - DAY - CLOSE SHOT - DR. BREWSTER
       AND SHERIFF

He looks at the Doctor bleakly.

                    SHERIFF
          Frank Stanley has confessed to
          murder and I have to act on it.
          It won't hurt him to ride out
          there with us.

                    DR. BREWSTER
                 (emphatically)
          I give you my word that it will!

                    SHERIFF
          That's too bad. But money and
          position don't rate him any
          better treatment than anyone
          else from me.

                                        CONTINUED

bm

189   CONTINUED

He looks off toward the Coroner.

                    SHERIFF
          Did he act crazy to you, Doctor
          Peters?

CAMERA PULLS BACK to BRING IN Peters.

                    DR. PETERS
          No-o... can't say that he did...
          a little irrational, maybe, same
          as anyone after committing murder.

                    SHERIFF
          You can come along if you like, Doc.
          If everything's all right, I'll turn
          him over to you and forget about the
          confession. That ought to be fair
          enough.

He starts away from the desk, CAMERA PULLING BACK as the
others follow him from the room.

                                        DISSOLVE TO:

190   EXT. DARK OAKS - DAY - MED. SHOT

It is not raining but the ground and trees are wet. The
Sheriff's big touring car with the Judge, Dr. Brewster,
Frank, the Deputy named Small. The Sheriff comes in and
stops before the porch steps. It is followed immediately
by a smaller car in which the Coroner and the Deputy, Sam
Arnold, are riding. They all get out and CAMERA PANS them
to the front door, which is blowing open and shut with the
gusty, wet wind.

191   EXT. DARK OAKS - DAY - MED. SHOT - AT FRONT DOOR

The Sheriff looks from the open door to Dr. Brewster
suspiciously. He pulls the old-fashioned bell which can
be HEARD JANGLING in the back of the house.

                    SHERIFF
          Funny they'd leave the door open
          on a day like this.

He steps in and the others follow, the two Deputies remaining on either side of Frank.

192   INT. DARK OAKS RECEPTION HALL - DAY - FULL SHOT

           The group comes in from the door, walks a little way along
           the hall.

                              SHERIFF
                            (calling)
                    Anyone here?...

           His voice reverberates eerily and there is no answer.
           He turns to Frank.

                              SHERIFF
                    Suppose you show us where you
                    were when you shot Katherine, and
                    where she and her husband were.

           Frank hesitates, a pitifully strained and worried look on
           his face.

                              DR. BREWSTER
                    There's nothing to worry about,
                    Frank. You go ahead and re-enact
                    what you _think_ happened.

           Frank turns to the sheriff.

                              FRANK
                    It was in the library.

           He starts down the hall with the others following, but
           Dr. Brewster manages to let the others go ahead. They
           all EXIT into the open library door, except the doctor,
           who continues quietly along the hall to the cellar door,
           and EXITS through it.

193   INT. CELLAR - DAY - MED. SHOT - AT STAIRS - DR. BREWSTER

           He descends to the cellar, then starts quickly toward the
           piled packing cases, CAMERA PANNING with him.

194   INT. CELLAR - DAY - MED. SHOT - DR. BREWSTER

           He comes into the chicken crate which is now empty, and
           moves around it to the space behind the cases where Count
           Alucard's chest was.

195   INT. CELLAR - DAY - MED. SHOT - SPACE BEHIND PACKING CASES

           Where the chest was, there is now only an empty space.

196   INT. CELLAR - DAY - CLOSE SHOT - DR. BREWSTER

        He stands looking into the space for a moment, a tired,
        defeated expression on his face. He turns slowly, and
        starts away.

197   INT. LIBRARY - DAY - FULL SHOT

        The group, excepting Dr. Brewster, are standing listening
        attentively to Frank.

                             FRANK
                    Then I think I fired at him again
                    and ran out that door.

        He points off to the french door.

                             SHERIFF
                    Show us where you ran.

        He leads the way over to the door, Frank and the others
        following. They EXIT as Dr. Brewster ENTERS from the
        hall and crosses to EXIT after them.

198   EXT. PORCH - DAY - MED. SHOT - GROUP

        They follow Frank across the porch and down to the wet
        garden. It is no longer raining, but the trees and shrubs
        are dripping. Frank stops and looks around. Dr. Brewster
        comes in and stands on the fringe of the group.

199   EXT. GARDEN - DAY - MED. SHOT - GROUP

        Frank turns to the sheriff.

                             FRANK
                          (doubtfully)
                    I seem to remember running to my
                    car... down by the gates.

                             SHERIFF
                    You didn't go very far in it.
                    You left it up the road a piece...
                    don't you remember? We passed it
                    coming in.

        Frank nods, appears to be straining now to recall the
        events of the night.

                                                        CONTINUED

199   CONTINUED

                            FRANK
                I don't think I even got into it.
                There was a - a dog or a wolf, and
                I ran (he points) that way I believe!

        They all start in that direction.

200   EXT. SERVANTS' CABINS - DAY - LONG SHOT

        The group comes in and is led by Frank through the space
        between cabins in the direction of the graveyard beyond
        them.

201   EXT. GRAVEYARD - DAY - LONG SHOT - GROUP

        In the f.g. are the mounds and markers of the graves that
        trail off toward the vault in the b.g., where the spade
        Alucard used is standing against the vault door. The
        group comes in from BEHIND CAMERA, walks a short distance
        and stops.

202   EXT. SERVANTS' GRAVEYARD - DAY - MED. SHOT - GROUP

        Frank, in the f.g. with the sheriff, looks around him with
        a bewildered expression.

                            FRANK
                I was here... but I can't remember
                anything after that.

        The sheriff nods, looks all around him and down at the
        nearby graves searchingly. He starts walking. CAMERA PANS
        with group as they all follow him until he stops again.

203   EXT. GRAVEYARD - DAY - MED. SHOT - GROUP

        The sheriff, with Frank standing beside him, looks around.
        His eyes fix on something o.s.

204   EXT. GRAVEYARD - DAY - MED. SHOT - SHERIFF'S ANGLE -
        THE SPADE

        against the vault door.

205   EXT. GRAVEYARD - DAY - MED. SHOT - GROUP

The sheriff looks at Frank obliquely.

                    SHERIFF
          Come over here, Frank.

CAMERA PANS them to near the vault door where the sheriff
stops on the edge of a water-filled hole in the ground.
He looks down at it for a moment, then takes a few steps
to the vault door, picking up the spade.

                    SHERIFF
          Remember this, Frank?

Frank shakes his head dully. The sheriff pokes at the
water-filled hole with the spade.

206   EXT. GRAVEYARD - DAY - CLOSE SHOT - DOWN ANGLE - ON WATER
FILLED HOLE

It is a small hole, a few feet square and from the length
of the spade that is in the water, is apparently only a
foot or so deep.

207   EXT. GRAVEYARD - DAY - MED. SHOT - GROUP

The sheriff prodding around in the hole with the shovel
has a puzzled expression. He suddenly jabs the spade
firmly in the hole and leaves it standing there. He looks
over to the vault door and crosses to it. He opens the
door and takes just a step or two inside, where he stands
looking down.

208   INT. VAULT - DAY - MED. CLOSE SHOT - ANGLING DOWN ON THE
FLOOR OF THE VAULT

A little trail of spilled earth leads over to the coffin
space in which Count Alucard placed Katherine.

209   INT. VAULT - DAY - MED. SHOT - THE SHERIFF

He is in the vault doorway with the others partly seen
in the b.g. behind him. He comes into the vault, looks
about, then seeing the trail of dry earth on the floor,
follows it to the coffin compartment. CAMERA TRUCKS BACK
as he crosses. He pulls away the wooden cover and looks
in. The others follow.

pg   78

210   INT. VAULT - _DAY_ - CLOSE SHOT - KATHERINE

       lying on the bed of soil in the coffin space. She is
       dressed as she was when Frank shot her, but with the
       stains showing on her gown.

211   INT. VAULT - _DAY_ - MED. CLOSE SHOT

       on sheriff and others all looking with reactions into
       the open coffin space. The sheriff lifts his eyes and
       turns to Brewster.

                         SHERIFF
                       (cynically)
              I think we'd better go back to
              the office, Doctor - while you
              do some explaining.

       They start out.

                                                 FADE OUT

       FADE IN

212   EXT. DR. BREWSTER'S HOME - NIGHT - MED. SHOT

       Dr. Brewster comes up on the porch, unlocks the door and
       EXITS into the house.

213   INT. DR. BREWSTER'S HALL - NIGHT - MED. SHOT

       The doctor takes off his hat and raincoat and is hanging
       them in the closet when Sarah comes hurrying along the
       hall. The doctor closes the closet door, turns to face
       her. She looks at him anxiously.

                         DR. BREWSTER
              Good evening, Sarah. Did
              Professor Lazlo arrive?

                         SARAH
              Yes, suh. He's been here all
              day... in and out.

       She appears to be bursting to ask him a dozen questions,
       but restrains herself with an effort and only asks:

                         SARAH
              Can I fix you somethin' to
              eat, Doctah? The Professor's
              had his dinner.

                                                 CONTINUED

213   CONTINUED

                              DR. BREWSTER
                    No, never mind, thanks.

        The door to his office opens and Professor Lazlo appears
        in it. The doctor crosses to him as Sarah EXITS down the
        hall.

214   INT. DR. BREWSTER'S HALL - NIGHT - CLOSE SHOT - DR.
        BREWSTER AND PROFESSOR

        They shake hands.

                              PROFESSOR LAZLO
                    I heard of the tragic events of
                    last night and I called at the
                    court house several times this
                    afternoon, but they wouldn't let
                    me see you.

        The doctor nods, puts his arm through the professor's and
        leads him back into the office.

215   INT. DR. BREWSTER'S OFFICE - NIGHT - MED. SHOT -
        DR. BREWSTER AND PROFESSOR

        The doctor draws up a chair for the professor and takes
        his own behind the desk. The doctor reaches for a
        cigarette. The professor brings out a pipe and tobacco
        pouch. CAMERA ADVANCES TO:

216   INT. DR. BREWSTER'S OFFICE - NIGHT - CLOSE SHOT - THE TWO

        The doctor lights his cigarette.

                              DR. BREWSTER
                    The sheriff believes I'm an
                    accessory after the fact in
                    the murder of Katherine...
                    and I can't say I blame him.

        The professor is tamping tobacco into the bowl of his
        pipe.

                              PROFESSOR LAZLO
                    Why?

                              DR. BREWSTER (continuing)
                    He can't believe I spoke to
                    Katherine after Frank shot her,
                    and because I urged him to stay
                    away from Dark Oaks until tonight,
                    he thinks I intended to hide her
                    body during the day.

                                                    CONTINUED

216   CONTINUED

                              PROFESSOR LAZLO
                    He didn't arrest you?

                              DR. BREWSTER
                    He questioned me most of the day,
                    but he's not quite ready to hold
                    me.

The professor pulls on his pipe nervously, then:

                              PROFESSOR LAZLO
                    Then you didn't tell him what
                    we believe?

                              DR. BREWSTER
                    The chances of convincing a
                    hard-headed sheriff he was dealing
                    with a vampire seemed pretty slim.

                              LAZLO
                         (nodding)
                    Very... and yet I am satisfied
                    such is the case. Alucard is
                    undoubtedly a vampire... probably
                    a descendant of Count Dracula.

Dr. Brewster shakes his head dubiously - not quite able
to accept the theory in toto.

                              DR. BREWSTER
                         (quizzically)
                    We're not letting our imaginations
                    run away with our common sense,
                    are we, Professor?

                              LAZLO
                    Can you suggest any other
                    explanation for the events of
                    the past few days?

                              DR. BREWSTER
                    No-o, but neither can I give a
                    very lucid explanation of a vampire.

                              LAZLO
                    Broadly speaking, a vampire is an
                    earth-bound spirit whose body comes
                    to life at night and scours the
                    countryside satisfying a ravenous
                    appetite for the blood of the living.
                    This it gets by sucking it from the
                    throat of the victim.

                                        CONTINUED

216   CONTINUED - 2

> DR. BREWSTER
> Nauseating thought. They're
> supposed to be immortal, no
> doubt.

> LAZLO
> Practically... so long as they
> return to their graves before sunrise.
> From then till sunset they remain in
> a sort of cataleptic state, during
> which they can be destroyed by two
> different means. At night, however,
> they are invulnerable.

> DR. BREWSTER
> You mean you actually believe Frank
> shot thru Alucard without hurting
> him?

> LAZLO
> Bullets would have had no effect
> on him.

> DR. BREWSTER
> It's strange to hear a man of
> science like yourself calmly admit
> belief in a superstition so
> fantastic.

> LAZLO
> I could spend days citing proofs that
> it is not mere superstition. My
> own homeland in the Carpathian hills
> where Count Dracula lived is sad
> testimony to its truth. What was
> once a happy, productive region is
> today a barren waste, villages
> depopulated, the land abandoned.

Dr. Brewster rises and steps to the window thoughtfully,
growing more and more convinced that Lazlo is not
mistaken.

> DR. BREWSTER
> Perhaps that's why he left it and
> came here to a younger country...
> stronger and more virile.

> LAZLO
>   (with conviction)
> Of course... and he will fasten on
> it and drain it dry just as he did
> his homeland... unless we can find
> his grave and destroy him in it.

> DR. BREWSTER
> His grave! That's some place in
> Hungary.. who knows where?

                                                CONTINUED

216   CONTINUED - 3

                              LAZLO
                          (quietly)
                I suspect he brought his grave
                with him.

        Dr. Brewster stares a second, then smiles skeptically.

                            DR. BREWSTER
                Come, come, Professor. That's
                stretching it a little too far!

                              LAZLO
                Not at all! You'll find one of the
                chests he brought contained a layer
                of soil from his birthplace. That
                constitutes a grave. Rest assured
                he has it hidden in some safe place
                and returns to it just before sunrise
                every morning.

                            DR. BREWSTER
                Then it seems to be our job to
                find that chest with him in it and
                destroy him!

                              LAZLO
                That won't be as simple as it
                sounds. The vampire can assume
                many forms at will.

217   INT. DR. BREWSTER'S OFFICE - NIGHT - MED. SHOT (SPECIAL
        EFFECT)

        on the office side of the hall door. Lazlo's VOICE
        continues OVER SCENE from off stage.

                            LAZLO'S VOICE
                Sometimes it appears as a bat,
                sometimes as a were-wolf,
                sometimes as a small cloud of
                swirling vapor.

        During the speech a thin cloud of vapor is seen slipping
        thru the thin crack of the door (of the crack under it.)
        As it forms into a sort of cloud, it DISSOLVES into
        Count Alucard who stands glaring off at the two men.

218   INT. DR. BREWSTER'S OFFICE - NIGHT - MED. SHOT

        on Brewster and Lazlo as Lazlo concludes his speech.

                                            CONTINUED

218   CONTINUED

                              LAZLO
                    In this way it can move unseen
                    among its enemies, learn their
                    plans and be in position to
                    outwit them.

Both men start nervously as Alucard's VOICE COMES OVER
from o.s.

                              ALUCARD'S VOICE
                    You are a very brilliant man,
                    Professor Lazlo! Perhaps too
                    brilliant for your own good
                    and Dr. Brewster's!

219   INT. DR. BREWSTER'S OFFICE - NIGHT - MED. SHOT

        on Alucard as he stands looking off at the other two men.
        Now he moves slowly toward them, CAMERA PANNING HIM till
        it brings the other two into scene with him. He stops
        and continues speaking.

                              ALUCARD
                    You are right... I am here because
                    this is a young and virile race,
                    not decadent and dry like ours,
                    Professor.

        He bows with mock deference to the professor who is
        watching developments with natural alarm, as also is
        Brewster. Alucard turns from Lazlo to Brewster and
        continues, but with his eyes shining fiercely now.

                              ALUCARD
                    It has what I want; what I need;
                    what I must have! I am not likely
                    to be balked by any human weakling!

        His voice rises and his attitude becomes more maniacally
        menacing as he speaks. In spite of himself, Brewster
        shrinks back a bit. At the end of the line, Alucard
        makes a sudden lunge at him, and catching him by the
        throat, is obviously about to throttle him to death when
        Lazlo springs forward toward the two men.

220   INT. DR. BREWSTER'S OFFICE - NIGHT - MED. CLOSE SHOT

        on the three. Alucard has Brewster's throat in the
        clutch of his strong, bony fingers as Lazlo springs into
        scene. Alucard lets go of Brewster with one hand and
        reaches for Lazlo. The hand never quite touches the
        professor's throat, for he shoves his hand with the palm
        open in front of Alucard's eyes. Alucard stops short and
        stares at what lies in the palm - a fair-sized crucifix.
                                                      CONTINUED

220   CONTINUED

His fingers relax their grip on Brewster and he drops to
the floor almost out. Alucard starts backing away.

221   INT. DR. BREWSTER'S OFFICE - NIGHT - CLOSE SHOT (SPECIAL
EFFECT)

Alucard's face and Lazlo's hand with the crucifix in the
palm. Alucard is staring fixedly at the cross, horrified.
Suddenly, Alucard is not there and in his stead is a small
cloud of vapor which swirls and floats off toward the hall
door.

222   INT. BREWSTER'S OFFICE - NIGHT - MED. SHOT (SPECIAL
EFFECT)

on office side of hall door. The cloud of vapor in the
scene pinches down and disappears thru the crack in the
door.

223   INT. DR. BREWSTER'S OFFICE - NIGHT - MED. SHOT

on Lazlo and Brewster. Lazlo stands with crucifix in hand
staring off toward the direction the vapor went. He now
turns to help Brewster up and into a chair. The doctor is
little the worse for wear except for his fright and a
certain amount of pinching about the throat. Lazlo hurries
from scene while Brewster works at his throat and tries to
regain his breath. Lazlo returns with a decanter and
glass, pouring a drink as he enters.

                         LAZLO
             Here... drink this.

Brewster takes the glass with a trembling hand and drains
it. He shakes his head and returns the glass.

                         DR. BREWSTER
             Thanks.

He closes his eyes tightly, then re-opens them and looks
up at the professor.

                         DR. BREWSTER
             This doesn't leave me much room
             to go on disputing your theories,
             Professor.

                                        CONTINUED

223   CONTINUED

Lazlo puts down the decanter and empty glass.

                        DR. BREWSTER (continuing)
              ... but what on earth did you
              do to drive him away?

                        LAZLO
                        (displaying crucifix)
              Showed him this.

                        DR. BREWSTER
                        (amazed)
              A simple cross?

                        LAZLO
                        (nodding)
              It would take too long to explain
              why they fear it, but they do!
              Keep this and wear it at all
              times... especially in your sleep.
              Dracula has you marked for death.

                        BREWSTER
              Not only me, but unsuspecting
              people throughout the district,
              who would not believe us if we
              tried to warn them!

He leans his elbows on the desk and holds his head be-
tweeen his hands.

                        DR. BREWSTER
              We've got to find a way to
              destroy him before...

He is interrupted by a light tapping on the hall door. He
and Lazlo look toward it.

224   INT. DR. BREWSTER'S OFFICE - NIGHT - MED. SHOT

at hall door. It opens and Sarah appears.

                        SARAH
              Excuse me, Dr. Harry, but it's
              Miz Land to see you.

Mrs. Land, who has been partially visible behind Sarah
now moves forward. In her arms she is carrying Tommy
who lies there very limp and white.

                        MRS. LAND
              It's about Tommy, Doctor. I can't
              imagine what's happened to him.

She is moving toward the doctor as she speaks.

225   INT. DR. BREWSTER'S OFFICE - <u>NIGHT</u> - MED. FULL SHOT

Dr. Brewster rises as Mrs. Land ENTERS carrying Tommy.
He takes the boy from his mother's arms, crosses with
him to the couch where he deposits him gently. Mrs. Land
follows, speaking as she goes.

                    MRS. LAND
          I sent him to my sister's on an
          errand tonight and he was gone
          so long I went after him.

Dr. Brewster lays the boy down and calls off to Lazlo.

                    DR. BREWSTER
          Bring my bag, will you, Professor?

The professor takes the bag and starts across with it.

226   INT. DR. BREWSTER'S OFFICE - <u>NIGHT</u> - MED. SHOT

at couch. Tommy lies on the couch with his eyes half
closed and looking very listless. Lazlo ENTERS with the
doctor's bag, and as Brewster starts opening it, Mrs.
Land continues her explanation.

                    MRS. LAND
          I found him beside the road just
          like this. He talked a little
          but it didn't make sense. He
          acted like he was scared foolish
          and said something about a foreign
          man in a fog... but there wasn't
          any fog tonight.

During this speech, the doctor has brought out some
smelling salts and waved it back and forth under Tommy's
nose. At mention of the foreign man and the fog, Dr.
Brewster abandons the salts and quickly bares the boy's
throat, Lazlo leaning over to watch.

227   INT. DR. BREWSTER'S OFFICE - <u>NIGHT</u> - CLOSE SHOT

on Tommy's throat on which are a couple of small wounds -
nothing that would be serious in themselves, but identical
with those we have previously seen on Katherine's throat.
OVER SCENE we hear Mrs. Land's VOICE.

                    MRS. LAND
          I noticed those little wounds on
          his neck, too. What are they....
          small animal bites?

228   INT. DR. BREWSTER'S OFFICE - NIGHT - MED. CLOSE SHOT

on group.   Brewster and Lazlo exchange significant glances.

                    BREWSTER
            No, I don't think so.   We can
            fix that very simply.

As he speaks he takes a small vial with a glass rod set
into a rubber cork.   He removes the cork and starts to
daub the small cuts.

229   INT. DR. BREWSTER'S OFFICE - NIGHT - CLOSE SHOT

on Tommy's throat.   The doctor's hand ENTERS SCENE and
paints the wounds with iodine, doing it in such a way that
he leaves a very obvious sign of the cross on the throat -
a protection against a return of Alucard.

230   INT. DR. BREWSTER'S OFFICE - NIGHT - MED. SHOT

Brewster finishes painting the wound.   He glances o.s.
toward the door and calls:

                    DR. BREWSTER
            Sarah!

                    SARAH'S VOICE
            Yes, Doctah Harry.

                    DR. BREWSTER
                 (to Mrs. Land)
            Tommy's had a severe shock.   We'll
            go into that later.   Right now you
            get him home and into bed.   Feed him
            all the rare steak he can eat and no
            school till I say so!

By now Sarah has entered.   Brewster continues to her:

                    DR. BREWSTER
            Help Mrs. Land to the car with
            Tommy, Sarah.   I'll be in to see
            him tomorrow, Mrs. Land.

Sarah and Mrs. Land EXIT with Tommy, leaving Lazlo and
Brewster together.

231   INT. DR. BREWSTER'S OFFICE - NIGHT - MED. FULL SHOT

Mrs. Land thanks Dr. Brewster as she and Sarah EXIT with

                                        CONTINUED

231   CONTINUED

Tommy. As the door closes behind them, Dr. Brewster
turns to Lazlo in f.g.

                    LAZLO
          Dracula's first victim! It's
          starting fast.

                    DR. BREWSTER
          Tell me.... Does this mean Tommy's
          in danger of becoming a vampire
          himself?

                    LAZLO
          No, only if Alucard had drained
          so much blood from him that he
          died.

                    DR. BREWSTER
                    (puzzled)
          What about Kay? Alucard didn't
          drain all her blood. She died
          from bullet wounds, but you
          implied she would become a vampire.

                    LAZLO
                    (nodding)
          Her case was different... her
          background was....

He hesitates uncomfortably, not knowing quite how to
proceed. Brewster fills in his unspoken thought.

                    DR. BREWSTER
          ..morbid. I know that. She had
          gone overboard on the subject of
          the supernatural... black magic and
          the like.

                    LAZLO
          Exactly. This is a frightful thing
          to say, but I rather suspect Miss
          Caldwell may have made the transition
          from choice.

                    DR. BREWSTER
                    (nonplussed)
          You don't know what you're saying!
          No one could choose to become a
          thing so loathsome... living on
          human blood... as it comes from
          the body.

                                        CONTINUED

ys

231   CONTINUED - 2

                              LAZLO
                            (eagerly)
              Don't forget the girl was morbid.
              That often means fear of death....
              and Alucard could guarantee her
              eternal life.

                              DR. BREWSTER

              Eternal life at such a price? It's
              unthinkable! Why do you think she
              is a vampire, anyway?

                              LAZLO
              The dirt which I understand had
              been dumped into her coffin.
              Who could have performed that
              service except Alucard.... **Count
              Dracula?**

                              DR. BREWSTER
                            (horrified)
              That means we have to destroy her
              as well?

                              LAZLO
              That should be relatively simple.
              Her sister has only to order her
              cremation while the body is still
              in the morgue.

         During the foregoing dialog, the two men have left the
         side of the couch and crossed to the doctor's desk,
         putting away the medicine bag, etc., during the con-
         versation.

232 .   INT. DR. BREWSTER'S OFFICE - NIGHT - MED. SHOT

         at Brewster's desk.

                              DR. BREWSTER
              I'd better call Claire and make
              arrangements.

         As he speaks the phone RINGS. He takes up the receiver
         and answers.

                              DR. BREWSTER
                            (into phone)
              Hello.... Oh, it's you, Claire.
              I was just about to call you.

         He listens a moment, then speaks into the phone.

                                                  CONTINUED

232   CONTINUED

> DR. BREWSTER
> Why, yes, I think it's perfectly
> safe. Professor Lazlo and I will
> stop by and pick you up... No,
> no trouble at all. In fact we've
> something we want to talk to you
> about. See you in a few minutes.

He hangs up and turns to Lazlo.

> DR. BREWSTER
> The sheriff's office just called
> her. Said Frank's still a bit
> irrational and insists on seeing
> her. While she's there she can
> leave orders for Katherine's
> cremation.

As he speaks he is rising and leading the way out.

DISSOLVE TO:

233   EXT. MORGUE - NIGHT - MED. SHOT

on the exterior of the morgue. This is a building about
large enough for a single large room. A gooseneck lamp
thrusts out from the wall above the door, illuminating
it enough to show that on it is fastened a bronze plaque.
CAMERA DOLLIES UP to the plaque close enough to read the
legend:

        COUNTY MORGUE

DISSOLVE TO:

234   INT. MORGUE - NIGHT - MED. FULL SHOT (SPECIAL EFFECT)

In the foreground is a coffin, over the head of which
hangs a shaded night light. As scene DISSOLVES IN, a
thin wisp of tenuous vapor oozes out from inside the
coffin along one edge of the lid. It takes no special
form but seems to be drawn out of scene PAST CAMERA
rather than blown out.

235   INT. MORGUE - NIGHT - MED. SHOT (SPECIAL EFFECT)

on door of morgue. The vapor of previous scene is drawn
in from CAMERA and disappears thru the crack of the door.

235   EXT. MORGUE - NIGHT - MED. SHOT (SPECIAL EFFECT)

        The thin seepage of vapor oozes into scene along one
        crack of the door and as it forms in a wispy cloud,
        DISSOLVES INTO a large bat which flutters a moment,
        then flies out PAST CAMERA CLOSE to the lens.

                                                DISSOLVE TO:

236   INT. FRANK'S CELL - NIGHT - MED. FULL SHOT

        showing Frank on the cot in a fitful sleep. The scene
        does not include the window. CAMERA PANS away from Frank
        to a MED. CLOSE SHOT of cell window. The big bat
        flutters INTO SCENE outside the bars of the window where
        it remains poised in mid-air on awkwardly fluttering wings.

237   INT. FRANK'S CELL - NIGHT - CLOSE SHOT

        on Frank. He is fully dressed but has unbuttoned his
        collar and loosened his tie. His hair is touseled and
        even though asleep, he is still struggling with the
        horror of the past twenty-four hours. He moves uneasily
        and mutters unintelligibly without waking.

238   INT. FRANK'S CELL - NIGHT - MED. FULL SHOT

        The bat is still at the window but is now inside the
        bars where it is fluttering to maintain its position.
        It now flits toward the cot, CAMERA FOLLOWING it to
        show it hover for a moment above Frank, then slowly
        settle on his breast and start working its way toward
        his throat. Frank stirs again but does not waken nor
        seem conscious of the bat.

239   INT. FRANK'S CELL - NIGHT - CLOSE SHOT

        on Frank as the bat drags itself a couple of inches
        across his chest and drops its head to a spot on his
        throat over the carotid artery with an intent which
        should be obvious.

                                                DISSOLVE TO:

240   INT. BREWSTER'S CAR - NIGHT - (PROCESS) (CITY STREET B.G.)

        Brewster driving with Claire and Lazlo beside him. They
        have evidently been discussing the business in hand, and
        Claire is quite obviously puzzled.

                                                CONTINUED

240   CONTINUED

                         CLAIRE
          I have no personal objection to
          ordering Kay's cremation, doctor.
          But I think you might explain why
          you're so insistent about it.

                         BREWSTER
                    (uncomfortably)
          I intend to, Claire, but this is
          hardly the time nor place.

                         LAZLO
          Believe me, Miss Caldwell, the
          doctor's reasons are valid... but
          for the time being you must take
          him on faith.

                         CLAIRE
          I've always done that... I don't
          see why I should stop now.

                         BREWSTER
          That, my dear, is the highest
          compliment I have ever received.

241   INT. FRANK'S CELL - NIGHT - MED. CLOSE SHOT

        on Frank as he lies on his cot with the vampire bat at
        his throat. Frank stirs uneasily - not in pain, merely
        restless. The bat moves away from its position and a
        couple of abrasions show on Frank's throat. The bat
        flutters out PAST CAMERA. Frank lies as before. After
        a moment, OVER SCENE COMES KAY'S VOICE, quietly - sooth-
        ingly.

                         KATHERINE'S VOICE
          Frank.

        Frank moves restlessly. He has heard, but reaction to
        the voice has not wakened him. The VOICE REPEATS:

                         KATHERINE'S VOICE
          Frank.

        At this he rouses and in a single action comes up on
        one elbow, but with his face turned away from the spot
        where the bat flew to.

                         FRANK
          Yes.

                                             CONTINUED

241   CONTINUED

Then, as if realizing that he is the victim of his own
imagination he runs his fingers up over his face and
pushes them through his hair with the futile gesture
of the defeated.

                    FRANK
          Why does it have to....

He leaves the sentence unfinished and rises for no special
reason... simply that he is unable to remain on the cot
in his frame of mind.

242   INT. FRANK'S CELL - NIGHT - MED. FULL SHOT

Frank rises from the cot, and still groping through the
fog of his sleep, walks a couple of paces away from the
cot toward the bars that define the corridor outside
his cell. He is stopped short by the third calling of
his name.

                    KATHERINE'S VOICE
          Frank...

He stops in his tracks, hesitates, then turns against his
will, and as if fighting the conviction that he is not
entirely sane and is hearing things. At what he sees
o.s. he reacts.

243   INT. FRANK'S CELL - NIGHT - FULL SHOT

Frank is standing transfixed, staring at Katherine who
stands near the cell window smiling easily and naturally
at him. There is no doubt about its being Katherine, but
there is something rather different about her - her skin
seems waxen, and her lips are a trifle fuller, more
sensual.
                    FRANK
                 (in a barely audible whisper)
          Katherine....

He covers his eyes with his hands as if to shut out what
he believes is an hallucination. With his eyes thus
covered he continues, still in a whisper as if trying to
convince himself:

                    FRANK
                 (continuing)
          No; it can't be!

                    KATHERINE
                 (quietly)
          Yes, Frank... I'm Katherine.

                              CONTINUED

243   CONTINUED

He removes his hands quickly from his eyes and stares
crazily at her. Kay starts quietly toward him. He
backs away from her, growing more and more convinced that
he is really losing his mind.

                         FRANK
                    (desperately)
               You can't be Katherine! She's
               dead! I know... I killed her!
               I saw her fall! I was with the
               sheriff when he found her body!
               And she was dead!

Katherine has come considerably closer during his speech.

                         KATHERINE
               You see me now, too...and I
               am alive.

                         FRANK
                    (unconvinced)
               Yes, but...

                         KATHERINE
                    (interrupting)
               Can you doubt the evidence of
               your own senses?

As she speaks she is close enough to reach him and she
quickly lays a hand on his arm, and with the other takes
hold of his coat as she moves closer, smiling up at him.

244   INT. FRANK'S CELL - NIGHT - MED. CLOSE SHOT

on the two as Katherine takes him by the arm. At the
move he instinctively shrinks away, then the obvious
feel of a human hand on his arm becomes something hard
to doubt. He looks incredulously down at the hand, then
a slow smile comes to his lips as his eyes move from the
hand to the girl's eyes. Now his face beams with a wild
look of delight at finding her really a fact instead of
another indication of his insanity.

                         FRANK
               Yes, it is you... and you are
               alive! Oh, Kathy!

As he speaks he impulsively takes her hands between his
own and draws her closer. Then his smile fades and a
look of doubt and uneasiness - almost repugnance - takes
its place.

                                        CONTINUED

(pickup middle of page 94)

KAY

You see me now,too.

FRANK

Yes, but ----

KAY

Do you doubt your own eyes?

FRANK

Yes, it is you - and you are alive. Oh, Kay!
What is it, Kay? You seem to have life but
your hands are cold.....you feel like death.
You seem to be Kay, but there is a strange difference.
I feel almost as if I didn't know you.

KAY

Does that mean you no longer love me?

FRANK

I'll always love you, Kay.

KAY

Enough to spend the rest of your life with me?

FRANK

You are married to Count Alucard.

KAY

I don't love xx him, Frank. I never did.

FRANK

I know, but you are married to him.

KAY

I had to, Frank. This was part of the plan I told
you about in the garden. I asked you to have faith
in me then - I beg you to have faith in me now.

FRANK

I don't understand.

KAY

Alucard is immortal. Through him I attained immortality.

CONTINUITY RECORD

RSAL PICTURES COMPANY, INC.

PICT. NO.

SCENE NO.	
DATE	
SOUND	SILENT
TAKES	PRINT
NIGHT	DAY

[CE]

                    FRANK
                   (aghast)
Do you mean you deliverately planned all this ----
married him --- so you would become a ----

                    KAY
                (interrupting)
So WE   could attain immortality -- yes!

                    FRANK
Even if it would work, am I suppose to agree to a
plan... so fantastic?

                    KAY
You have no choice. I all ready took the first step
before I woke you.

                    FRANK
No, Kay, - I can't do it!

                    KAY
                  (hardening)
I've all ready explained, you have no choice.
        (she moves across to him and continues with
               a smile)
An eternity together is better than a few years
of ordinary life.

                    FRANK
                (half convinced)
Yes... yes, I suppose it is.

(he turns and walks away thoughtfully -
 apparently beginning to be sold)

                    KAY
               (taking quick advantage)
There is one thing you must do while you are
still in your present form.

        (as per script to bottom of pg. 98)

                    FRANK
There is not way I could keep him from his grave.

CONTINUITY RECORD

IVERSAL PICTURES COMPANY, INC.

LE]	
	PICT. NO.
QUENCE]	

SCENE NO.	
DATE	
SOUND	SILENT
TAKES	PRINT
NIGHT	DAY

gs   95

244   CONTINUED

                              FRANK
                   What is it, Kay? You seem to
                   have life - but there is the
                   feel of death in your touch!

His eyes drop again to her hands. She draws them hastily
away from him.

                              KATHERINE
                   Nonsense! Of course I am
                   alive.

He takes her by the shoulders and stares curiously into
her eyes.

                              FRANK
                   You seem to be Katherine... there
                   is a strange difference. I feel
                   almost as if I don't know you.

Katherine's eyes harden as she looks up into his face.

                              KATHERINE
                   Does that mean you no longer
                   love me?

                              FRANK
                         (quietly)
                   I don't think I need to answer
                   that.

He again draws her closer.

                              KATHERINE
                   Enough to leave here and trust to spend
                   the rest of your life with me?

Frank moves her a bit farther from him as he says
gravely:
                              FRANK
                   Have you forgotten you are married
                   to Count Alucard?

                              KATHERINE
                         (persuasively)
                   I don't love him, Frank. I never did.

                              FRANK
                   Nevertheless, you are married to
                   him.

                                        CONTINUED

~~Yes this was part of the plan.~~

I said to FRANK, — this was a part
of plan I told you about in the garden —
I asked you to have faith in me then —
I ~~asked~~ you to have faith in me know
^leg

Alucard is immortal —
thru him is attained —
immortality — thru me
you will do the same, —
and we shall spend
eternity together. —

244   CONTINUED - 2

> KATHERINE
> I had to marry him to get immortality
> for you and me...so we could spend
> eternity together.

Frank regards her with growing bewilderment, wondering
whether he is hearing aright, or whether he is really
insane.

> FRANK
> I'm afraid I don't understand
> Kay.

> KATHERINE
> Alucard is immortal. You know that.
> You shot thru him without hurting him.

> FRANK
> (smiling tolerantly)
> I think you'll find I missed him.

> KATHERINE
> You didn't miss him. You can't
> kill him by ordinary means. He
> is immortal!

> FRANK
> Of course, I never studied those
> things as you have, but that sounds
> pretty ridiculous to me.

> KATHERINE
> It may not sound so ridiculous
> when I tell you his name is not
> Alucard. It is Dracula.

She watches his face for reaction. For a moment he looks
puzzled.

> FRANK
> Dracula? I seem to know something
> about that name...Dracula.

He continues searching his memory for an association of
ideas with the name.

> KATHERINE
> Of course you do. Everybody has
> read about Count Dracula.

Frank has moved a couple of paces away. At mention of
Count Dracula, he turns quickly and looks searchingly at
the girl.

CONTINUED

gs

244   CONTINUED - 3

                         FRANK
            Count Dracula! ~~You mean~~ the
            Hungarian that's supposed to have
            become a....

                         KATHERINE
                      (interrupting)
            Don't use that word, Frank. We
            don't like it. Say rather that
            we are un-dead -- immortal.

Frank comes closer, eyeing her incredulously.

                         FRANK
            Are you seriously telling me there
            is truth in that old fairy tale?

                         KATHERINE
                       (smiling)
            Can you explain the fact that
            bullets didn't hurt him? How
            can you explain my being here
            although you know I was killed?

                         FRANK
                       (aghast)
            ~~Are you saying~~ you deliberately   *Do you mean*   *planned all this*
            ~~cultivated him so you could become~~
            ~~a...~~ *married him so you would have a* --- *yes!*

                         KATHERINE   *we*
            So ~~I~~ could attain immortality ~~and~~
            ~~pass it on to you. Our love need~~
            ~~never die now. That is the plan I~~
            ~~mentioned to you the night of the~~
            ~~reception. Remember?~~

            Even if
                         FRANK
            ~~Assuming~~ it would work, am I supposed
            to agree to a plan so...so fantastic?

                         KATHERINE   *took*
            You have no choice. I ~~was~~ already ~~taken~~   *before & while*
            the first step ~~while you were sleeping~~   *you...*

She touches his throat at the point where the bat was
seen working. Frank springs to a small mirror on the wall
above a washbasin and stares into it examining the tiny
wounds.

                         FRANK
            But I'd rather die a hundred times
            than go thru with a plan so loathesome.

                                        CONTINUED

244   CONTINUED - 4

KATHERINE

That's a foolish human prejudice.
You'll forget it once you've made
the change.

FRANK

No, Kay! ~~I don't intend to make the change.~~ *I can't do it!*

KATHERINE
(hardening)
I've explained you have no choice.

She moves across to him and continues with a smile:

~~You always wanted to marry me.~~
~~Isn't~~ An eternity together *is* better
than t~~he~~ few years of ~~an average~~ *ordinary*
life~~time~~?

As she speaks she puts her hands on his shoulders and
smiles up into his eyes. For a moment he stands unde-
cided; then he gives a little shake of the head.

FRANK *(half-conscious)*
~~(with a wry smile)~~
~~I must admit you make it sound~~ *yes -- yes, I*
~~rather tempting~~ *suppose it is.*

He turns and walks away thoughtfully, apparently beginning
to be sold.

KATHERINE *(taking quick advantage)*
There is one thing you must do
while you're still in your present
form.

FRANK

What's that?

KATHERINE
Get rid of Dracula.

FRANK
(with a short laugh)
I tried that once! ~~He handled me~~
~~like a kitten!~~

You never felt happy

KATHERINE
There is one advantage all humans
have over us. You can move about
in the daytime. We can't. During
the day, we must remain in our graves.
If we're not there by sunrise, we
are destroyed.

245   INT. FRANK'S CELL - <u>NIGHT</u> - CLOSE SHOT

on Frank with part of Katherine's SPEECH COMING OVER as
he listens with keen interest to this bit of data.

                        FRANK
~~I don't know any way~~ I could keep
him from his grave.

There is no way

246   INT. FRANK'S CELL - <u>NIGHT</u> - MED. SHOT

on the two.

                        KATHERINE
You don't have to. You can destroy
him while he's in ~~his grave~~ in one
of two ways; either drive a wooden
stake thru his heart, ~~or cremate him.~~

                        FRANK
                    (thoughtfully)
~~It might be worth going thru with
it just to get rid of that Alucard.~~

He crosses to the cot, and sitting down, leans his chin
in his cupped hands, thinking. Katherine drops down beside him and slips an arm thru his.

247   INT. JAIL - <u>NIGHT</u> - MED. FULL SHOT

Jailer sitting sidewise to a flat-top desk reading a
magazine. Lying on the desk near his elbow is a ring
of keys. The jailer looks up over the top of the magazine as an o.s. door opens. Then, with a little smile,
he rises. Claire, Brewster and Lazlo enter.

                        JAILER
Hello, Miss Caldwell. It got so
late I wasn't sure you'd come
tonight.

                        CLAIRE
I thought you might have told
Frank, and I didn't want to
disappoint him.

                        DR. BREWSTER
I don't suppose we're allowed to
see him, too, are we?

                        JAILER
Sheriff says no.

                                        CONTINUED

247   CONTINUED

                              DR. BREWSTER
                             (to Claire)
                    Find out if he knows where Count
                    Alucard keeps himself in the daytime.

                              CLAIRE
                    I'll try.

         CAMERA PANS jailer and Claire as he leads her to a heavy
         door opening into the jail corridor.

248   INT. JAIL CORRIDOR - NIGHT - MED. SHOT

         at jail office door. Jailer pushes the door open and
         points along the corridor.

                              JAILER
                    He's in number three on the
                    right.

                              CLAIRE
                    Thank you.

         She EXITS PAST CAMERA. The jailer leaves the door open
         and returns to the office.

249   INT. FRANK'S CELL - NIGHT - MED. FULL SHOT (SPECIAL
         EFFECT)

         Frank still seated on the cot in thought. Katherine
         stands near him, watching. At sound of the voices in
         foregoing scene, Kay turns and looks off in that direction,
         then disappears. Frank lifts his head too late to see the
         disappearance and reacts in huge surprise at finding her
         gone. Then he hears the approaching sister and gets to
         his feet.

250   INT. JAIL CORRIDOR - NIGHT - MED. FULL SHOT

         Frank's cell is downstage. Claire is approaching it.
         Frank is moving to the bars.

                              CLAIRE
                             (approaching)
                    Hello, Frank.

                              FRANK
                    Hello, Claire. It was good of
                    you to come here, after...everything.

                                                      CONTINUED

250   CONTINUED

> CLAIRE
> I can only stay a few minutes,
> but I wanted to tell you I know
> it was an accident.

251   INT. FRANK'S CELL - NIGHT - MED. SHOT

on Claire and Frank talking thru bars.

> FRANK
> That makes me feel better. Kay
> understands, too.

Claire makes a quick takeum on this before she can catch
herself, then:

> CLAIRE
> (gently)
> I'm sure she does.

> FRANK
> I know it. She's been...

He stops short, as he realizes what this must sound like
to anyone not in the know. Then he continues:

> FRANK
> Would you think I was losing my
> mind if I said she's been here
> to talk with me?

> CLAIRE
> (dissembling)
> I'd be more likely to say you'd
> been dreaming.

> FRANK
> But I know she...you're probably
> right. I must have dreamed it.

252   INT. JAIL OFFICE - NIGHT - MED. SHOT

on jailer, Brewster and Lazlo.

> JAILER
> They'll never convict Stanley of
> that killin'.

> BREWSTER
> No?

CONTINUED

252   CONTINUED

                              JAILER
                         (shaking his head)
                No; he's nutty as a filbert. He's
                been back there a long time talkin'
                to some dame that wasn't there.
                First he'd talk in his own voice
                and then answer in the woman's voice.

        Dr. Brewster and Lazlo look quickly at one another.

                              LAZLO
                Did you overhear anything that was
                said?

                              JAILER
                That'd be a fine way to spend a
                rainy evening...eavesdropping on
                a goof talking to himself in two
                voices. Some fun.

253   INT. JAIL CORRIDOR - NIGHT - MED. SHOT

        on Claire and Frank talking thru bars.

                              CLAIRE
                Dr. Brewster is doing all he
                can for you, Frank.

                              FRANK
                All he can do is get me off on an
                insanity plea...
                         (he laughs bitterly)
                that shouldn't be hard.

                              CLAIRE
                You mustn't even think such things.

                              FRANK
                Why not? I can't be sane. I really
                believe Kay has been here and talked
                to me. If that's not crazy...

        He ends with a little shake of the head. Claire is
        caught with no reply for the moment. Frank changes the
        subject.

                              FRANK
                When are they going to hold the
                funeral?

                              CLAIRE
                We haven't been able to contact
                Count Alucard so far. Do you
                happen to know where he stays
                during the day?

g5

254   INT. FRANK'S CELL - NIGHT - CLOSE SHOT

        on Frank. He looks searchingly at Claire as the possible
        significance of this line strikes him.

                            FRANK
                  Why during the day?

255   INT. JAIL CORRIDOR - NIGHT - MED. SHOT

        on the two. Frank watches closely for a sign to tip him
        off. Claire answers casually.

                            CLAIRE
                  It's an unpleasant trip out there
                  at night and there's no phone.

                            FRANK
                  Why would anyone think I knew?

                            CLAIRE
                  You said you saw him meet Kay on
                  the road once. I wondered if
                  you saw where he came from.

                            FRANK
                  Sorry; I don't know a thing.
                  You'll bury her at Dark Oaks, I
                  suppose.

                            CLAIRE
                  Yes, I think so. At least her
                  ashes will be taken there.

                            FRANK
                  Her ashes!

                            CLAIRE
                  Yes; I'm going to leave an order
                  for her cremation.

                            FRANK
                  But you can't do that! If you
                  cremate her, it'll kill her!

                            CLAIRE
                            (gently)
                  You seem to forget, Frank...She
                  is already dead!

256   INT. JAIL OFFICE - NIGHT - MED. SHOT

   on jailer, Brewster and Lazlo. They listen as OVER SCENE
COMES FRANK'S VOICE raised excitedly.

                    FRANK'S VOICE
          She is not dead! I know! She's
          been here talking to me! If you
          cremate her, you'll kill her!

During the speech, the jailer hops to his feet and hurries
out into the jail corridor.

257   INT. JAIL CORRIDOR - NIGHT - MED. FULL SHOT

   Claire and Frank facing each other thru the bars. Frank
is holding Claire by the arm.

                    FRANK
          I won't let you burn her...now
          that she's attained immortality.

                    CLAIRE
                    (gently)
          You mustn't excite yourself this
          way. You've got to reconcile
          yourself to the fact that Kay is
          dead!

                    FRANK
          I say she isn't! She is...

                    JAILER
                    (entering)
          Let her go, Stanley!

As he speaks he grabs Frank's wrist. Frank relaxes his
grip on Claire and backs away from the bars.

                    JAILER
                    (to Claire)
          I think you'd better leave.

Claire nods and hurries along the corridor.

                    JAILER
                    (to Frank)
          You'd better try to get some sleep.

                    FRANK
          But I...

                              CONTINUED

257   CONTINUED

                            JAILER
                          (interrupting)
              I said you'd better sleep.

                            FRANK
                          (more quietly)
              I'll try.

The jailer EXITS back toward the office. Frank looks
after him, then turning, begins to call softly:

                            FRANK
              Kay!.....Katherine! Where are
              you?

258   INT. FRANK'S CELL - NIGHT - MED. FULL SHOT (SPECIAL EFFECT)

        as Katherine suddenly appears in front of Frank. At sight
        of her he hurries to her.

259   INT. FRANK'S CELL - NIGHT - MED. CLOSE SHOT

        on the two.

                            FRANK
              Did you hear what she said?
              They're going to cremate you!

                            KATHERINE
                          (furiously)
              I heard! That means Dr. Brewster
              has guessed the truth. We may have
              to get rid of him and Claire.

                            FRANK
              You couldn't do that...not your
              sister! ~~enemy best friend~~

                            KATHERINE
              They are not sister and friend when
              they interfere with me!

                            FRANK
              They can't cremate you! You don't
              have to leave your body in the morgue
              for them to find, do you?

                            KATHERINE
              Of course not. I'll go to Dark Oaks
              tonight. But Dr. Brewster will talk
              and we'll never be safe while he's
              alive.

Frank walks a few paces away and turns back.

260   INT. JAIL OFFICE - <u>NIGHT</u> - MED. SHOT

        on jailer. He has taken up his book, but has it lying
        on his lap and is in a listening attitude, evidently
        having heard the voices from the cell down the corridor.
        Now he gets up quietly, and going to the corridor door,
        he opens it a crack and listens.

        260A

261   INT. FRANK'S CELL - <u>NIGHT</u> - MED. SHOT

        as Frank turns back and says:

                          FRANK
                Our first worry is Alucard. If
                you could get me out of here I'd
                start hunting for him.

                          KATHERINE
                        (smiling)
                I can get you out of here ---
                and you don't have to hunt for
                Alucard. I know where he can
                be found in the daytime.

                          FRANK
                Where?

                          KATHERINE
                You remember the old drainage
                flume at the edge of the swamp
                near Zimba's cabin?

                          FRANK
                Of course.

                          KATHERINE
                That's the place... but be
                sure you don't get there
                until the sun is up.

262   INT. JAIL CORRIDOR - <u>NIGHT</u> - MED. SHOT

        at office door. The door is ajar and the jailer is
        listening. OVER THIS we PLAY A PART OF THE DIALOGUE OF
        PRECEDING SCENE. Now he throws the door wide and starts
        down PAST CAMERA to talk to Frank.

263   INT. FRANK'S CELL - <u>NIGHT</u> - MED. SHOT

        Frank and Katherine hear the jailer coming o.s. Frank
        leaves her and walks to the cell door. CAMERA PANS him
        and loses Kay.

pg   107

264   INT. JAIL CORRIDOR - NIGHT - MED. FULL

        at Frank's cell. No one is in it but Frank. The jailer
        enters to the cell door.

                              JAILER
                    I told you to go to sleep.

                              FRANK
                    I couldn't. I had company.

                              JAILER
                    Sure... but they're gone now
                    so I'll douse the lights.

        He EXITS along the corridor and the lights suddenly flash
        off, leaving the corridor in semi-darkness.

265   INT. JAIL OFFICE - NIGHT - MED. SHOT

        at desk. One of the drawers opens. Papers inside are
        rustled around. The drawer is closed and another opens
        by unseen hand which brings out a gun and closes the
        drawer again. Now the ring of keys is picked up, and
        together with the gun, they move out of scene as if
        carried by someone.

266   INT. JAIL CORRIDOR - NIGHT - MED. SHOT

        at office door. The jailer enters from CAMERA and goes
        thru the doorway to the office. The ring of keys and the
        revolver carried by unseen hands come thru the door from
        the office and EXIT PAST CAMERA.

267   INT. JAIL CORRIDOR - NIGHT - MED. SHOT

        at Frank's cell. The keys and gun COME INTO SCENE. The
        gun stops before the door. The keys separate, and one of
        them is thrust into the lock of the door. It turns, and
        the door opens. The gun is taken by Frank who now starts
        up the corridor toward the office. During the business
        we hear the following dialog.

                              KATHERINE'S VOICE
                    How are you going to get to the
                    swamp?

                              FRANK
                    The sheriff left my car parked down
                    the street.

                              KATHERINE'S VOICE
                    I'll wait for you at the Oaks...
                    in the playroom Claire and I used
                    to have up in the attic. I'll be
                    safe there for one day.

        Frank hurries quietly up the corridor.

268   EXT. COURT HOUSE - NIGHT - MED. SHOT

on Dr. Brewster's car. Claire, Brewster and Lazlo
discovered in the parked car where they have been
discussing what took place in the jail. Evidently the
men intend to let Claire take the car while they remain,
for she is under the steering wheel. She is summing up
her conclusions.

                    CLAIRE
          He was so positive Kay's alive
          and has been to see him! I'm
          afraid he's definitely not sane.

                    DR. BREWSTER
          Certainly doesn't sound normal.

                    LAZLO
          Miss Caldwell, did you happen to
          notice if he had any slight
          abrasions or small wounds on his
          throat.....about here?

He indicates a spot on his own throat. Claire seems
surprised.

                    CLAIRE
          Now that you mention it, I
          believe he did. Why do you ask?

                    DR. BREWSTER
                    (smiling)
          Professional secret. You run
          along home. We'll try to talk
          the sheriff into letting us
          see Frank.

As he speaks, he and Lazlo are starting to climb out of
the car. Claire steps on the starter.

269   EXT. COURT HOUSE - NIGHT - MED. SHOT

at curb. Dr. Brewster and Lazlo climb out of car which
starts off.

                    LAZLO
          I'm afraid there is no doubt now.
          Kay has been to see Frank in his
          cell... and for one definite purpose.

                    BREWSTER
                    (nodding)
          To form a loathesome, maniacal
          alliance, preying on the peaceful
          countryside till they've laid it
          waste like your own homeland!

                                        CONTINUED

pg   109

269   CONTINUED

                              LAZLO
                    We've simply got to find where
                    Dracula's hidden his coffin.

                              DR. BREWSTER
                    And even if we have to burn down
                    the morgue, we must cremate Kay...
                    before she destroys her own
                    immortal soul and Frank's.

        They start toward the court house.

270   INT. JAIL OFFICE - NIGHT - MED. SHOT

        on jailer at desk reading. His back is more or less
        toward the o.s. door to jail corridor. Suddenly he lifts
        his head as if he hears a little noise. He holds the pose
        listening a moment, then having determined the direction
        of the sound, he turns toward the corridor door. What he
        sees causes him to start to his feet defensively. At the
        same time, CAMERA PANS to include Frank who is approaching
        stealthily and is nearly upon him. He strikes down with
        the barrel of the gun Kay has given him. The jailer
        throws up a hand and catches his wrist, warding off the
        blow.   Wild-eyed, Frank struggles to get the gun free.
        In the struggle the gun is fired harmlessly. With a
        furious wrench, Frank gets his gun hand free and clubs the
        jailer with the gun. As the jailer slips to the floor,
        Frank turns and runs for the outer door, gun in hand.

271   INT. COURT HOUSE CORRIDOR - NIGHT - MED. FULL SHOT

        at entrance to jail. Dr. Brewster and Lazlo hurry in
        from CAMERA. As they reach the door, Frank opens it from
        inside and bursts out on them. He makes a swipe at one
        with the gun and as the man ducks, he straight-arms the
        other and races out PAST CAMERA. Brewster calls after
        him.

                              DR. BREWSTER
                    Frank! Frank Stanley!

272   INT. COURT HOUSE CORRIDOR - NIGHT - MED. SHOT

        at sheriff's office. The door opens and the sheriff
        comes out with a couple of deputies following, all
        obviously puzzled by the sound of commotion. They have
        been too late to see Frank, but seeing Brewster and Lazlo
        o.s., they hurry to them, CAMERA PANNING THEM.

                                                CONTINUED

gs   110

272   CONTINUED

                              SHERIFF
            What's happened?

                              DR. BREWSTER
            Frank Stanley just escaped! We met
            him at the door but couldn't stop
            him. He's armed!

As he speaks he is helping Lazlo to his feet from where
Frank hurled him.

                              SHERIFF
                         (to his deputies)
            Get after him! If you have to
            shoot, do it!

The deputies beat it for outside. Sheriff, Brewster and
Lazlo hurry into the jail.

273   EXT. CITY STREET - NIGHT - MED. FULL SHOT

It has stopped raining long since, but the streets are
still wet and glistening. Frank runs in from CAMERA and
across the courthouse lawn to the curb where he jumps
into a car, starts it and drives rapidly out. As he gets
under way, the two deputies run in FROM CAMERA, fire after
him, then run out presumably to get a car and give chase.
(THIS INTERCUTS WITH:)

274   EXT. COURTHOUSE - NIGHT - MED. SHOT

        at front door as the two deputies run into scene from
        inside, look about for Frank, see him o.s., and chase
        after him.

275   INT. JAIL - NIGHT - MED. SHOT

on Sheriff, Brewster, Lazlo and jailer. They have picked
up the dazed man and put him in his chair at the desk.
Brewster is giving him a drink of cold water. The man is
regaining consciousness, but things are still a bit foggy.

                              SHERIFF
            What happened, Mac? How did he
            get out?

                              JAILER
            I can't guess, Sheriff! The keys
            were on the desk as usual...now they're
            gone and so is Stanley! I tried to stop
            him and...

                                                CONTINUED

275   CONTINUED

He grimaces and puts his hand gingerly to his head. The
sheriff whirls on Brewster.

                         SHERIFF
               Did you have anything to do with
               this break, Doctor Brewster?

                         BREWSTER
               Of course not! We'd just entered
               the building when we heard the shot!

                         LAZLO
               We're as anxious as you to keep him
               locked up!

                         BREWSTER
                         (testily)
               More so!

He turns to the jailer and continues:

               Did you hear him do any more
               talking to that girl?

                         JAILER
                         (surprised)
               How did you know?

                         SHERIFF
                         (puzzled)
               What girl?

                         LAZLO
               Katherine Caldwell.

                         SHERIFF
               Are you crazy?

                         JAILER
                         (explaining)
               It's some sort of trick Stanley
               pulls. He pretends to be talking
               to a girl...first in his own voice,
               then in hers!

                         SHERIFF
                         (to Brewster)
               What is it, a trick you put him
               up to so he'd sound crazy?

Dr.Brewster ignores the Sheriff and continues to the jailer.

                                        CONTINUED

190

275   CONTINUED - 2

                              DR. BREWSTER
               Did you listen in as we asked
               you to?

                                JAILER
                              (nodding)
               For a couple of minutes...but it
               was too crazy to bother with.

                               BREWSTER
               For instance.

                                JAILER
               Oh, the girl's voice said something
               about getting him out of jail and...

                                LAZLO
               That wasn't so crazy, was it? He
               is out!

     Apparently the coincidence strikes the jailer for the
     first time.

                                JAILER
               That's right...I never thought
               of it! Do you really think there
               was someone in there with him?

                              DR. BREWSTER
               Never mind that. What else did
               you hear...however crazy it sounded.

                                JAILER
                              (struggling to remember)
               Something about she'd wait for him
               at Dark Oaks in some kid playroom.

                               BREWSTER
               I know where it is. What else?

                                JAILER
               Some goofy stuff about killing Count
               Alucard...

                                LAZLO
                              (interrupting)
               Did he say kill him or destroy him?

                                JAILER
                              (trying to remember)
               Come to think, I believe he did say
               "destroy"...shove a stake thru him
               or something.

                                        CONTINUED

275   CONTINUED - 3

                              SHERIFF
              Shove a stake thru him! We're
              dealing with a madman!

                              DR. BREWSTER
              Obviously!

Now he turns again to the jailer.

              Did he say anything that would
              give us an idea where he expected
              to find Alucard?

                              JAILER
              Yeah; but that really was silly.
              He said something about a drainage
              tunnel from the swamp that opened
              off it about...

                              DR. BREWSTER
              I know where that is, too!

                              SHERIFF
              Good! We'll get out there and warn
              Alucard before Frank gets there!

                              DR. BREWSTER
              You're not going to warn him...not
              if we have to lock you in your own
              jail!

                              SHERIFF
              What's that?

                              BREWSTER
              There's a lot to this that you don't
              understand, Sheriff! If you don't
              believe it, let's go take a look in
              the morgue!

                              SHERIFF
              What's the morgue got to do with it?

                              DR. BREWSTER
              Never mind! It's all getting as clear
              as day, isn't it, professor?

                              LAZLO
              It has been to me for some time.

                              DR. BREWSTER
              All right. Let's take a look at
              the morgue.

As the three men start out,

                                        WIPE TO:

276   EXT. MORGUE - <u>NIGHT</u> - MED. SHOT

The door now stands open, the lock broken. The Sheriff,
Lazlo and Brewster ENTER FROM CAMERA. The door stands
before them, an opening into a black hole.

                         SHERIFF
              Someone's forced the door!

He leads the way inside.

277   INT. MORGUE - <u>NIGHT</u> - MED. FULL SHOT

The set is dark save for such night light as falls in
thru a high barred window. The indistinct forms of the
Sheriff, Brewster and Lazlo fumble their ways thru the
darkness to a stone slab where the Sheriff reaches up for
the drop-light he knows hangs from the ceiling. He finds
the switch and snaps it, flooding the slab beneath with
a dazzling light. The slab stands unoccupied - coffin and
body are both gone.

                         SHERIFF
              The corpse is gone...coffin and
              all!

                         LAZLO
              Of course!

The Sheriff turns on the two men savagely.

                         SHERIFF
              You sound as if you expected it!

                         LAZLO
              We did.

                         SHERIFF
              What's your part in all this?
              How is it you know in advance
              what's happening?

                         DR. BREWSTER
              We'd better get out to where Alucard
              is hiding. We'll try to explain it
              to you on the way!

                         SHERIFF
              I thought you weren't going to warn
              Alucard about Frank!

                         DR. BREWSTER
              We're not! We may have to save
              Frank from the Count...and from
              his own madness!

                                        CONTINUED

The scene described on the next page and a half of the script was presumably filmed, given the existence of this photo. Both the script and the Continuity Breakdown call for dead leaves (on the porch and ground), showing that Dark Oaks has already started to "slip" just in the few days since Col. Caldwell's death and the servants' flight.

277   CONTINUED

                              SHERIFF
              The farther we go the crazier you
              sound!

          As he speaks the three are on their way to the door.

                                        DISSOLVE TO:

278   EXT. DARK OAKS - NIGHT - MED. SHOT

          on porch. The house is without lights and the door stands
          open. A few wet leaves are scattered about the porch,
          blown there during the few days the place has been with-
          out a caretaker. From the dark depths of the entrance
          hall comes the SOUND of Alucard's VOICE.

                              ALUCARD'S VOICE
              I'm not sure it was wise of you
              to come here, my dear. It is the
              first place they will look.

                              KATHERINE'S VOICE
              They won't find me the first day,
              and by the second day I'll have
              chosen a hiding place they will
              never find.

          Toward the end of her line she and Alucard appear from
          inside walking side by side, her hand resting on his arm.
          They come out onto the porch where they stand, Alucard
          letting his eyes roam appreciatively about the grounds.

                              KATHERINE
              I shall hate to leave all this,
              Anthony...after planning so care-
              fully to remain here forever.

          Alucard continues to look off at the grounds. His eyes
          darken as he nods.

279   EXT. DARK OAKS GROUNDS - NIGHT - MED. FULL PAN SHOT

          The moss on the trees and the dark shadows between patches
          of brilliant moonlight lend the place an eerieness,
          heightened by the SOUND of tree toads and crickets. OVER
          SCENE COMES ALUCARD'S VOICE with definite venom in it.

                              ALUCARD'S VOICE
              We should never have had to leave,
              except for the blundering of that
              fool, Stanley! We would have been
              safe from intrusion...free to follow
              our own devices.

280   EXT. DARK OAKS - <u>NIGHT</u> - MED. CLOSE SHOT

        on Alucard and Katherine. He continues.

                        ALUCARD
                Someday I shall think of a punishment
                for him to fit the injury he has done
                us!

        Katherine reacts with a quick look of alarm which she
        covers.

                        KATHERINE
                Of course, but...

        She stops and listens as from a distance comes the faint
        SOUND of a ROOSTER CROWING. She continues:

                I'm afraid you'd better leave,
                Anthony. It must be nearly dawn.

                        ALUCARD
                Goodnight, my dear.

        He apparently is about to take her in his arms, but she
        beats him to punch by holding out her hand. He takes it,
        hesitates a second, then bends low to touch his lips to it.

                                                WIPE TO:

281   EXT. SWAMP - <u>NIGHT</u> - MED. FULL SHOT

        This is somewhere along the trail we first saw Katherine
        following on the way to Queen Zimba's cabin. Frank is
        seen coming toward CAMERA from the shadows between moss-
        festooned growth. He jumps from hummock to hummock, slips
        and continues his uncertain way till he nears CAMERA where
        he pauses to regain his breath and brush the perspiration
        from his forehead. In one hand he carries a battered five
        gallon oil can. He looks off toward the east.

282   HORIZON SHOT

        with the sun not far below the earth's edge.

283   EXT. SWAMP - <u>NIGHT</u> - MED. SHOT

        on Frank. He laughs rather crazily, takes up his oil can
        and hurries PAST CAMERA. CAMERA PANS him on his way as he
        goes on slipping and rising to hurry on into the shadows.

                                                WIPE TO:

284   EXT. ROAD - NIGHT - MED. SHOT (PROCESS)

on sheriff, Brewster and Lazlo in the sheriff's car, the
sheriff driving. The road is winding and heavily wooded.
The sheriff is listening to Lazlo with a dry grin that
says plainly it all sounds like twaddle to him.

                    LAZLO
          If my theory is right we have only
          today between sunrise and sunset to
          safeguard the region from a fate too
          horrible to describe.

                    SHERIFF
          Do you expect me to believe all
          that flub-dub?

                    LAZLO
          Certainly not... but I shall let
          you explain what we shall find
          in the drainage flume.

The sheriff gives him a quick look as if he doesn't like
this calm acceptance of something he would like to pooh-
pooh.

                    DR. BREWSTER
          Better park, sheriff. We go afoot
          from here.

The sheriff turns the wheel to bend the car to the brush
at one side of the road.

285   EXT. SWAMP ROAD - NIGHT - MED. FULL SHOT

The sheriff's car pulls over to the cane-brake beside the
road and stops. The three men get out.

286   EXT. SWAMP ROAD - NIGHT - MED. SHOT

at sheriff's car as the men climb out.

                    SHERIFF
          What is it you expect to find in
          the flume?

                    DR. BREWSTER
          If Frank gets there before sunrise,
          you'll find something I'd rather
          not think about. This way.

The last two words as he starts down toward the swamp's
edge. CAMERA PANS the three men as they reach the swamp
and start along it to follow to the drainage flume some-
where o.s.

                                          WIPE TO:

287   EXT. SWAMP'S EDGE - NIGHT - MED. FULL SHOT

Frank is hurrying toward CAMERA with the oil can and making
heavy work of it. CAMERA PANS with him as he passes and
it shows him reaching the open end of a heavy beam tunnel
leading into a low hill. The bottom of the tunnel entrance
is practically on a level with the swamp water and was presumably constructed originally to drain off swamp water
in time of high water. The structure has now fallen
somewhat into decay. Brush has grown partly over it from
above and from the sides and a timber or two have rotted
and fallen across a part of the entrance. Frank looks
off toward the east again.

288   ANOTHER SHOT OF A SUNRISE SKY

somewhat brighter than the previous.

289   EXT. DRAINAGE FLUME - NIGHT - MED. SHOT

Frank peers into the dark interior, then with a quick look
about on all sides, he hurries in as if anxious to get
his job over with.

290   INT. DRAINAGE FLUME - NIGHT - FULL SHOT

The flume is covered, but the covering is broken here and
there to allow the entrance of light thru irregular openings. The plank walls are bulged in from pressure of
loose ground outside and in places have broken. The
bottom of the tunnel is covered in spots with pools of
water an inch or so deep. The walls are damp and here
and there there is a dropping of water from above. At
the far end, the tunnel makes a gradual bend so wo cannot
see how far it runs. On a pile of ground that has fallen
in from a side wall stands Alucard's coffin, six or eight
inches above the floor level. Frank ENTERS FROM CAMERA,
hesitates, glances back, then moves on to the coffin
where he stops.

291   INT. DRAINAGE FLUME - NIGHT - MED. CLOSE SHOT

on Frank beside the coffin. Near the coffin is a chicken
crate with the lid thrown back and several birds lying
about dead and mutilated. Frank seems pretty much on edge
now that he has got right down to his job. With growing
apprehension he lifts the lid of the coffin as if expecting to find something inside to menace him. The coffin
is empty but contains a thin layer of earth. Leaning the
cover back against the wall, Frank starts slopping oil
over the coffin inside and out.

mn

292   EXT. SWAMP - <u>NIGHT</u> - MED. FULL SHOT

From the shadows of trees upstage a bat flies its strange
erratic course out PAST CAMERA.

293   INT. DRAINAGE FLUME - <u>NIGHT</u> - MED. FULL SHOT

SHOOTING TOWARD opening. Frank enters FROM CAMERA, turns
and looks back at what he has done, then with a half-crazy
laugh he hurries on toward the tunnel mouth.

294   EXT. DRAINAGE FLUME - <u>NIGHT</u> - FULL SHOT

SHOOTING PAST tunnel opening in f.g. The big bat disc.
flying toward the CAMERA from upstage. It drops behind
a low bush and as it disappears, Alucard suddenly appears
in its place. He starts downstage intending to enter the
flume. Within a few feet of it, Frank suddenly comes out
from inside. Both men stop short at sight of each other.
They hold it motionless for a moment.

295   EXT. DRAINAGE FLUME - <u>NIGHT</u> - MED. CLOSE SHOT

on Alucard. His eyes are burning as he regards Frank o.s.
Then a slow menacing smile comes to his lips.

                    ALUCARD
          It is not often my enemies are so
          accomodating. How did you learn
          where to find me?

296   EXT. DRAINAGE FLUME - <u>NIGHT</u> - MED. SHOT

on the two, shooting PAST Alucard toward Frank.

                    FRANK
          I know all about you! I know you
          are not Count Alucard, but Count
          Dracula... one of the un-dead--
          a loathesome thing,--- human in
          form only, surviving on the blood
          of the living. I came here to
          destroy you.

                    ALUCARD
          If you had known more about me
          you would not have come here till
          after sunrise. As it is, it is not
          <u>I</u> who will be destroyed!

As he speaks he is moving closer to Frank. Frank does not
attempt to run. Alucard's line times so that as he ends it
he reaches out and clutches Frank's shoulder.

                              CONTINUED

mn

296   CONTINUED

                           FRANK
          Don't be too sure till you look
          inside.

Alucard looks into the tunnel and reacts with a horror
almost impossible to overdo.

297   INT. DRAINAGE FLUME - NIGHT - FULL SHOT

from Alucard's ANGLE. The coffin on its slight elevation
at the upstage end of set is blazing high. Frank has
lighted it before coming out.

298   EXT. DRAINAGE FLUME - NIGHT - MED. SHOT

on Alucard and Frank. Alucard still has Frank by the arm
and is staring into the tunnel horrified.

                        ALUCARD
             (wildly - crazily)
      No... you can't! My grave... I must
      be inside by sunrise! Put it out!

By the time he reaches the end he is screaming. Spinning
Frank around, he heaves him headlong into the tunnel and
follows after.

299   INT. DRAINAGE FLUME - NIGHT - MED. FULL SHOT

SHOOTING TOWARD the burning coffin upstage. Frank is
hurled headlong into scene from CAMERA. He falls to the
floor. Alucard follows him in and drags him to his feet,
screaming.

                        ALUCARD
      Put it out! If the fire touches
      me, it is the end! Get up!

It is useless. Even if Frank wanted to obey, he cannot.

300   INT. DRAINAGE FLUME - NIGHT - MED. CLOSE SHOT

on Alucard. He is really insane. He must be inside the
coffin by sunrise and he can't get in it because the fire
will cremate him - rob him of his supernatural powers.

                        ALUCARD
      With all eternity before me, I will
      not be stopped by a fool and a match!

He springs out toward the fire.

301 INT. DRAINAGE FLUME - NIGHT - MED. SHOT

on Alucard as he grabs a broken plank in the wall and
wrenches it loose. Using this as a shovel he starts
trying to smother the fire by throwing loose earth on
it. The fire seems to burn all the higher.

302 INT. DRAINAGE FLUME - NIGHT - MED. CLOSE SHOT

on Frank lying where Alucard threw him. He comes to,
the flicker of fire light and Alucard's o.s. ranting
bring him to a consciousness of where he is. He starts
easing his way out toward the end of the tunnel. CAMERA
PANS and sees him get to his feet and stagger toward the
opening.

303 INT. DRAINAGE FLUME - NIGHT - MED. SHOT

on Alucard as the flames drive him back from them. He
turns and sees Frank o.s. escaping. He runs out after
him.

304 INT. DRAINAGE TUNNEL - NIGHT - MED. SHOT

on Frank making for the entrance. He hears Alucard coming.
Though he knows it is useless, he still draws the revolver
and fires off at the approaching menace. Alucard storms
in and grabs him by the throat.

305 EXT. SWAMP TRAIL - NIGHT - MED. FULL SHOT

as sheriff, Brewster and Lazlo stop in f.g., looking off
PAST CAMERA.

                    DR. BREWSTER
          Those shots sound as if we're
          too late!

306 INT. DRAINAGE FLUME - NIGHT - MED. CLOSE SHOT

on Alucard and Frank. Alucard has him by the throat.

                    ALUCARD
                  (crazily)
          You would destroy a Dracula?
          Then we'll both have company
          on our plunge into....

He leaves the sentence unfinished as he hurls Frank out
of scene toward the flaming coffin.

307   INT. DRAINAGE FLUME - <u>NIGHT</u> - MED. FULL SHOT
       (SPECIAL EFFECT)

       Frank is hurled staggering toward the blazing coffin. He
       plunges headlong into its open maw. Almost immediately he
       is up again staggering crazily out of the flames, his
       clothing afire. He stumbles toward CAMERA and throws him-
       self full length into the shallow pool of muddy water.

308   INT. DRAINAGE FLUME - <u>NIGHT</u> - MED. SHOT

       on Frank as he lands in the pool and rolls about ex-
       tinguishing the flames. Alucard's roaring laugh SOUNDS
       crazily OVER SCENE - then his VOICE.

                           ALUCARD'S VOICE
               You'd be wiser to get it over quickly!

       With this he bends and drags Frank to his feet. CAMERA
       TILTING up with them.

                           ALUCARD
                 This time you will stay!

       He is about to hurl Frank to the flames again, but before
       he can consumate the act a sudden sharp burst of light
       floods the scene from the direction of the tunnel's mouth.
       Alucard stops short frozen - terrified. Forgetful of
       Frank and revenge he holds him and turns to face the
       strong light.
                           ALUCARD

               THE SUN!

       He lets go of Frank who falls OUT of SCENE. Alucard at
       the same time covers his eyes with his hands and backs
       away toward the burning coffin. CAMERA PANS with him. A
       few paces away, he slows down, sways, clutches at the
       wall for support, then slowly collapses.

309   INT. DRAINAGE FLUME - <u>DAY</u> - MED. FULL SHOT

       SHOOTING TOWARD entrance. Frank ENTERS SCENE pulling
       himself up to his feet by clawing at the wall. He looks
       back at Alucard over his shoulder as he reaches the en-
       trance and disappears in the direction of Dark Oaks.

310   INT. DRAINAGE FLUME - <u>DAY</u> - MED. SHOT

       on Alucard lying on the floor. The rays of the sun cut a
       sharp line along the wall of the tunnel with Alucard in
       the shadow. Theoretically it is not yet sunrise where he
       lies which accounts for his being in the same physical
       condition as before. As the o.s. sun climbs higher, the
       hot streak on the wall drops down the slimy boards until
       the light falls full on Alucard. For a moment, nothing
       happens, then his features begin to fade, his clothing
       disintegrates and there remains only a skeleton. One
       hand lies on his chest and on the index finger is the
       ring by which he has been identified earlier. Now a
       shadow falls across the scene from the direction of the
       entrance

311   INT. DRAINAGE FLUME - <u>DAY</u> - MED. FULL SHOT

        The skeleton lies as before. Upstage the coffin is still
        burning. Brewster leads the way in, followed by Lazlo and
        the sheriff.

                            BREWSTER
                This is one thing we didn't foresee,
                professor.

                            LAZLO
        No.
                            SHERIFF
        What's happened?

                            BREWSTER
        Alucard had to be in his coffin
        by sunrise. Frank fixed it so he
        couldn't.

                            SHERIFF
        And?

                            BREWSTER
                The end of Count Dracula.

        He indicates the skeleton.

                            SHERIFF
                That's going to take some proving.

                            LAZLO
        Take a look at the ring on his hand.

        The sheriff kneels down to do as suggested.

                            SHERIFF
                It's his ring...but where's Stanley?

                            BREWSTER
                At Dark Oaks, I suspect.

                                                WIPE TO

312   INT. DARK OAKS - UPPER HALL - <u>DAY</u> - MED. FULL SHOT

        Frank, his clothing burned and generally in a pitiable
        condition, stumbles in FROM CAMERA, makes his way along
        the hall to the far end where he stops at a small door.

313   INT. DARK OAKS - UPPER HALL - <u>DAY</u> - MED. SHOT

        at door. Frank leans against the door to get his breath,
        then opening the door, discloses a flight of steps up
        which he climbs.

314   INT. ATTIC - <u>DAY</u> - MED. FULL SHOT

        on a small door. It opens and Frank ENTERS as from down-
        stairs. He looks about the room, CAMERA PANS him from
        the door to another door in a partition. The room is
        littered with the usual attic accumulation of broken
        furniture, etc. Frank reaches the partition and opens a
        concealed door through which he EXITS.

315   INT. KATHERINE'S PLAYROOM - <u>DAY</u> - MED. FULL SHOT

It is a small room with a single window. It is furnished
chiefly with children's furniture and toys. At the end
away from the door is a small stage for kid theatrics,
raised perhaps two feet above the floor level. The curtains are drawn aside. On the platform rests Kay's
coffin. Frank ENTERS and crosses uncertainly to the stage.
There he lifts the coffin lid and draws it back.

316   INT. KATHERINE'S PLAYROOM - <u>DAY</u> - MED. CLOSE SHOT

on Frank as he looks down at Kay lying like marble in the
coffin before him. After a moment he reaches down and
gently touches the tiny scars on her throat, then as he
looks off thoughtfully his hand wanders to the scars on
his own throat as he half whispers:

                         FRANK
            Eternity!

He remains lost in thought for a moment, evidently turning
over the possibilities of the proposition she made to him
in his cell.

317   EXT. DARK OAKS - <u>DAY</u> - MED. FULL SHOT

as Sheriff's car pulls up at the open door. Sheriff,
Lazlo and Brewster go into house.

318   INT. KATERINE'S PLAYROOM - <u>DAY</u> - MED. CLOSE SHOT

on Frank beside open coffin, looking off speculatively.
Now he turns back to Katherine. Her hands lie across
her breast. He lifts the left one and takes a wedding
ring from it. This he lays carefully on the coffin lid.
Now he removes a ring from one of his own fingers and
places it on the finger.

                         FRANK
            It is much better this way, Kathy.

Gently he replaces the coffin lid, leaving the ring on it
where he placed it.

319   INT, DARK OAKS - <u>DAY</u> - UPPER HALL - MED. FULL SHOT.

Sheriff, Brewster and Lazlo ENTER and Brewster leads them
to door at rear of hall which stands open. They start
up the stairs.

320   INT. KATHERINE'S PLAYROOM - <u>DAY</u> - MED. FULL SHOT

on door in partition. Frank backs in from coffin, his
eyes on it. He moves through the door and stands staring
off at the little theatre.

321   INT. ATTIC - <u>DAY</u> - MED. FULL SHOT

Frank stands at the open door looking into the playroom.
He becomes conscious of Brewster, sheriff and Lazlo only
after they have moved into SCENE behind him and stand
looking through the door with him. Turning, he faces them.

                    FRANK
          I had to take things into my own
          hands, Harry. I couldn't stand to
          think of her as she wanted it to be.

322   INT. ATTIC - <u>DAY</u> - MED. SHOT

on group in f.g. with the open door to playroom behind
them. Through the door may be seen the children's stage
with Kay's coffin on it. The drapes that mask the lower
part of the rostrum have been lighted and the flames have
by now spread to the full stage.

                    BREWSTER
          We understand.

                    FRANK
          I destroyed Dracula...in the old
          drainage flume.

                    BREWSTER
          I know...we just came from there.

Frank turns back to the door, takes one last look within
the room, then closes the door on the SCENE, putting a
sort of finis to the whole business. He now turns back
and faces the sheriff.

                    FRANK
          I had to do what I thought best,
          sheriff. Now I'm ready to go back and
          take whatever the law wants to give
          me.

                    SHERIFF
          For what, Frank?

                    FRANK
          For killing Kay.

The sheriff looks rather shamefacedly at Brewster and Lazlo.

                    SHERIFF
          Dr. Brewster says he talked to Miss
          Caldwell several hours after you
          thought you shot her. There isn't a judge
          in the state who'd question his word.

The SOUND of the o.s. FIRE is now increasing. The sheriff
continues:

                    SHERIFF
          Now let's get out o' here and let
          this cussed old mausoleum burn down!

As the men start for the stair door,
                                              FADE OUT

                    T H E   E N D

THE UNIVERSAL PRESSBOOK

A UNIVERSAL PICTURE

Copyright 1943, Universal Pictures Co., Inc.

LIKE FATHER— LIKE $ON!

"SON OF DRACULA"

brings to the screen all the power...all the thrill-after-thrill terror of its spectacular predecessor...plus the great selling value of the screen's master character creator... LON CHANEY....as Count Dracula...and in a role that has no compare for sensationalism...a revelation in loveliness...LOUISE ALLBRITTON... as Dracula's vampire bride! "SON OF DRACULA" was sired by a box-office champion...back it up with a

CHAMPIONSHIP CAMPAIGN!

CREDITS

Universal Pictures
presents
"SON OF DRACULA"
with
Louise Allbritton - Robert Paige
Evelyn Ankers - Frank Craven
J. Edward Bromberg
Samuel S. Hinds
and the screen's master character
creator
LON CHANEY
as Count Dracula

Screen Play	Eric Taylor
Original Story	Curtis Siodmak

Director of Photography, George Robinson, A.S.C.; Art Direction, John B Goodman, Martin Obzina; Director of Sound, Bernard B Brown; Technician, Charles Carroll; Set Decorations, R A Gausman, E R Robinson, Associate Producer, Donald H Brown; Film Editor, Saul Goodkind; Gowns, Vera West; Assistant Director, Melville Shyer; Music Score H J Salter.

Directed by	Robert Siodmak
Produced by	Ford Beebe

THE CAST

Frank Stanley	Robert Paige
Katherine Caldwell	Louise Allbritton
Claire Caldwell	Evelyn Ankers
Doctor Brewster	Frank Craven
Professor Lazlo	J. Edward Bromberg
Judge Simmons	Samuel S. Hinds
Madame Zimba	
	Adeline DeWalt Reynolds
Sheriff Dawes	Patrick Moriarity
Sarah	Etta McDaniel
Colonel Caldwell	George Irving
LON CHANEY as Count Dracula	

SYNOPSIS

(Not for Publication)

At their plantation, Dark Oaks, Colonel Caldwell (George Irving) and his daughter Katherine (Louise Allbritton), are entertaining Count Alucard (Lon Chaney), whom Katherine had met in Budapest. Katherine's fiance, Frank Stanley (Robert Paige), finds that "Alucard" is an alias and her friend Doctor Brewster (Frank Craven) suspects Alucard, whose name is "Dracula" spelled backward, of relationship to the infamous vampire.

Suddenly the Colonel is found dead and evidence indicates he has been attacked by a huge bat. Meanwhile, Katherine marries Alucard.

Firing a gun at his rival, Frank sees the bullets pass through him and kill Katherine. Later, Dr. Brewster goes to Dark Oaks and finds Katherine alive and presumably well; but soon after, her body is found in the family vault at Dark Oaks.

Doctor Brewster calls in Professor Lazlo (J. Edward Bromberg) for consultation. They agree that Alucard is a vampire—a bloodsucking creature which lives only by night and can assume the form of a bat.

While Alucard unsuccessfully attacks the two men, Katherine has also become a vampire. She reassumes human form and persuades Frank to destroy Alucard and then join her in "immortality." After a desperate struggle, Alucard is destroyed.

Frank decides that the best course is to destroy Katherine as well. He sets fire to the house and Katherine's remains are cremated in the smouldering ruins.

'SON OF DRACULA' BRINGS FEARSOME HORROR LEGEND TO LIFE ON SCREEN

Lon Chaney, as the vampire, finds a beautiful victim in the person of Louise Allbritton in Universal's absorbing horror classic, "Son of Dracula."

(Mat 11)

"Son of Dracula," Universal's sensational horror thriller, features (L to R) Robert Paige, Louise Allbritton and Evelyn Ankers. Lon Chaney, the screen's master character creator, has the title role.　(Mat 21)

Colorful Player Group Enacts Vampire Drama

(Advance)

Horrendous happenings are scheduled to take place on the screen of the .... Theatre ...., when Universal's latest scare-film, "Son of Dracula," will begin its long-awaited engagement. The new shudder-drama, said to contain the same chilling fascination of the original "Dracula" film, features Louise Allbritton, Robert Paige, Evelyn Ankers and Frank Craven. Lon Chaney, known as the screen's master character creator, appears in the title role.

ACTOR MENACED BY BAT IN APARTMENT

(Current)

Working with a bat during the making of Universal's "horror" drama, "Son of Dracula," reminded J. Edward Bromberg of the occasion on which he batted a bat around a New York apartment. The actor related the experience to his co-players in the new shudder-film which is now playing at the .... Theatre.

Several years ago, Bromberg spent a night in a seventh floor apartment belonging to friends, but which had been vacant for some time.

Just after retiring, the actor heard a whirring noise. He turned on the light, to discover a bat floating around the apartment.

Remembering the superstition that bats always light on a person's head, Bromberg grabbed the nearest hat, which happened to be a pith helmet. Then he went to bat—with a broom.

Garbed in pith helmet and pajamas, Bromberg swung the broom until he finally connected with the bat, and dropped the creature out the window.

"I must have been a ridiculous sight," the actor recalled. "But I was never so scared in my life."

"Son of Dracula," with Lon Chaney in the title role, has a notable cast which includes Louise Allbritton, Robert Paige, Evelyn Ankers, Frank Craven and other cinema favorites. The director was Robert Siodmak.

Reviving one of the eeriest of all ancient legends, "Son of Dracula" deals with the ghoulish activities of a descendant of the "vampire" man. Chaney portrays the weird character, a blood-sucking creature which lives only by night and can assume the form of a bat, a werewolf or a wisp of vapor.

Locale of the new drama is an isolated country estate. The mysterious action begins with the arrival of a strange visitor. Deaths follow and the clues point to the telltale marks of the vampire.

Striking Portrayal

Miss Allbritton is said to give a striking character portrayal of the vampire's victim who returns from the tomb to haunt her fiance, portrayed by Paige. Other killings are attempted before the menace is finally destroyed in the blazing ruins of the old mansion.

The cast, which includes J. Edward Bromberg and Samuel S. Hinds, is said to be one of the best ever assembled by Universal for a horror picture. This studio, makers of the "Frankenstein" and other chill movies, has become famous for this type of entertainment.

"Son of Dracula," an original story by Curtis Siodmak, was prepared as a screen play by Eric Taylor. George Robinson was the photographer and the picture was directed by Robert Siodmak. Ford Beebe was the associate producer.

Robert Paige Earns Role in Scare-Film

(Advance)

Singing star of a dozen outstanding musical films, Robert Paige, steps out of the swing field into his first dramatic role as leading man in Universal's horror drama, "Son of Dracula," coming .... to the .... Theatre.

Paige's all-round training in radio and diversified musical screen roles are evidenced in his strong portrayal in the dramatic film. The story finds him coming into conflict with the infamous Count Dracula, after the latter has brought Paige's fiance under his sinister influence.

Lon Chaney has the Dracula role and Louise Allbritton is the girl.

Paige is an Indiana boy who received his schooling in California and began his professional career as a jack-of-all-trades on the air in Los Angeles. He not only sang on his first radio programs but also assumed another identity as the announcer.

Robert Paige
(Mat A)

Louise Allbritton, popular and talented film player, has the most important role of her screen career in Universal's chill-drama, "Son of Dracula," in which Lon Chaney portrays the fearsome legendary vampire. Other movie notables in the picture's cast include Robert Paige, Evelyn Ankers, Frank Craven, J. Edward Bromberg and Samuel S. Hinds. Robert Siodmak directed under the associate producership of Ford Beebe.

(Mat 12)

The actor came to pictures from radio, after a brief period as a salesman, and his singing roles on the screen range as far as the lead in Olsen and Johnson's eccentric hit, "Hellzapoppin."

Paige stepped easily into his first serious role, in "Son of Dracula," in which his fellow-players also include Evelyn Ankers, Frank Craven, J. Edward Bromberg and Samuel S. Hinds. Robert Siodmak was the director.

PICTURE CALLED BLOOD-CURDLING

(Current)

The blood-curdling "vampire" legend which has plagued the imagination for centuries past, is revived again in Universal's "Son of Dracula" now playing at the ...... Theatre. Appearing in the new horror drama are Louise Allbritton, Robert Paige, Evelyn Ankers, Frank Craven, J. Edward Bromberg and Samuel S. Hinds. Lon Chaney, known as the screen's master character creator, has the title role.

"Son of Dracula," an original story by Curtis Siodmak, was scenarized by Eric Taylor. The picture was directed by Robert Siodmak under the associate producership of Ford Beebe.

Lon Chaney, the screen's master character creator, appears as Count Dracula in Universal's "Son of Dracula."

(Mat 13)

SOLDIERS HONOR EVELYN ANKERS

(Current)

Soldiers at Camp Kohler near Sacramento, Calif., have elected Evelyn Ankers, Universal actress, "the girl we'd most like to see in camp."

Miss Ankers was notified of the honor in a letter she received during the making of "Son of Dracula," the new horror film now at the .... Theatre. The letter was written by Pvt. Albert J. De Long and was signed by 25 men from Barracks 56.

The actress, incidentally, is in private life the wife of a U. S. Navy yeoman. Her husband is Richard Denning, former actor, who is in the service.

Appearing with Miss Ankers in "Son of Dracula" are Louise Allbritton, Robert Paige, Frank Craven and over screen favorites. Lon Chaney has the title role and the picture was directed by Robert Siodmak.

'SON OF DRACULA' IS CHILL-PACKED

(Advance)

"Son of Dracula," hailed as one of the most potent screen shockers of recent seasons, comes ...... to the ...... Theatre. The new picture is presented by Universal, makers of the "Frankenstein," "Wolf Man" and other chill dramas including the original "Dracula" film which is still rated one of the outstanding screen thrills of all time.

Lon Chaney has the title role in "Son of Dracula." Louise Allbritton, Robert Paige, Evelyn Ankers and Frank Craven appear in exciting characterizations and the cast is further enhanced by J. Edward Bromberg and Samuel S. Hinds.

Based on the age-old vampire legend, "Son of Dracula" was directed by Robert Siodmak. The associate producer was Ford Beebe.

VAMPIRE MYTH STRIKES NEW TERROR IN 'SON OF DRACULA,' FILM SHOCKER

New Horror Production Has Louise Allbritton

Robert Paige and Louise Allbritton have impressive romantic roles in Universal's horror drama, "Son of Dracula."

(Mat 14)

CHANEY DESCRIBES EERIE FILM ROLE

(Current)

When Lon Chaney's wife wanted to see him in make-up for his role in Universal's horror drama, "Son of Dracula," the actor gave a simple demonstration.

In the new film, Chaney plays a descendant of Dracula, who is able to change himself into various forms, including a wisp of smoke. The actor handed his wife a cigarette and a match.

"Light up, dear," Lon told Mrs. Chaney, "and see me in character."

"Son of Dracula," now at the .... Theatre, is a movie dramatization of the age-old vampire legend. Appearing with Chaney in the special cast are Louise Allbritton, Robert Paige, Evelyn Ankers, Frank Craven, J. Edward Bromberg and Samuel S. Hinds.

Robert Siodmak directed and the associate producer was Ford Beebe.

USE GRAVEYARD FOR MOVIE SET

(Advance)

Hungarian inscriptions on tombstones in a graveyard set for Universal's "horror" drama, "Son of Dracula," aroused the curiosity of Robert Paige during production of the picture in which he has hectic battles with a werewolf and a bat.

Paige asked Director Robert Siodmak to translate one of the inscriptions.

"That means 'Rest in peace,'" Siodmak explained.

"Rest in peace?" echoed Paige. "Not on this set!"

"Son of Dracula," featuring Lon Chaney in the title role comes ..... to the .... Theatre. Louise Allbritton, Evelyn Ankers, Frank Craven and other notables are in the distinguished cast.

(Review)

Most fearsome monster of the horror archives, the "vampire," came yesterday to the screen of the .... Theatre. The picture, "Son of Dracula," an outstanding event in the shudder cycle, was made by Universal, the studio which became famous for the "Frankenstein," "Wolf Man" and other creepy sensations. Universal made the original "Dracula" film, the spectacular success of its day. The current production will unquestionably achieve the distinction of the earlier project.

Lon Chaney, rightfully heralded as the screen's major character creator, has the title role in the new shocker. Appearing with him in highly dramatic roles are Louise Allbritton, Robert Paige, Evelyn Ankers and Frank Craven. Other distinguished players in the cast are J. Edward Bromberg and Samuel S. Hinds.

Although "Son of Dracula" is not a "continuation" of the previous thriller, it is based mainly on the same ghoulish legend of the vampire, "the terror that goeth by night" to suck the blood of its victims.

Ominous Surroundings

A lonely country estate is the scene of the vampire's depredations and Miss Allbritton is seen as one of his victims. Paige has the role of her fiance. Driven to desperation over her weird demise and mysterious return from the dead, he ends a series of killings by finally destroying the "bat man."

Expert direction by Robert Siodmak and effective photography by cinematographer George Robinson, plus impressive performances by the entire cast, give the picture its gripping, logical appeal. The screen play by Eric Taylor is "strong stuff," excellently done.

Special credit for "Son of Dracula" must be handed to associate producer Ford Beebe.

STUDIO IS FAMOUS FOR HORROR FILMS

(Advance)

Home of "Frankenstein," "Dracula," the "Invisible Man," the "Wolf Man" and other "horror" hits, Universal studio presents its latest super-shocker, "Son of Dracula" ..... at the .... Theatre.

Lon Chaney, title player in "The Wolf Man" who re-created the role in "Frankenstein Meets the Wolf Man," has another outstanding "horror" role in the new film, which has perhaps the strongest cast yet lined up for a chiller-diller.

Two feminine leads are played by Louise Allbritton, important candidate for stardom who has just completed the headline role in "Good Morning, Judge," and Evelyn Ankers, the feminine lead in three previous "horror" dramas.

Robert Paige has the chief romantic role. The supporting cast is headed by three well-known character actors, Frank Craven, J. Edward Bromberg and Samuel S. Hinds.

Robert Siodmak directed "Son of Dracula." Ford Beebe was the associate producer, while George Robinson handled the camera.

Evelyn Ankers (L) and Louise Allbritton have gripping dramatic roles in Universal's latest horror production, "Son of Dracula" in which they are menaced by the sinister "vampire man."

(Mat 22)

Movie Doors Now Open To Taller Actresses

(Advance)

Measuring up to a screen role has become a physical as well as a professional qualification of Hollywood's leading women.

Statistics show that the average player today is taller than her predecessor of several years ago. Wartime movie manpower shortages find more important roles going to actresses and height has become almost a prerequisite for those parts.

For example, there are two feminine leads—Louise Allbritton and Evelyn Ankers in Universal's "Son of Dracula," a horror drama which once would have been considered exclusively a male province. The new film, featuring Lon Chaney in the title role, comes .... to the .... Theatre.

In casting feminine principals together, there are several problems. First, they must not look too much alike, lest the audience become confused. No problem there, however, in the case of "Son of Dracula."

Second, it is preferable not to cast two blondes or two brunettes together, and the Misses Allbritton and Ankers are both blondes. This worry was solved when Louise volunteered to don a black wig, both for contrast to her fellow-player and because dark hair is better suited for her vampirish "psychological" role.

Third, the two must be equal or nearly equal in height. There can

"Son of Dracula," Universal's new screen shocker, features (L to R) Louise Allbritton, Lon Chaney and Robert Paige.

(Mat 23)

be no compromise on this, because the camera exaggerates, rather than equalizes, differences in stature to the definite disadvantage of the shorter girl. Miss Allbritton is five feet, seven inches tall and Miss Ankers only an inch shorter.

In Tall Company

Their height makes Louise and Evelyn well-qualified to appear opposite Chaney and Robert Paige, male principals, who stand six feet, three and one-half inches and six feet, two, respectively. Their comparatively lofty measurements also give the girls a physical advantage in today's trend toward pictures featuring women in important roles —because a girl has to be tall to move in today's feminine film circles.

Take Katherine Hepburn, at five feet, eight inches, the tallest feminine star. Hedy Lamarr and Alexis Smith are each five feet, seven inches, and Maria Montez and Lucille Ball both stand five feet six and one-half inches.

Story Based On Myth

Both Miss Ankers and Miss Allbritton appear in the most exciting scenes of "Son of Dracula." The story, based on the fantastic vampire myth of the middle ages, reveals the sinister activities of a "bat man" who menaces the occupants of a lonely country estate.

"Son of Dracula" was directed by Robert Siodmak. The associate producer was Ford Beebe.

Lon Chaney

(Mat B)

Evelyn Ankers

(Mat C)

LON CHANEY VIVIDLY THRILLING AS EVIL SPECTRE IN 'SON OF DRACULA'

PLAYER SHOCKED BY MORGUE SCENE

(Current)

Irish comedian Pat Moriarity received the scare of his life in a realistic morgue scene during production of Universal's new horror drama, "Son of Dracula." The picture is now at the .... Theatre.

Director Robert Siodmak instructed Moriarity, who plays a sheriff, to cross the morgue, lift the lid of a coffin and look inside.

It was Pat's first sequence in the picture, and he gave the initial rehearsal a rousing climax. He lifted the coffin lid, emitted a yell and fled from the set.

Siodmak had neglected to inform the actor that the coffin contained Louise Allbritton, wearing deathly-pale make-up and lying in complete repose.

Lon Chaney has the title role in "Son of Dracula." The cast also includes Evelyn Ankers, Robert Paige, Frank Craven, J. Edward Bromberg and Samuel S. Hinds. The associate producer was Ford Beebe.

Evelyn Ankers, blonde beauty of the cinema, is a featured player in Universal's "Son of Dracula," sensational horror drama based on the vampire legend.

(Mat 15)

Sensational Role Goes To Louise Allbritton

(Current)

Versatility is expected of a full-fledged star, but versatility on the part of a screen newcomer can mean only two things.

It may be that the young player really has what it takes to be a top box-office personality.

It may also mean that something is lacking on the romantic side, because the usual build-up for feminine stardom begins with a half-dozen or more straight "heart interest" leads. If there's any versatility to be displayed, it comes later —else cynical experts, or vice versa, are suspicious.

In the case of Louise Allbritton, one of the more versatile newcomers to the screen, the question has already been raised—and answered. The tall blonde actress appeared in only seven pictures. She has played, among other things a woman lawyer, aviatrix, interior decorator, radio writer and an enemy agent.

Louise Allbritton
(Mat D)

That Louise lacks nothing romantically was demonstrated when Universal chose her as the girl to take John Wayne away from Marlene Dietrich in "Pittsburgh."

As the result of her refusal to confine herself to romantic roles, Miss Allbritton is well on her way to cinematic importance after only

seven starts. She willingly faced her greatest test with a difficult "psychological" role in her eighth picture, Universal's "horror" drama, "Son of Dracula." The new chill-movie is now at the .... Theatre.

Robert Siodmak, director of the film, advances two reasons for the versatility of the 22-year-old actress. Siodmak is something of a versatile person himself, having been an actor, producer, director, writer and film editor.

"First, Louise has natural adaptability," Siodmak asserts. "Secondly, she has all-round stage experience behind her. At the Pasadena Community Playhouse, an excellent training ground, she played leads in ten productions as widely varied as 'The Merchant of Venice' and 'The Little Foxes.'"

Praised By Director

Siodmak will make no predictions as to the outcome of Miss Allbritton's present effort, the vampirish role in "Son of Dracula." He did say, however, that "I know of no other actress of her age and experience to whom I would have entrusted the characterization."

Lon Chaney has the title role in "Son of Dracula." Other well known performers in the picture are Robert Paige, Evelyn Ankers, Frank Craven, J. Edward Bromberg and Samuel S. Hinds.

Ford Beebe officiated as associate producer.

Film Actor Lauded As Ace Character Creator

(Current)

Lon Chaney has now completed the cycle of the four outstanding "horror" roles of modern motion pictures.

The four most shuddery characterizations, by any standards, are the "Frankenstein Monster," "Dracula," "The Mummy," and "The Wolf Man."

Chaney has played them all, to distinguish himself as the most versatile character actor since the reign of his late father, Lon Chaney, Sr.

His performance as the "Mummy" in "The Mummy's Tomb" won Chaney his present Universal contract. He played the "Monster" in "The Ghost of Frankenstein," originated "The Wolf Man" and portrayed the part again in "Frankenstein Meets the Wolf Man." Now he plays the title role of the vampire in "Son of Dracula." The new horror film, based on the age-old "vampire" legend, is playing currently at the .... Theatre.

Roles Are Punishing

Only a giant of Chaney's proportions—six feet, three and one-half inches, and weighing 220 pounds—could have absorbed the physical punishment his "horror" assignments have entailed, as well as the tedious hours spent in the studio make-up chair.

In "The Ghost of Frankenstein," for example, Chaney toted 64 pounds in make-up and costume. He was painfully burned, and out of the picture for a week, as a result of

an allergy to sponge rubber used in the "Monster" make-up.

Chaney was clubbed with a heavy cane in a fight scene for "The Wolf Man" and was knocked out when a falling crossbeam on the set of "Son of Dracula" struck him on the head.

In comparing the various roles, Chaney himself feels that "Dracula" is more potentially horrifying even than those which required more gruesome make-up. He wears only a bluish-gray grease paint on his face for this role.

Monster Described

" 'Dracula' is seen most of the time in human form, although he can change form at will," Chaney states. "I feel that a human monster, with his crafty human mind, is more terrifying than a semi-human beast."

Seen with Chaney in the new screen shocker are Louise Allbritton, Robert Paige, Evelyn Ankers, Frank Craven, J. Edward Bromberg and Samuel S. Hinds. The picture was directed by Robert Siodmak under the associate producership of Ford Beebe.

Home-Towns

Louise Allbritton .... Oklahoma.. City, Okla.
Robert Paige .... Indianapolis, Ind.
Evelyn Ankers .... Valparaiso, Chile
Frank Craven .... Boston, Mass.
J. Edward Bromberg ...... Temesvar, Hungary
Samuel S. Hinds .... Brooklyn, N. Y.
Lon Chaney .... Oklahoma City, Okla.

BLONDE CHANGES TO BRUNETTE IN DRAMA

(Current)

Blonde Louise Allbritton goes brunette for the first time in her brief screen career to play the feminine lead in Universal's "Son of Dracula" now at the........Theatre.

A dark wig was ordered for Miss Allbritton partially as a contrast to blonde Evelyn Ankers, who plays her sister, but primarily because she enacts a "psychological" role in the 'horror' drama.

A graduate of the Pasadena Community Playhouse, and recently named to the exclusive "Star Ring of 1943," Miss Allbritton is one of the most serious-minded members of the group. She agreed with Ford Beebe, associate producer, that her new dramatic role was better suited for a brunette than a blonde.

"Besides," she added, in feminine fashion, "I'm told it looks very attractive in tests."

"Son of Dracula," in which Lon Chaney plays the title role, also features Louise Allbritton, Robert Paige, Frank Craven, J. Edward Bromberg and Samuel S. Hinds. The picture was directed by Robert Siodmak.

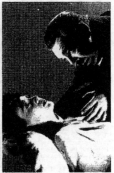

Louise Allbritton and Lon Chaney in Universal's "Son of Dracula."
(Mat 16)

FRANK CRAVEN IS INTUITIVE ACTOR

(Current)

Two Broadway plays turned down by Frank Craven failed, demonstrating the veteran actor's ability to pick his stage roles expertly.

Trying to outguess the footlight public is a hazardous business at best, but Craven is known as a shrewd judge of prospective Broadway material.

In recent months Craven has been pressed to appear in two likely Broadway vehicles, but he refused both offers. One "flopped" in its New York debut while the other folded after a Boston tryout.

Craven is appearing currently in Universal's much-talked-about horror drama, "Son of Dracula," now at the........Theatre. Lon Chaney has the title role and the cast includes Louise Allbritton, Robert Paige, Evelyn Ankers, J. Edward Bromberg and Samuel S. Hinds.

Based on the ancient "vampire" legend, "Son of Dracula" was directed by Robert Siodmak. The associate producer was Ford Beebe.

Lon Chaney, the screen's master character creator, gives his most spectacular performance as the sinister "vampire man" in Universal's "Son of Dracula."
(Mat 24)

UNUSUAL LOBBY

For a "different" lobby piece blow up still No. 4 to life size, cut out and mount the figures before the witch's table. Replace the pictured bowl with a real bowl of drab pottery or scarred metal. In the story this is a bowl of blood over which the witch tells fortunes. In your bowl use dry ice in water so that vapor rises, color the water red to look as much like blood as possible. In large letters spot the following copy (from the script) in cut-out balloon to show that the witch speaks them:

"I SEE YOU MARRYING A CORPSE AND LIVING IN A GRAVE!"

Elsewhere on the display use the following selling copy:

Over a bowl of blood the old witch saw the coming of terror! Will this beautiful girl marry the "SON OF DRACULA" ? ? ?

Spot other sales lines from the display lines on this page as space affords.

NATIONAL SCREEN

has made a trailer that's a seat selling shock!

MAKE BAT DISPLAYS

The bat is the insignia of the vampire. Out of black coated cardboard your sign shop can cut many winged figures to represent these creatures. Two strange eyes should be painted in green, and voluptuous mouth in scarlet in the shape of kissing lips. Hang these around the rim of your marquee, and suspend a number from the ceiling. Hidden fan can make them move. By attaching a few to a continuous line from top of your entrance doors to corner of marquee, and attaching line to a motor, you can get the effect of bats flying around above your box office.

v v v

ORIGINAL 'DRACULA' BOOK

Although this is an original story, the action of which has nothing to do with the original book by Bram Stoker, your book dealer should be interested in taking advantage of your date to merchandise the original title.

Tell him this is an opportunity to move unsold copies of "Dracula" off his shelves. Copy angle for a co-op window should read:

THE 'SON OF DRACULA' CARRIES ON THE TRADITION OF HORROR INTRODUCED IN THE ORIGINAL BOOK (ETC.)

A CONTEST IN WHICH CRITIC ASKS READERS TO PREDICT THE FUTURE OF A HOLLYWOOD STAR

The screen presents many new characters to your audiences. The majority of them climb to stardom thru the familiar qualities of Beauty, Personality or Ability. LOUISE ALLBRITTON possesses all three of these. And she adds a fourth . . . a deep and realistic quality of MENACE!

"Son of Dracula" gives her a wider scope for this ability. Critics viewing her work in this film predict future characterizations that will be more realistic and hardbitten than any female star has heretofore attempted. "Allbritton," say the critics, "is born for menacing roles."

All of which suggests a piece of promotion that should appeal to a local dramatic critic.

Pick a critic who is interested in predicting the futures of new stars. Let him read the above comments on Allbritton and be sure you have along a number of Allbritton stills and portraits. Suggest that he conduct a contest (as part of his column or on the drama page) in which he asks the public to make their guess concerning the future of this unusual star.

He should discuss Allbritton, taking his cue from the introductory remarks above. He can follow with discussion of his own predictions in the past. He should repeat the predictions (given above) that Allbritton is destined to become the screen's leading exponent of "hardbitten" roles. THEN HE SHOULD ASK HIS READERS WHO HAVE SEEN ALLBRITTON IN "SON OF DRACULA" (or in other roles) TO MAKE THEIR GUESS AS TO THE FUTURE OF THIS NEW STAR.

Post prizes for the most interesting predictions. Make them of sufficient inducement to appeal to the columnist. This idea will not only be of general interest but it will focus attention on his column.

v   v   v

Scenes From Screen's Weirdest Thrill . . . "SON OF DRACULA"

Put over to the readers of your daily newspaper the thrilling highlights of "SON OF DRACULA"
with this six column series of captioned mats. Order from your Universal Exchange Exploitation Mat No. SOD-1.

"I see you marrying a ghastly thing that thirsts for blood," the old witch tells Kay (Louise Allbritton) as she foretells the coming of the Son of Dracula to Dark Oaks, a ghostly plantation on the edge of the swamplands.

The presence of Dracula on the plantation is heralded by murder. While Frank and Claire (Robert Paige and Evelyn Ankers) watch Dr. Brewster (Frank Craven) attend the victim, Kay alone knows the trail of terror has just begun.

Irresistibly drawn back to the swampland, Kay holds her first rendezvous with Dracula (Lon Chaney) and agrees to be his mate. With his kiss she too becomes a vampire, cursed with the thirst for blood.

As the murders increase Frank is accused and jailed. He is dazed when Kay, one of the supposed victims, slips like a phantom into his cell. Can she change form? Can she live only at night? Is she a kiss-killer?

Nights of creeping horror leave their trail of mystery . . . the throats of sleeping beauties blazed with the crimson kiss of doom. In Claire's bedroom Dr. Brewster discovers a ghastly clue . . . the mark of bloody lips!!

A pale of horror envelops it! A pall of terror follows it! Can man cope with the supernatural? Can a vampire live forever? The screen's newest and greatest thrillshocks await you in "SON OF DRACULA."

ALLBRITTON LOBBY PIECE

ALLBRITTON *means* ALL OUT MENACE!

UNIVERSAL PRESENTS
THE SCREEN'S NEW
TEMPTRESS of TERROR

Louise Allbritton
is a fitting partner for
LON CHANEY
in
SON OF DRACULA

The sinister aspect of Louise Allbritton's unusual role in this picture is Box Office Bonanza and should be played up to the hilt. (See stunt headed "CONTEST IN WHICH CRITIC ASKS READERS TO PREDICT FUTURE OF MISS ALLBRITTON").

One way of merchandising this angle is to make a lobby piece along the lines indicated in the accompanying sketch. The photo shot used is a blowup of a still in your regular Exchange Set. Tint it with cold blues, purples and greens for added effect. For a more elaborate display get a selection of Allbritton portraits and stills from other Universal pictures in which she has appeared and, of course, add stills from "Son of Dracula."

∇

DICTIONARY TIE UP

Make a novel tie-up with your leading book store combining a display of dictionaries with still and production material from "SON OF DRACULA."

In center and up front close to the window glass, place the largest type of dictionary they sell. Open it to the page describing . . . Vampire. It will read something like this: "A fabulous ghostly being that sucks the blood of the living while they sleep. One who preys on his or her fellow men." Cut-out a square of cardboard to fit the page with a single window so that only the description of this one word can be read by passersby. If necessary, hang a magnifying glass above the copy so as to make it legible from the sidewalk.

Book dealer's tie-in copy naturally deals with the average person's need to look up the meaning of many words.

Your copy ties in with this angle by a headline over your display reading:

WHAT IS A VAMPIRE?

Ribbon leads from this to the definition in your displayed dictionary open at the word. Around this is banked your production stills, using many with the background of the bat . . . and sales copy as follows:

A VAMPIRE'S BRIDE

Red lips thirsting for redder blood!
Pale hands caressing for ghastly love!
Enslaved by the kiss of doom to . . .

"SON OF DRACULA"

∇

TEASER GIVE-AWAY

Teaser cards for give-aways will intrigue the imagination if made up according to the sketch herewith. The lips are to be printed in blood red, the wings and copy in black. Copy is as follows:

**RED LIPS THIRSTING FOR REDDER BLOOD
BLACK WINGS HOVERING for GHASTLY LOVE**

Night-pouncing horror . . . the
Vampire strikes with the
KISS OF DOOM

**CAN YOU STAND SHOCK?
CAN YOU TAKE TERROR?**

see . . .

"SON OF DRACULA"

∇

STREET BALLY

For your bally we suggest two figures, one dressed as Lon Chaney in black flowing cape, black trousers, black shoes, and possibly a black hood with bat wings; the other dressed as Miss Allbritton in long white flowing dress. Girl's face should be absolutely white (make up can kill all complexion, eyebrows, etc.) Her lips however should be livid red. She should be led around with her eyes closed as if in a trance. Copy covering the show can appear on man's back.

∇

SILK SCREEN ACCESSORIES

Silk screen means SEAT SELLING SOCK . . . those extra specialty items such as 10x60's, 30x40's, 24x60's and other sizes and shapes, all built for that extra take. See them on display at your local NATIONAL SCREEN EXCHANGE. Ordering them in addition to your regular, dependable, Universal items means additional B.O. insurance!

ACCESSORY ORDER
"SON OF DRACULA"

ITEMS	Unit Price	Quan.	Amount
One Sheet	.15 ea.		
Three Sheet	.45 ea.		
Six Sheet	.90 ea.		
24 Sheet	2.40 ea.		
22 x 28 (Full Co'or)	.40 ea.		
Eight 11 x 14's	.75 set		
14 x 36 Insert	.25 ea.		
Midget Window Card	.03½ ea.		
Regular Window Card	.07 ea.		
40 x 60 Gelatin	1.00 ea.		
6 x 9 Herald	2.25 M.		
Regular 8x10 Stills	.10 ea.		
		TOTAL	

Manager

Theatre

Address

6x9 HERALD ONE COLOR $2.25 PER M.

BRIDE OF A VAMPIRE! TEMPTRESS OF TERROR!
Cursed by the kiss of her monstrous mate . . . to live forever . . . to kill forever . . . a beautiful beast!

SON of DRACULA

with
Louise ALLBRITTON   Robert PAIGE
Evelyn ANKERS   Frank CRAVEN
J. EDWARD BROMBERG   SAMUEL S. HINDS
and
LON CHANEY
as Count Dracula

Screen Play by Eric Taylor   Original Story by Curtis Siodmak   Directed by ROBERT SIODMAK   Produced by FORD BEEBE   A UNIVERSAL PICTURE

TWENTY-FOUR

ONE

EIGHT 11x14's

22x28

SIX

THREE

40x60

14x36

REGULAR WINDOW CARD

MIDGET WINDOW CARD

Printed in U.S.A.

A UNIVERSAL PICTURE
Ad No. 1F—1 Col. Mat 15c

A UNIVERSAL PICTURE
Ad No. 2B—2 Col. Mat 30c

A UNIVERSAL PICTURE
Ad No. 1A—1 Col. Mat 15c

A UNIVERSAL PICTURE
Ad No. 1G—1 Col. Mat 15c

REALART REISSUE PRESSBOOK
(courtesy of William Armstrong)

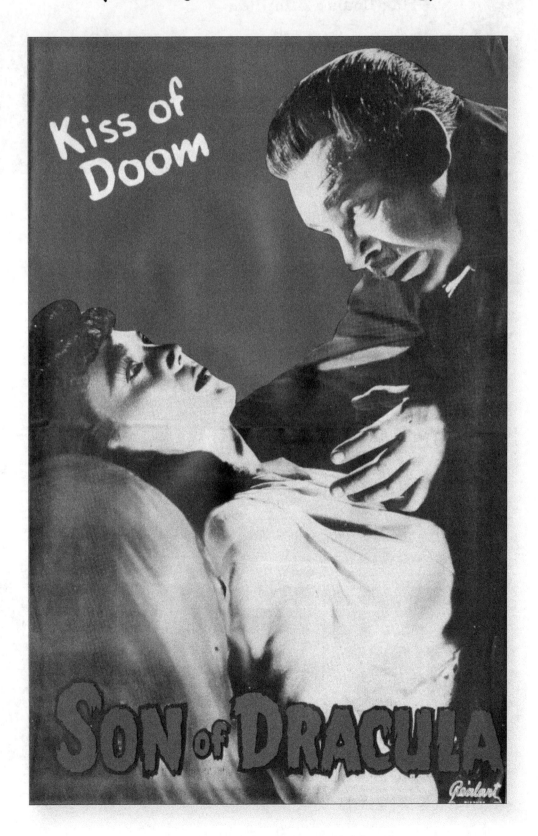

'SON OF DRACULA' BRINGS FEARSOME HORROR LEGEND TO LIFE ON SCREEN

Horror Production Has Louise Allbritton

(Review)

Robert Paige and Louise Allbritton have impressive romantic roles in the Realart horror drama, "Son of Dracula".

1 Col. Scene Mat No. 1B

Most fearsome monster of the horror archives, the "vampire," came yesterday to the screen of the..............Theatre. The picture, "Son of Dracula," an outstanding event in the shudder cycle, is being released through Realart Pictures, the company who has just brought you the spine-tingler, "The Ghost of Frankenstein". "The Son of Dracula" unquestionably will keep theatre audiences glued to their seats in thrilling expectation, just as the original film story, "Dracula", did.

Lon Chaney, rightfully heralded as the screen's major character creator, has the title role in the shocker. Appearing with him in highly dramatic roles are Louise Allbritton, Robert Paige, Evelyn Ankers and Frank Craven. Other distinguished players in the cast are J. Edward Bromberg and Samuel S. Hinds.

Although "Son of Dracula" is not a "continuation" of the previous thriller, it is based mainly on the same ghoulish legend of the vampire, "the terror that goeth by night" to suck the blood of its victims.

Ominous Surroundings

A lonely country estate is the scene of the vampire's depredations and Miss Allbritton is seen as one of his victims. Paige has the role of her fiance. Driven to desperation over her weird demise and mysterious return from the dead, he ends a series of killings by finally destroying the "bat man."

Expert direction by Robert Siodmak and effective photography by cinematographer George Robinson, plus impressive performances by the entire cast, give the picture its gripping, logical appeal. The screen play by Eric Taylor is "strong stuff," excellently done.

Special credit for "Son of Dracula" must be handed to associate producer Ford Beebe.

CHANEY DESCRIBES EERIE FILM ROLE

(Current)

When Lon Chaney's wife wanted to see him in make-up for his role in Realart's horror drama, "Son of Dracula," the actor gave a simple demonstration.

Lon Chaney

In the film, Chaney plays a descendant of Dracula, who is able to change himself into various forms, including a wisp of smoke. The actor handed his wife a cigarette and a match.

"Light up, dear," Lon told Mrs. Chaney, "and see me in character."

"Son of Dracula," now at the .... Theatre, is a movie dramatization of the age-old vampire legend. Appearing in the special cast are Louise Allbritton, Robert Paige, Evelyn Ankers, Frank Craven, J. Edward Bromberg and Samuel S. Hinds.

SYNOPSIS

(Not for Publication)

At their plantation, Dark Oaks, Colonel Caldwell (George Irving) and his daughter Katherine (Louise Allbritton), are entertaining Count Alucard (Lon Chaney), whom Katherine had met in Budapest. Katherine's fiance, Frank Stanley (Robert Paige), finds that "Alucard" is an alias and her friend Doctor Brewster (Frank Craven) suspects Alucard, whose name is "Dracula" spelled backward, of relationship to the infamous vampire.

Suddenly the Colonel is found dead and evidence indicates he has been attacked by a huge bat. Meanwhile, Katherine marries Alucard.

Firing a gun at his rival, Frank sees the bullets pass through him and kill Katherine. Later, Dr. Brewster goes to Dark Oaks and finds Katherine alive and presumably well; but soon after, her body is found in the family vault at Dark Oaks.

Doctor Brewster calls in Professor Lazlo (J. Edward Bromberg) for consultation. They agree that Alucard is a vampire—a bloodsucking creature which lives only by night and can assume the form of a bat.

While Alucard unsuccessfully attacks the two men, Katherine has also become a vampire. She resumes human form and persuades Frank to destroy Alucard and then join her in "immortality." After a desperate struggle, Alucard is destroyed.

Frank decides that the best course is to destroy Katherine as well. He sets fire to the house and Katherine's remains are cremated in the smouldering ruins.

CREDITS

Realart Pictures
presents

"SON OF DRACULA"

with

Louise Allbritton - Robert Paige Evelyn Ankers - Frank Craven J. Edward Bromberg Samuel S. Hinds

and the screen's master character creator

LON CHANEY
as Count Dracula

Screen Play .... Eric Taylor
Original Story ...... Curtis Siodmak
Director of Photography, George Robinson, A.S.C.; Art Direction, John B. Goodman, Martin Obzina; Director of Sound, Bernard B. Brown, Technician, Charles Carroll; Set Decorations, R. A. Gausman, E. R. Robinson; Associate Producer, Donald H. Brown; Film Editor, Saul Goodkind; Gowns, Vera West; Assistant Director, Melville Shyer; Music Score H. J. Salter.

Directed by .... Robert Siodmak
Produced by .... Ford Beebe
Running Time: 80 minutes.

THE CAST

Frank Stanley	Robert Paige
Katherine Caldwell	Louise Allbritton
Claire Caldwell	Evelyn Ankers
Doctor Brewster	Frank Craven
Professor Lazlo	J. Edward Bromberg
Judge Simmons	Samuel S. Hinds
Madame Zimba	
	Adeline DeWalt Reynolds
Sheriff Dawes	Patrick Moriarity
Sarah	Etta McDaniel
Colonel Caldwell	George Irving

LON CHANEY as Count Dracula

Colorful Player Group Enacts Vampire Drama

(Advance)

Horrendous happenings are scheduled to take place on the screen of the................Theatre..............when Realart Pictures scare film, "Son of Dracula", will be in its long-awaited engagement. The shudder-drama, said to contain the same chilling fascination of the original "Dracula" film, features Louise Allbritton, Robert Paige, Evelyn Ankers and Frank Craven. Lon Chaney, known as the screen's master character creator, appears in the title role.

(Current)

The blood-curdling "vampire" legend which has plagued the imagination for centuries past, is revived again in Realart's "Son of Dracula" now playing at the ...... Theatre. Appearing in the horror drama are Louise Allbritton, Robert Paige, Evelyn Ankers, Frank Craven, J. Edward Bromberg and Samuel S. Hinds. Lon Chaney, known as the screen's master character creator, has the title role.

Reviving one of the eeriest of all ancient legends, "Son of Dracula" deals with the ghoulish activities of a descendant of the "vampire" man. Chaney portrays the weird character, a blood-sucking creature which lives only by night and can assume the form of a bat, a werewolf or a wisp of vapor.

Locale of the drama is an isolated country estate. The mysterious action begins with the arrival of a strange visitor. Deaths follow and the clues point to the telltale marks of the vampire.

Striking Portrayal

Miss Allbritton is said to give a striking character portrayal of the vampire's victim who returns from the tomb to haunt her fiance, portrayed by Paige. Other killings are attempted before the menace is finally destroyed in the blazing ruins of the old mansion.

The cast, which includes J. Edward Bromberg and Samuel S. Hinds, is said to be one of the best ever assembled by Hollywood for a horror picture. Robert Siodmak, director of many spine-tingling chill movies, has become famous for this type of entertainment.

"Son of Dracula," an original story by Curtis Siodmak, was prepared as a screen play by Eric Taylor. George Robinson was the photographer and the picture was directed by Robert Siodmak.

Ford Beebe was the associate producer.

Lon Chaney, the screen's master character creator, gives his most spectacular performance as the sinister "vampire man" in Realart Pictures, "Son of Dracula."

2 Col. Scene Mat No. 2A

Movie Doors Now Open To Taller Actresses

(Advance)

Measuring up to a screen role has become a physical as well as a professional qualification of Hollywood's leading women.

Statistics show that the average player today is taller than her predecessor of several years ago. Wartime movie manpower shortages found more important roles going to actresses and height had become almost a prerequisite for those parts.

Evelyn Ankers

For example, there are two feminine leads—Louise Allbritton and Evelyn Ankers in Realart's "Son of Dracula," a horror drama which once would have been considered exclusively a male province. The film, featuring Lon Chaney in the title role, comes .... to the .... Theatre.

In casting feminine principals together, there are several problems. First, they must not look too much alike, lest the audience become confused. No problem there, however, in the case of "Son of Dracula."

Second, it is preferable not to cast two blondes or two brunettes together, and the Misses Allbritton and Ankers are both blondes. This worry was solved when Louise volunteered to don a black wig, both for contrast to her fellow-player and because dark hair is better suited for her vampirish "psychological" role.

Third, the two must be equal or nearly equal in height. There can be no compromise on this, because the camera exaggerates, rather than equalizes, differences in stature to the definite disadvantage of the shorter girl. Miss Allbritton is five feet, seven inches tall and Miss Ankers only an inch shorter.

In Tall Company

Their height makes Louise and Evelyn well-qualified to appear opposite Chaney and Robert Paige, male principals, who stand six feet, three and one-half inches and six feet, two, respectively. Their comparatively lofty measurements also give the girls a physical advantage in today's trend toward pictures featuring women in important roles—because a girl has to be tall to move in today's feminine film circles.

Take Katherine Hepburn, at five feet, eight inches, the tallest feminine star. Hedy Lamarr and Alexis Smith are each five feet, seven inches, and Maria Montez and Lucille Ball both stand five feet six and one-half inches.

'SON OF DRACULA' IS CHILL-PACKED

(Advance)

"Son of Dracula," hailed as one of the most potent screen shockers of recent seasons, comes .... to the .... Theatre. The picture is presented by Realart, distributors of "The Ghost of Frankenstein," which is rated one of the outstanding screen thrills of all time, as well as many other chill dramas.

Lon Chaney has the title role in "Son of Dracula." Louise Allbritton, Robert Paige, Evelyn Ankers and Frank Craven appear in exciting characterizations and the cast is further enhanced by J. Edward Bromberg and Samuel S. Hinds.

Based on the age-old vampire legend, "Son of Dracula" was directed by Robert Siodmak. The associate producer was Ford Beebe.

Beautiful Louise Allbritton and sinister Lon Chaney are shown in one of the blood-curdling scenes from the Realart film, "Son of Dracula".

1 Col. Scene Mat No. 1A

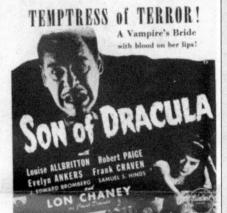

THREE SHEET

POSTERS and LOBBIES

ONE SHEET

22 x 28

ONE SET OF 8 11x14's
IN BEAUTIFUL FULL **COLOR**

22 x 28

DICTIONARY TIE UP

Make a novel tie-up with your leading book store combining a display of dictionaries with still and production material from "SON OF DRACULA."

In center and up front close to the window glass, place the largest type of dictionary they sell. Open it to the page describing . . . Vampire. It will read something like this: "A fabulous ghostly being that sucks the blood of the living while they sleep. One who preys on his or her fellow men." Cut-out a square of cardboard to fit the page with a single window so that only the description of this one word can be read by passersby. If necessary, hang a magnifying glass above the copy so as to make it legible from the sidewalk.

Book dealer's tie-in copy naturally deals with the average person's need to look up the meaning of many words.

Your copy ties in with this angle by a headline over your display reading:

WHAT IS A VAMPIRE?

Ribbon leads from this to the definition in your displayed dictionary open at the word. Around this is banked your production stills, using many with the background of the bat . . . and sales copy as follows:

A VAMPIRE'S BRIDE

Red lips thirsting for redder blood!
Pale hands caressing for ghastly love!
Enslaved by the kiss of doom to . . .
"SON OF DRACULA"

TEASER GIVE-AWAY

Teaser cards for give-aways will intrigue the imagination if made up according to the sketch herewith. The lips are to be printed in blood red, the wings and copy in black. Copy is as follows:

**RED LIPS THIRSTING FOR REDDER BLOOD
BLACK WINGS HOVERING for GHASTLY LOVE**

Night-pouncing horror . . . the
Vampire strikes with the
KISS OF DOOM

**CAN YOU STAND SHOCK?
CAN YOU TAKE TERROR?**

see . . .

"SON OF DRACULA"

V

STREET BALLY

For your bally we suggest two figures, one dressed as Lon Chaney in black flowing cape, black trousers, black shoes, and possibly a black hood with bat wings; the other dressed as Miss Allbritton in long white flowing dress. Girl's face should be absolutely white (make up can kill all complexion, eyebrows, etc.) Her lips however should be livid red. She should be led around with her eyes closed as if in a trance. Copy covering the show can appear on man's back.

MAKE BAT DISPLAYS

The bat is the insignia of the vampire. Out of black coated cardboard your sign shop can cut many winged figures to represent these creatures. Two strange eyes should be painted in green, and voluptuous mouth in scarlet in the shape of kissing lips. Hang these around the rim of your marquee, and suspend a number from the ceiling. Hidden fan can make them move. By attaching a few to a continuous line from top of your entrance doors to corner of marquee, and attaching line to a motor, you can get the effect of bats flying around above your box office.

V V V

ORIGINAL 'DRACULA' BOOK

Although this is an original story, the action of which has nothing to do with the original book by Bram Stoker, your book dealer should be interested in taking advantage of your date to merchandise the original title.

Tell him this is an opportunity to move unsold copies of "Dracula" off his shelves. Copy angle for a co-op window should read:

**THE 'SON OF DRACULA'
CARRIES ON THE TRADI-
TION OF HORROR IN-
TRODUCED IN THE
ORIGINAL BOOK (ETC.)**

Litho in U. S. A.

APPENDIX 1:
"THE TEMPTRESS WHO VAMPED COUNT ALUCARD: LOUISE ALLBRITTON"
By Gregory William Mank

The legend goes that, one day at Universal, early in 1943, the *Son of Dracula* company enjoyed an unforgettable practical joke.

Director Robert Siodmak set up the scene—the discovery of the body of Southern belle Katherine Caldwell, resting in the family vault, actually under the spell of vampirism. Romantic lead Robert Paige, veteran character player Frank Craven and other actors rehearsed; the actress playing the vampire was already in her coffin, the lid closed.

"Action!" called Siodmak—and Paige grimly opened the coffin lid.

And there in the casket—wearing only her black wig and a sly grin—was *Son of Dracula's* "vampire bride," Louise Allbritton.

Some versions claim Louise was wearing a flesh-tinted body stocking; a few say that infamous "outtake" still lurks deep in Universal's vaults. A few cynics opine that, considering the rapid pace necessary to shoot *Son of Dracula*, there probably was no time for such a practical joke at all.

Yet it's a perfect anecdote to accompany a performance which—along with Ingrid Bergman of *Dr. Jekyll and Mr. Hyde*, Simone Simon of *Cat People*, Ilona Massey of *Frankenstein Meets the Wolf Man* and Linda Darnell of *Hangover Square*—is one of the sexiest performances of 1940s horror.

Trained in Shakespeare at the Pasadena Playhouse, noted for her "screwball," Carole Lombard – style performances in Universal comedies, the blonde, blue-eyed, 5'7½" Louise threw herself into the macabre spirit of *Son of Dracula* the same way she approached everything: from her pursuit of an acting career (in fiery defiance of her wealthy Texas father), to sports, to being a Hollywood "playgirl" (her off-screen flirtation with one

> This chapter is an expanded version of the chapter "Louise Allbritton" in Mank's book *Women in Horror Films, 1940s* (McFarland & Co., 1999).

noted Hollywood "heavy" reportedly contributing to his self-destructive demise), to, finally, matrimony (to famed reporter Charles Collingwood, for whom she sublimated her career—and to whom she stayed married until her death in 1979).

She was sleek, energetic and sophisticated, both on screen and in life. And in the canon of Universal horror, Louise Allbritton achieved a wonderful, sex-reversal status: She played the woman who seduced Count Dracula.

Louise Allbritton was born in Oklahoma City on July 3, 1920. The family moved to Wichita Falls, Texas; her mother Caroline died when Louise was a child, and Louise grew up waging affectionate war with her father, L.L. Allbritton, whom one Hollywood columnist later described as "a big shot Texan with a temper." In 1942, United Press Hollywood columnist Frederick Othman described Louise thusly:

> She is the lady who helped her father run for mayor of Wichita Falls. She helped him with his speeches and gave him a lot of good advice. He lost.

Mr. Allbritton, who had eventually bought a 100,000-acre Texas ranch, hoped his daughter would pursue her early flair as a writer and cartoonist. After an English teacher got Louise hooked on acting by having her read aloud from the classics, Allbritton sent his daughter to the University of Oklahoma. She retaliated by taking every drama course the college offered, and—after two years—running away to California to join the famous Pasadena Playhouse.

When Louise arrived at Pasadena, she weighed 165 pounds. She energetically lost 40 pounds via an apple diet, morning running and steam baths. From June of 1939 into March of 1942, she appeared in over two

Louise Allbritton as Portia, one of Shakespeare's greatest heroines, in *The Merchant of Venice* at Pasadena Playhouse. It's Portia who, disguised as a male lawyer, recites the classic "The quality of mercy is not strained" soliloquy, which saves the title character from having to provide Shylock his "pound of flesh." (Photos courtesy of Ross Clark, Pasadena Playhouse Archives)

dozens productions at Pasadena Playhouse. Among her plays and roles: *The Merchant of Venice* (as Portia, opening night March 25, 1941), *Dinner at Eight* (as Millicent Jordan, the role played by Billie Burke in the 1933 screen version, July 7, 1941) and *The Little Foxes* (as the sinuous Regina Giddens, the role played in the 1939 Broadway production by Tallulah Bankhead and the 1941 film by Bette Davis, January 13, 1942). Her final play at Pasadena was *The Philadelphia Story* (March 10, 1942), in which Louise played Liz the photographer, the part played in the 1940 film by Ruth Hussey.

After her father learned of her success, he slashed her allowance. As Doug McClelland reported in his *Screen Facts* profile of Louise, "Allbritton's landlady staked her—even to long-distance calls to Wichita Falls to sound off her defiance." Yet, as Louise later remembered of her relationship with her volatile dad:

> When things looked blackest,
> I always said to myself, "Listen,
> Louise. What's the worst thing
> that can happen? Only that you'll
> wind up back on a lovely ranch,
> very comfortably off."

But she wouldn't go back to the ranch; Louise aggressively campaigned for a movie offer. When she realized how tall she looked in casting offices while standing beside her 5'4" agent, Louise mandated that the agent wear lifts while she wore flats. Finally, Columbia offered *Not a Ladies' Man* (1942), which presented a faint prophecy of Louise's horror celebrity to come: The star was *King Kong*'s Fay Wray and the director was *The Raven*'s Lew Landers. She followed at Columbia with *Parachute Nurse* (1942), directed by Charles (*Abbott and Costello Meet Frankenstein*) Barton.

"I played the parachute, I think," quipped Louise afterwards.

Then Universal made an offer. The try-out: *Danger in the Pacific*, a 60-minute potboiler in which Louise had the lead role of an aviatrix. The cast included

Don Terry, Andy Devine, Leo Carrillo, Edgar Barrier and Turhan Bey. Horror fans, however, will be most interested in the scene where Louise meets (and looms over) Dwight Frye, the erstwhile Renfield of *Dracula* and Fritz of *Frankenstein*, here reduced to the unbilled bit part of a hotel clerk. If stardom was on the horizon for Louise, who now won a Universal contract, it was long forsaken by Frye, who would die a year after *Danger in the Pacific*'s release.

Universal paired Louise and Patric Knowles as the romantic leads in Abbott and Costello's *Who Done It?* (1942), then cast the new contractee in *Pittsburgh* (1942), with Marlene Dietrich, John Wayne and Randolph Scott; it afforded her PR as the actress "successful in winning John Wayne away from the glamorous Dietrich." By the end of 1942, Louise Allbritton was a Hollywood star; Harriet Parsons, in her "Keyhole Portrait" column (November 29, 1942), introduced Louise to her readership:

> Off-screen she's Miss Perpetual Motion, a human dynamo, a young cyclone … when she undertakes anything, whether it's losing five pounds or learning a new dive, she wants to do it all at once. … whatever is worth doing, she thinks, is worth doing hard … which explains why she's broken her nose three times … first time was at 13 during a scrimmage with the grade school football team … second time was when she tried to do a perfect jack-knife dive and hit the springboard instead of the water … third (and final she hopes) break was the result of a little error in judgment while high-diving … she ploughed into the side of the pool … "It's a wonder I don't look like Maxie Rosenbloom," she says … but despite so much smacking around, the Allbritton pan is a very pleasant sight … when she breezes across the lot, the boys whistle … even though she's usually wearing blue jeans and pull-over sweater and travelling almost too fast for the naked eye to see … on her way to the commissary the other day, she passed Abbott and Costello in high gear … Costello did a double take and cracked, "If Universal could find some way of

Louise Allbritton, Universal star and Hollywood playgirl, circa 1943.

> tapping that girl for energy they could padlock the powerhouse for the duration."

Within a year at Universal, Louise Allbritton had become a marquee name. The studio's award was something Louise never expected.

"I see you marrying a corpse! Living in a grave!"

--prophecy of Queen Zimba (Adeline DeWalt Reynolds) to Kay Caldwell (Louise Allbritton) in *Son of Dracula*

Like so many of the Universal horror films, *Son of Dracula* had its own peculiar genesis and behind-the-scenes dynamics:

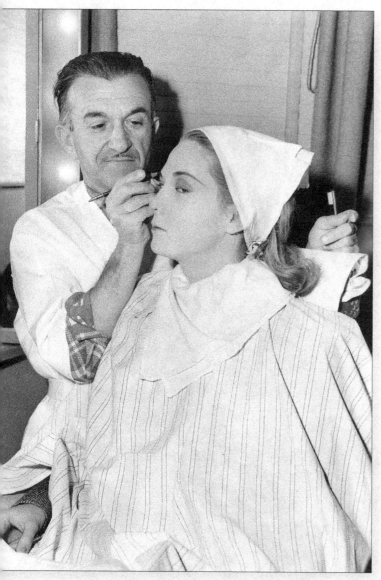

From the back-of-still snipe: "Louise Allbritton is unrecognizable as Jack Pierce, Universal studio makeup chief, prepares the actress for her 'psychological' role in *Son of Dracula*. Miss Allbritton appears in the film as a brunette for the first time, and wears a deathly-pale makeup in latter sequences."

After European émigré Curt Siodmak attained a bit of clout at Universal, following his classic scripts for *The Wolf Man* and *Frankenstein Meets the Wolf Man*, he asked the front office a favor: "Please—give my brother Robert a job." Curt's older brother was a superbly stylist director, whose 1928 *Menschen am Sonntag* virtually started the careers of six people: directors Billy Wilder (who, according to Robert, his roommate at the time, worked "about an hour" on the screenplay), Edgar G. Ulmer, Fred Zinnemann, cinematographer Eugen Schufftan—and Curt and Robert Siodmak. Robert

went on to films like *Sturme der Leidenschaft*, starring Emil Jannings and featuring one of Robert's pet themes: betrayal of a man by a woman. In fact, Robert was so adept at sexual tension in his films that Goebbels labeled him "a corruptor of the German family"— and he (and Curt) fled to Paris.

In France, Robert directed *La Crise est finie* (Curt worked on the screenplay) and *Pièges*, a tale of French police employing a girl who tricks an old man (Pierre Renoir) into proving he's the ripper who's been slaying prostitutes; the cast included Eric von Stroheim and, in a non-singing role, Maurice Chevalier! Curt, meanwhile, had gone to London, then Hollywood; Robert fled Paris the day before the German troops arrived. By the time Robert reached Hollywood, Curt—working at Paramount on *Aloma of the South Seas*—persuaded the studio to give his émigré brother a director's job.

It hadn't worked out. Robert made Paramount Bs like *West Point Widow* (1941) and *My Heart Belongs to Daddy* (1942); the studio also loaned him out to Fox and Republic; and after Robert (according to Curt) denounced the work as "Paramount shit," the studio fired him. Once again, Curt came to the rescue: Universal signed Robert and assigned him *Son of Dracula*, for which Curt had written the story.

Lon Chaney, meanwhile, had played the Wolf Man, the Frankenstein Monster and the Mummy; Universal probably figured the role of Dracula was the latest jewel in the crown of the actor they billed as "The Screen's Master Character Creator." But Lon wasn't so pleased; the role he really wanted was the Phantom of the Opera, so he could emulate and (in his dreams) top his father's classic 1925 performance. Universal awarded the Phantom role to Claude Rains in its Technicolor, $1,750,000 spectacular, which would start shooting less than two weeks after *Son of Dracula*'s start date. (Actually, the part Chaney wanted most of all was the real-life one of marine cook, and the 36-year-old alcoholic actor was trying very hard to get into the military throughout the shooting of *Son of Dracula*.)

Alan Curtis, then licking his wounds from his divorce from Ilona Massey, was assigned the romantic lead role in *Son of Dracula*—only to suffer a knee injury a week into the shooting. Universal replaced him with Robert Paige.

Finally, there was the casting of Katherine "Kay" Caldwell, the Southern belle whose morbid fascinations lead her to become the bride of Count Dracula (or of his son, depending on how one interprets the script). Eric Taylor, who wrote the screenplay dated

December 23, 1942, might have had Louise in mind when he described Katherine:

> The girl is beautiful, tall, statuesque, and appears rather eager as she peers off into the darkness…

Louise allowed Jack P. Pierce to crown her with a sultry black wig—which not only gave Louise a striking femme fatale look but contrasted nicely with blonde Evelyn Ankers, who played Katherine's "better-adjusted" sister Claire. Production began January 7, 1943. Robert Siodmak finalized shooting plans and, at a tryout director's salary of $150 per week, began shooting *Son of Dracula*.

From her first entrance in *Son of Dracula*—on the veranda of her plantation, Dark Oaks, in the bayous—Allbritton makes a sexy, sinister impression. In her black wig and flowing Vera West gown which looks like a shroud, she makes Katherine Caldwell a vampiric Scarlett O'Hara. In the course of this remarkably morbid film, Louise subtly dominates, playing Delilah to Chaney's porcine count (called "Count Alucard"—Dracula spelled backwards, of course). Siodmak stages wonderful episodes:

In the book *Universal Horrors*, Michael Brunas said of Kay Caldwell, "It's far and away the best female role in a Universal horror movie since the sad, sinister Countess Zaleska in *Dracula's Daughter*."

🦇 There is *Son of Dracula*'s (probably) most famous vignette, in which Kay stands on the bank of a marshy body of water as one of Alucard's baggage boxes rises to the surface; vapor seeps out of it and morphs into Alucard, who levitates over to Kay. He weds her that night as lightning flickers, winds howl and thunder crashes outside the door of the justice of the peace.

🦇 There's the sequence in which Frank (Robert Paige), Kay's childhood friend and fiancé, shows up at Dark Oaks and tries to shoot Dracula. The bullets pass through the vampire—and Dracula's bride (standing behind him) falls gracefully to the floor. While no special effects were necessary for this scene, it's wonderfully effective.

🦇 There's Dr. Brewster's call at Dark Oaks, after Frank insists he has killed Kay; the doctor finds her sitting up in a four-poster bed, clearly alive but frighteningly pale as she insists they have no daytime visitors.

🦇 Katherine's plan is a sly one: She has married Count Dracula, only to betray him. In the jail cell where Frank has been incarcerated, she outlines her evil plan: Frank is to destroy Dracula, and Frank and Kay will be immortal. And when Kay's sister Claire announces plans to cremate her sister's body, Kay's plan becomes even more wicked: She wishes to destroy her own sister, as well as Dr. Brewster and Prof. Lazlo (a potato dumpling version of Prof. Van Helsing).

Of course, the *Son of Dracula* climax is the most unusual feature. In Robert Siodmak style, Chaney's Dracula meets a degrading fate, courtesy of the woman he loved: Frank sets fire to Alucard's lair in the drainage tunnel, and a bellowing Chaney—caught in the sun—plops into the muck, his skeletal hand jutting

Still, high spirits prevailed (as well as that famous gag with Louise naked, or in body-stocking, in the coffin). When shooting wrapped early in February 1943, the cast principals signed Robert Siodmak's script:

My dear Siodmak—With all your faults, I love you still—old song. With sincere good wishes,
Frank Craven

Thanks, Bob, for everything. You gave me a lot, including a great deal of respect for your "touch." Best of luck and happiness!
Louise Allbritton

I can't wish all foreigners luck but I do for you.
Lon
[see illustration to the left]

With best wishes and appreciation for your swell direction!   *Evelyn Ankers*

To Robert—With thanx and all of the best.
Joe Bromberg

from the water with Universal's famous Dracula ring on one bony finger. Then Frank keeps his rendezvous with Kay, in the attic playroom where they had spent time as children. As she sleeps, he places his ring on Kay's finger. And, in a surprisingly grim finale, beautifully scored by Hans J. Salter, the heroes arrive to find the attic in flames. Frank has cremated Kay, to free her soul from the curse of vampirism.

Son of Dracula plays as one of the most morbid horror films of '40s Universal. The episode in which Dracula, in bat form, chases Frank to the graveyard under a full moon, crawls upon the unconscious man's neck, then flees when the shadow of a graveyard cross falls upon him, is masterfully staged. Kay also visits Frank's jail cell, in bat form, and Siodmak has the camera linger as the bat almost sensually begins feeding on the sleeping man's throat. One of the top ironies is that Evelyn Ankers, who most fans would guess was on hand to dry Robert Paige's tears and walk off with him in the finale, is nowhere in sight at the end.

Son of Dracula had its problems. Curt Siodmak has oft told the story of Chaney, in a violent drunken mood, sneaking up behind the fastidious Robert Siodmak and smashing a vase over his bald head. Also, as Robert Paige remembered, Louise sometimes left the stage in tears and fled to her dressing room. While this might partly have been due to her discomfort in so atypical a role, Paige claimed it was primarily because she was so emotional an actress, so caught up in the Gothic romance that she often just lost control.

Son of Dracula opened at New York's Rialto on November 5, 1943. In Hollywood, the shocker opened at the Hawaii Theatre on November 10. It was a smash hit at both theaters. Many horror fans perennially lament Chaney's miscasting as Dracula (or, as Bromberg says in the film, "possibly a descendant of Count Dracula"); indeed, it's fun to imagine how much more effective *Son of Dracula* would be had the vampire been played by Lugosi (who had just completed *Frankenstein Meets the Wolf Man* at Universal) or John Carradine (who had just completed his first Universal horror movie, *Captive Wild Woman*). Yet Siodmak handles Chaney very well—and the true menace of *Son of Dracula* is Louise Allbritton. In a genre trademarked by domination of females, she out-vamps Dracula himself, foreshadowing the sexy vampires of the Hammer films and sparking *Son of Dracula* with an exotic charm all its own.

Miss Allbritton not only checks in a slick performance but also makes it quite evident that she's on her way to being one of Hollywood's top comediennes if given the right material. –
New York Journal-American review of Universal's *San Diego, I Love You* (November 10, 1944)

(Above) Queen Zimba tries to deter Kay from her morbid course. When a witch using a bowl of rooster blood as a crystal ball tells you to clean up your act, it's time to consider the possibility that you've crossed a line.

(Below) Sleeping Cutie: Queen Zimba foresaw Kay marrying a corpse and living in a grave. She may be an ol' swamp cat but prediction-wise she's two for two!

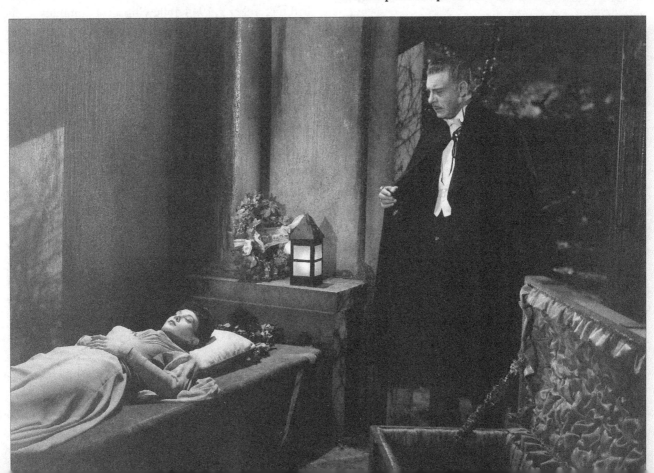

Thanks to *Son of Dracula*, Robert Siodmak became a major director at Universal; 1944 saw the release of his noir piece *Phantom Lady* (starring Ella Raines), *Cobra Woman* (with Maria Montez as good-and-bad twins) and *Christmas Holiday* (which Deanna Durbin later called her "only worthwhile film"). He later scored with Universal's *The Suspect* (starring Charles Laughton, 1944) and RKO's *The Spiral Staircase* (1946); he returned to Europe in the 1950s, living on the shore of Lake Maggiore in Switzerland, toying in the stock market and real estate and directing various European films. He died in 1971.

LA's work in *Son of Dracula* didn't earn her such rewards. She was, however, Universal's top farceur in such films as *Her Primitive Man* (1944), which starred Louise as "bring-'em-back-alive" anthropologist-lecturer Sheila Winthrop, who falls (temporarily) for *Son of Dracula* co-star Robert Paige's riotous, war-painted impersonation of a Lupari headhunter. *This Is the Life* (1944), starring Donald O'Connor and Susanna Foster (following her hit performance in *Phantom of the Opera*) found both O'Connor and Patric Knowles in love with Foster, and O'Connor delivering the incredible line, "We both have a yen for the same wren"; Louise was Harriet, whose "more mature allure" (as the New York newspaper *PM* put it) eventually captured Knowles. It was based on a play by Fay Wray and Sinclair Lewis, *Angela Is 22*. *San Diego, I Love You*, directed by horror specialist Reginald LeBorg, gave Louise her favorite role: Virginia McCooley, beauty in a house full of eccentrics, who tries passionately to sell her father's collapsible life raft. As Doug McClelland wrote in *Screen Facts*, "[A]ppearing in almost every scene, the star kept the picture afloat with her energetic, airy performance in a particularly Carole Lombard–ish role (pratfalls, black eyes, dunkings, etc.)." Also in 1944, Louise was a member of Universal's Hollywood Victory Committee (i.e., the virtual contract roster) in *Follow the Boys*, and was a very glamorous Lillian Russell, singing "Under the Bamboo Tree" in the studio's *Bowery to Broadway*.

Meanwhile, off-screen, Louise proved a dynamo in the gossip columns. Between late October of 1943 and early January of 1944, she was reported to be seriously romancing a major, a private and a lieutenant (with whom she reportedly almost eloped to Las Vegas). In February of 1944, she was touring the Mediterranean war zone in a USO show (headlined by George Raft until he was forced to come home with a sinus condition); Louise gained six pounds on G.I. food, and told the *Los Angeles Examiner* upon her return:

It was the most unforgettable experience of my life. At Cassino, we were taken within a mile of the front to play for men who had been pulled out of battle for a few hours' rest. The American artillery was behind us and several times the noise of our 240-mm. guns stopped the show. But there was no time for the men to be moved further back for the show. They see movies under the same conditions—sitting in the rain, with gunfire drowning out the soundtrack.

As soon as I have made one picture, I want to go again!

There was one area where Louise's high energy was, perhaps, misdirected. Laird Cregar, star of *The Lodger* (20th Century–Fox, 1944), had everybody talking about the young actor's powerhouse Jack the Ripper portrayal. More sophisticated audiences gossiped about the effeminate touches that Cregar (rumored to be a homosexual in Hollywood) gave the Ripper. Louise supposedly made a bet with her Hollywood playgirl friends that she could seduce Laird (who was a fellow Pasadena Playhouse alumnus) and "bring out the man" in him. According to mere gossip, she tried, and he responded—but without full success. It reputedly became one of the many private and professional woes that propelled Cregar to diet mercilessly during the fall 1944 shooting of *Hangover Square*, believing a weight loss would be a panacea for his many torments. Instead, he died December 9, 1944, following an abdominal operation, his heart fatally weakened by the diet regime; he was 31 years old. If true, in all fairness, Louise's worldly bet was just one of many agonies that brought on the self-destruction of this brilliant and tragically complex actor.

On September 11, 1944, Louise guest-starred on radio's *Globe Theatre* in "Phantom Lady," an adaptation of the noir thriller Robert Siodmak had directed for Universal. She played the role Ella Raines had portrayed in the film.

Louise starred in two Universal 1945 comedy releases. *Men in Her Diary* cast her as Isabel Glenning, an insanely jealous wife who discovers the "dream romance" diary of her husband's (Jon Hall) scraggly secretary (Peggy Ryan). The *New York Herald Tribune* critiqued, "Peggy Ryan plays the ugly duckling role as though she were dodging old eggs and cabbages; Jon Hall reaches a new high in 'phony' acting as the boss, and Louise Allbritton plays the boss' wife with her tongue halfway through her cheek." The supporting cast included Alan Mowbray, Virginia Grey, Ernest Truex and "Slapsie Maxie" Rosenbloom. *That Night with You* (1945) boasted

Susanna Foster, Franchot Tone, David Bruce and Louise, the last as Sheila Morgan, a comic secretary.

Louise's only 1946 Universal release was *Tangier*, a Maria Montez espionage saga. George Waggner, who had made his mark at Universal as director–associate producer of *The Wolf Man* and producer of *The Ghost of Frankenstein*, *Frankenstein Meets the Wolf Man* and *Phantom of the Opera*, ended his Universal sojourn as director of this film—which saw Louise and Preston Foster falling to their deaths in an amok elevator.

Louise Allbritton's big news of 1946 was her marriage. On May 13, she married Charles Collingwood, the famed news commentator, at the Little Church Around the Corner in New York City. Louise had met Collingwood during her USO tour in North Africa; the adventurous radio correspondent had gone on to land at Utah Beach two hours after the D-Day invasion, traveling on through France and Germany to the fall of Berlin. The groom was 29, the bride 25. "I'm very, very happy," Louise told Louella Parsons.

After the marriage, Louise cut back on her career activity, and the 1940s saw her in only five more films. Universal's merger with International might have ended in bankruptcy but for *The Egg and I* (1947), the giant box office hit based on the Betty MacDonald bestseller, starring Fred MacMurray and Claudette Colbert, and introducing Marjorie Main and Percy Kilbride as Ma and Pa Kettle. Louise was delightful as the vampy neighbor, who tries to lure MacMurray with her "new machinery." *Sitting Pretty* (20th Century–Fox, 1948) gave moviegoers Clifton Webb, winning a Best Actor Academy Award nomination as Mr. Belvedere; Louise played Maureen O'Hara's gossipy sister.

Louise was back as "the other woman" in United Artists' *Don't Trust Your Husband* (1948), with Fred MacMurray and Madeleine Carroll. She was a Russian-speaking "red herring" in Columbia's FBI semi-documentary *Walk a Crooked Mile* (1948), with Dennis O'Keefe and Louis Hayward, and stayed at Columbia for what would be her last film for 15 years, *The Doolins of Oklahoma* (1949), a Randolph Scott oater with Louise as Rose of Cimarron.

In 1946, Louise was an attraction of the radio show *Hollywood Jackpot*, and in the late 1940s played summer stock in *Love from a Stranger*. Come 1949, she moved to Washington, D.C., with husband Collingwood, where he was the CBS Capitol correspondent until 1952. He later headed CBS news offices in London and Paris, and he and Louise enjoyed a very social life in what Doug McClelland later described as "the best international circles."

But ham was in Louise's blood, and she often grabbed chances to act. She toured stock and "the Caribbean circuit" in such plays as *The Philadelphia Story*, *There's Always Juliet*, *Affairs of State* and *A Roomful of Roses*. On May 27, 1952, she and Dana Andrews were guest stars on radio's *Cavalcade of America* in "Valley of the Swans." On November 6 that same year, she opened in New Haven in the pre–Broadway tryout of *Rise by Sin*, but it never made it to New York. On November 2, 1953, Louise made her Broadway debut, replacing vacationing Neva Patterson for two weeks as the wife in *The Seven Year Itch*. In 1955, she starred on the NBC daily soap *Concerning Miss Marlowe*.

"They've talked and talked about our having a husband-and-wife show," said Louise at this time, as Collingwood worked at CBS, "but I'm too stupid."

"And I'm a lousy actor," said Collingwood. In December 1955, Louise appeared in Broadway's *Third Person*, a play about homosexuality, starring Bradford Dillman. It ran 84 performances, and *The New York Times* saluted Louise as "a handsome woman with a fine figure and winning manners." The same month that it opened, *The New York Post* reported that a thief had "escaped with $5000 to $8000 worth of jewelry" (including Louise's platinum wedding ring) from the Collingwoods' three-floor apartment at 120 East 65th Street. Surprised by the housekeeper, the thief had left behind another $15,000 in jewelry and $10,000 worth of furs.

From 1957 to 1959, the Collingwoods lived in England, where Louise made her London stage debut in 1958 in *A Touch of the Sun*, with no less than Sir Michael Redgrave and Lady Diana Wynyard.

Back in the U.S., Charles Collingwood hosted TV's *Person to Person* (1959-61) and was anchorman of *Eyewitness to History* (1962-63). One of his best-remembered engagements was accompanying First Lady Jacqueline Kennedy on her famed tour of the White House, televised Valentine's Day of 1962.

Louise wanted the role in *Breakfast at Tiffany's* that Patricia Neal nabbed. Her swan song came in 1964, when TV director David E. Durston (who had known Louise at the Pasadena Playhouse) cast her in the juicy role of the wealthy widow of a famed humanitarian who blames herself for his accidental death and becomes an alcoholic recluse, in the romantic mystery *Felicia*, filmed in Puerto Rico. The film—her first in color—was never released.

Once again the Collingwoods returned to London, where they lived from 1964 to 1975. Before Charles and Louise came back to New York, Queen Elizabeth named Collingwood an honorary commander of the Most Excellent Order of the British Empire. Louise traveled the world with her husband of many honors, enjoying her reputation as one of New York's most popular hostesses, and living fully and elegantly.

On February 16, 1979, the 58-year-old Louise died of cancer at a hospital in Puerto Vallarta, Mexico, where she and Collingwood enjoyed a resort home. There was a memorial service at St. James Episcopal Church in New York City.

"Film fans remember Louise as the beautiful star of *Pittsburgh, Sitting Pretty* and *The Egg and I*," wrote columnist Liz Smith. "But some of us simply remember her as a great friend who will be sorely missed."

The star horror fans remember so vividly for *Son of Dracula* was cremated, and her husband of almost 33 years scattered her ashes near their Puerto Vallarta home. Charles Collingwood died in New York City on October 3, 1985.

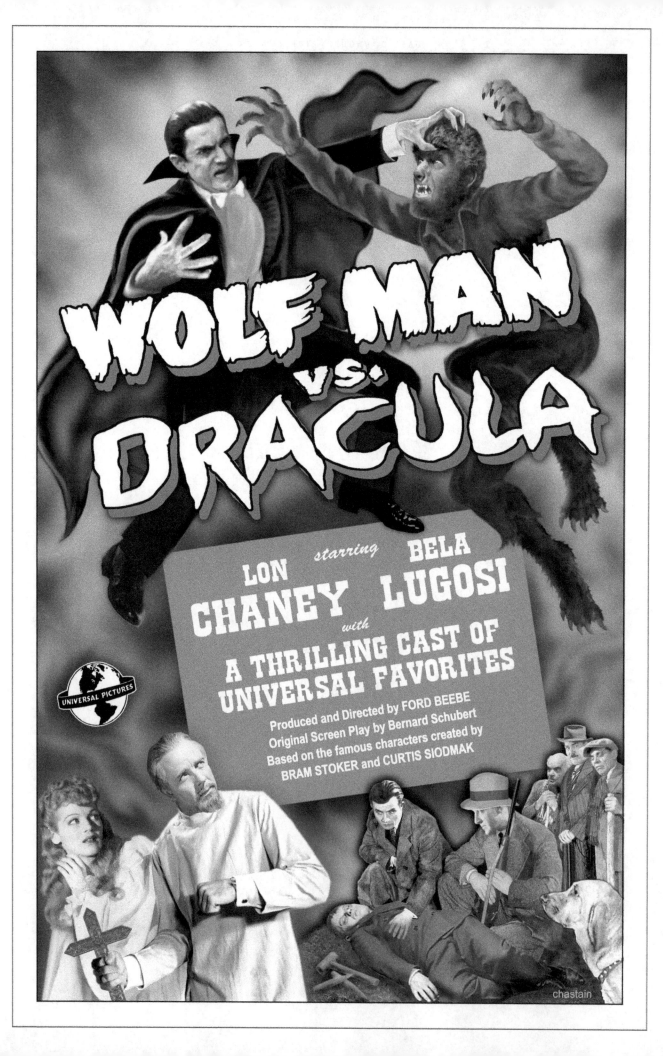

APPENDIX 2:
WOLFMAN VS. DRACULA

On December 1, 1944, Universal sent the Production Code Administration (PCA) the script of their planned (but never made) film *Wolfman vs. Dracula*. That same day, C.R. Metzger of the PCA read it and drafted a synopsis for his superiors to read. Metzger categorized it as a "usual horror story." Below is the synopsis he prepared:

The story opens in a Bohemian city during a full moon. A peasant leads a group of men into the country where he has discovered the skeleton of a woman, and beside it, the body of a man. There is no decay as to the man's body and a doctor suggests this may be suspended animation.

The man's body is taken to town where the doctor removes a silver bullet which had been pressing against the heart and the man, Larry Talbot, is restored to life. Talbot is resentful toward the doctor and, under the influence of the spell of the full moon, kills the doctor's assistant and flees.

The next day Talbot arrives at the farm home of a peasant, Anatole, who is shunned because he is the public hangman. Talbot tells Anatole he is bewitched and begs Anatole to kill him with a silver bullet (the only kind that is effective against a werewolf) but Anatole refuses. Anatole has a daughter, Yvonne, who is courted by a Dr. Draulac (really Dracula) who lives in a ruined castle nearby. Dracula changes form to a bat, etc., and the only thing of which he is afraid is a crucifix.

Yvonne likes Talbot and they slip away and are married, and are quite happy for several weeks. Talbot suspects Dracula and knows that Dracula sleeps some-

where by day, in a coffin, and can only be killed by driving a consecrated piece of wood through his heart. Talbot searches the castle but cannot find the coffin where Dracula spends his days.

Dracula tells Talbot that he can cure Talbot of being a werewolf but he demands as payment the small crucifix which Yvonne wears around her neck. While Yvonne is asleep, Talbot gets this crucifix for Dracula. However, Dracula assumes the form of a bat and puts the mark of the undead people on Yvonne's neck, and tells her to come to him at the castle the next day. Talbot and Anatole come to Yvonne's bedroom and see the marks of the bat on her throat. When she regains consciousness she is like a sleep walker. It is also close to the full moon again and Talbot realizes he will assume the form of the werewolf and become a menace. He asks Anatole to prepare a silver bullet to be used in case of emergency.

The afternoon before the full moon, Talbot goes to the castle. To it comes Yvonne in a trance to find Dracula. Talbot gets a wooden cross and drives this through Dracula's heart, while Dracula is still asleep in his coffin. Dracula is destroyed and turns to a skeleton. Then Talbot topples a brick wall over the coffin so it will not be disturbed and Dracula restored to life again.

Then Talbot returns to Yvonne, who has fainted, and sees on her hand the dreaded mark of the pentegram [*sic*] which means she is to be his next victim when he again becomes a werewolf. Anatole has secured the assistance of the police and they come to the castle. Talbot becomes a werewolf and battles with the police and then flees to Yvonne with the idea of destroying her. Anatole is handy with his silver bullet and wounds Talbot fatally. As he is dying, Talbot thanks Anatole for wounding him and keeping him from killing Yvonne with whom he had known brief happiness. Talbot dies and Anatole takes Yvonne home.

(Left) A make-believe movie poster for the never-made *Wolf Man vs. Dracula*, created for this book by artist **George Chastain.** You can see other examples of George's amazing art at his website, egorschamber.com/portfolio/

After the PCA's Joseph I. Breen examined the *Wolf Man vs. Dracula* script, he wrote this letter to Universal's Maurice Pivar:

December 4, 1944

Mr. Maurice Pivar
Universal Pictures Co., Inc.
Universal City, California

Dear Mr. Pivar:

We have read *Wolfman vs. Dracula*, and are pleased to report that the basic story seems to comply with the provisions of the Production Code.

It is imperative that you exercise the greatest restraint at all times in avoiding excessive gruesomeness and horror angles, not only to comply with the provisions of the Production Code relating to these points, but further to avoid considerable deletions by political censor boards.

Please send us lyrics and translations of various folk songs you intend to use.

We call your attention to the following details:

With reference to specific places where excessive gruesomeness must be avoided, note the following:

Page 5, scene 9 continued; page 11, scene 19; page 18, scenes 34, 35; page 65, scenes 134, 138; page 67, scene 146; page 85, scene 197; page 103, scene 268, where you must omit the sounds of the stake being driven into the body and the "ear-splitting scream;" page 116, scene 333, where again the "wild screams" should be omit-

ted; page 117, scenes 338, 340. It is imperative also that gruesomeness must be avoided as to the showing of any dead bodies or any wounds.

Page 13: In scene 21, we request that you rephrase the first sentence to read "He was <u>apparently</u> dead," inserting the underscored word. On this page in scene 22, please make this read "You <u>appeared</u> dead." Both of these changes should be made to avoid offense to persons of sincere religious convictions.

Page 26: In scene 49, the Doctor's speech beginning with "Most of it belongs back in the Dark Ages.....," should be rephrased to make it quite clear that the Doctor doesn't believe in religion than such a general statement as now appears. This also to avoid offense to persons of sincere religious convictions.

Page 40: In scene 76 there should be no unacceptable exposure of Yvonne's person, and we request further that she put on some sort of a bathrobe at this point.

Page 107: In scene 284, instead of having the words "Oh, God" come through, we request this be changed to something else, possibly "Merciful heaven."

Page 114: As now written, scene 318 will probably be deleted by most political censor boards. This action should be modified. In both scenes 319 and 320 the clunking should be suggested out of scene. Otherwise, this will be deleted by numerous political censor boards.

You understand, of course, that our final judgment will be based upon the finished picture.

Cordially yours,
Joseph I. Breen

APPENDIX 3:
COUNT-DOWN TO DRACULA:
LON CHANEY PRESS CLIPPINGS

Compiled by Bill Kaffenberger

Lon Chaney's Son Seeks Film Parts, Wants Own Name

Hollywood, Cal., Jan. 27 (P).— The matter of a name, apparently, is all that is keeping Creighton Chaney from following in the footsteps of his famous father, portrayer of weird screen roles.

The question is, shall Creighton start his film career under his own name or as Lon Chaney, jr.?

An agreement between the late star's 23-year-old son, who has been manager of the service department of his father-in-law's water heater business here for several years, and the R. K. O. studio has been drawn up, it became known today.

But a hitch developed when young Chaney demanded that the studio use his own name, an injunction urged, Hollywood hears, by the boy's stepmother.

The five-year contract, naming the terms at $250 a week and graduating to three thousand dollars a week, and specifying the billing as "Lon Chaney, jr.," requires the formalities of signing to make it effective, Edward Small, Chaney's agent, admitted.

"If I go in the movies I'll use my own name, not that of my father," Creighton told the Associated Press.

January 27, 1932

On the following pages, enjoy reproductions of a random sampling of Lon Chaney Jr. press clippings, from 1932 (the year his first movie was released) to 1942 (a *Wolf Man* clipping).

Anti-Suicide Club Formed to Save Gamblers From Act

Monte Carlo, Monaco – (U.P) – An "anti-suicide" club has been formed here to prevent unlucky gamblers from taking their losses too seriously.

Persons of all nationalities who try their luck at the casino, are being asked to join. Similar clubs are being formed at other gambling resorts on the Riviera. A series of suicides prompted the idea.

Monte Carlo has long been notorious for its supposedly large number of suicide cases. To kill this unfavorable impression, casino authorities have gathered statistics to prove that the suicide rate here is the lowest in the world.

They claim that the suicide rate in Monte Carlo is 10 per 1,000 of population each year, compared with 13 per 1,000 in the United States.

Two Chaneys

The rather handsome young man shown above in the straight picture is Creighton Chaney, son of the character player Lon Chaney. Creighton, who has recently signed a contract with R. K. O., says that he has no intention of trying to copy his famous father. Three character pictures of Lon are also shown. On the upper left Lon is shown as the hypnotist in the picture of the same name; lower left shows him in the title role of "Mr. Wu," one of his many Chinese characterizations, and lower right as Fagin in "Oliver Twist."

Late Chaney's Son Enlists In Films

Crighton Chaney's proposed camera debut will place him in the rather select rank of Hollywood's "second generation" in pictures. Others in this rank are Douglas Fairbanks, Jr., the only son of a star to become a star in his own right; Phillips, son of Taylor Holmes; Russell, son of James and Lucile Gleason; Constance and Joan, daughters of Richard Bennett, and Helene and Dolores, daughters of Maurice Costello.

Young Chaney's screen work, of course, will not attempt to follow the example set by his late father, but will be of the conventional juvenile type. He is 23, and has never acted before. He is to be admired for insisting that his screen debut be under his own name

February 20, 1932

February 26, 1932

Lon Chaney's Son Thinks Modestly Of His Talents

THE late Lon Chaney made "a thousand faces" familiar to moviegoers. Now Creighton Chaney, 23-year-old son of the famous character actor, is trying to make the public accept his. He's a good looking boy, better looking than Lon, though no matinee idol.

Creighton admits he doesn't know anything about acting, but he wants to learn. He says he had a secret yearning for the profession even when he was a boy, but his father thought one actor in the family was enough. So young Chaney went into other work. "I've had almost every kind of job," he says. "My father didn't want his success to spoil me, and insisted on my doing things for myself."

Creighton married when he was 19, and has been with his father-in-law's water heater company since. He has two children, Lon, 3, and Ronald, not quite 2.

"I'm not sure yet what type of parts I want to play," he says of his new career. "I want to succeed, and whatever they give me to do will be fine with me. But I think trying character parts right at first would be unwise, considering my inexperience. It takes a real actor to do those."

The young Mrs. Chaney approves of his screen venture. Creighton grins, "If she didn't, I wouldn't be taking it up."

March 3, 1932

Son Of Great Lon Chaney To Bow In Films

CREIGHTON CHANEY

HOLLYWOOD, March 24.—(U.P.)—Creighton Chaney, son of the great Lon, has been given his first role since signing recently for a screen career with R. K. O. He will portray an athletic youth in The Bird Of Paradise.

Along with young Chaney and Noah Beery, Jr., Bill Reid, son of the late Wallace Reid, is the most recent to follow the footsteps of illustrious parents. He will appear in a picture which his mother has financed.

March 24, 1932

Chaney Jr. Is Latest to Try Wings Alone

By Louella O. Parsons
Universal Service Wire

LOS ANGELES, April 23
Will Creighton Chaney, the son of the beloved Lon, make a success on the screen?

The odds are against him. This is a rather bitter thing to say at the very beginning of a career, but I say the odds are against him because it's the most difficult thing in the world for a child of a famous star to carve a name for himself or herself in the same line of work.

Outsiders who cannot get into the studios will look at young Chaney with envy; with the feeling that he is trading on his father's name. He will have to be just a little better than if he hadn't had Lon Chaney for a father. It's true he might never have had his opportunity at Radio Studio if he had not been born the son of Lon Chaney, but once in the studio the going is not easy.

April 24, 1932

May 4, 1932

SCREEN ODDITIES
by Captain Roscoe Fawcett

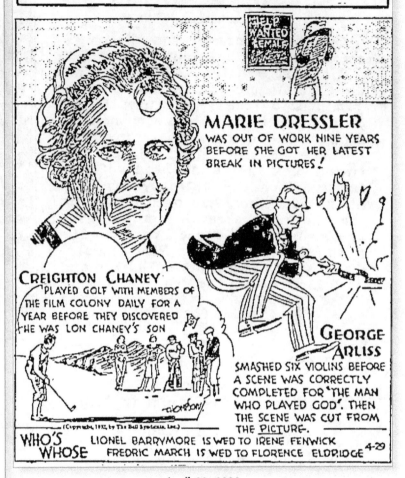

MARIE DRESSLER WAS OUT OF WORK NINE YEARS BEFORE SHE GOT HER LATEST BREAK IN PICTURES!

CREIGHTON CHANEY PLAYED GOLF WITH MEMBERS OF THE FILM COLONY DAILY FOR A YEAR BEFORE THEY DISCOVERED HE WAS LON CHANEY'S SON

GEORGE ARLISS SMASHED SIX VIOLINS BEFORE A SCENE WAS CORRECTLY COMPLETED FOR 'THE MAN WHO PLAYED GOD'. THEN THE SCENE WAS CUT FROM THE PICTURE.

WHO'S WHOSE LIONEL BARRYMORE IS WED TO IRENE FENWICK FREDRIC MARCH IS WED TO FLORENCE ELDRIDGE 4-29

April 29, 1932

Lon Chaney Grandson Hurt by Lawn Mower

Special to The Chronicle
HOLLYWOOD, May 3 — Lon Chaney II, 4-year-old grandson of the late motion picture star, and son of Creighton Chaney, actor, was removed to Hollywod Emergency Hospital today with injuries suffered when he walked into a lawn mower as he watched a gardener at work. His injuries are not serious.

Creighton Chaney To Be in Serials

Creighton Chaney, son of the famous Lon, has been signed to star in "The Last Frontier," R-K-O Radio's first serial picture, which is to be produced by the Van Beuren Corporation under the supervision of Fred McConnell, veteran serial expert.

Chaney, a strapping youth six feet two inches tall, and head of the family since the untimely death of his noted father, has been on the lot for the past several months being groomed for his screen career. His first role was in "The Bird of Paradise," which has Dolores Del Rio and Joel McCrea in the leading roles.

July 3, 1932

A dramatic director goes into action. Albert Lovejoy giving a few pointers to Rochelle Hudson and Creighton Chaney regarding the intricacies of the drama

August 7, 1932

CHANEY EXPERT HORSEMAN

Film Actor Learns Much in Long Rehearsal Period.

Months and months of riding instruction is hard work—take it from Creighton Chaney, handsome young star of "The Last Frontier," the RKO Van Beuren 12-chapter serial. Chaney's role demanded many horseback stunts—bucking, running, swimming, jumping across chasms and off cliffs and inclines. He didn't have a fall.

When he started rehearsals he was not an adept horseman. When he finished the picture, he rode with the best of the champion bronco busters in the cast. Reason? His tutors were Yakima Canutt, world's champion rider, roper and shooter; Pete Morrison, equally as famous; William Desmond, western star, and Dorothy Gulliver, an expert equestrienne.

September 18, 1932

CREIGHTON CHANEY

Lon Chaney's Son Rumored for Part in 'King of the Jungle'

By Harrison Carroll

HOLLYWOOD, Oct. 24.—After looking at a screen test made by Creighton Chaney, Paramount is hot to get this young actor to play the lead in the much publicized "King of the Jungle."

Several details remained to be straightened out, but the chances are two to one that R-K-O will change its plans for Chaney and allow him to accept the role.

Literally dozens of persons have been tested for this picture. Once Bob Hall, the football player, almost had the part. Then it was Norman Ross, the swimmer, and only two days ago Georges Carpentier was mentioned as a likely candidate.

If the choice really falls on Chaney it will be his biggest assignment since he decided to give up business and follow in his father's footsteps. Put under long term contract by R-K-O, he played a part in "The Bird of Paradise" and recently completed a serial.

October 25, 1932

CREIGHTON CHANEY AT ADA MEADE SATURDAY

Seventy-four inches of handsome young manhood. Two hundred pounds of athletic brawn. A bit of a resemblance to Valentino, a bit to Clark Gable—and a whole lot of what is just himself. A new, virile, red-blooded star at the age of 21! Creighton Chaney!

His first starring picture, a 12-chapter, thrill-packed modern talkie serial based on Courtney Ryley Cooper's famous story, "The Last Frontier," produced for RKO by the Van Beuren Corporation, is coming to the Ada Meade theater Saturday.

As his famous last name indicates, Creighton is the son of the immortal Lon Chaney.

He was born in Oklahoma City, Okla., while his parents were "barn-storming." Raised to boyhood and educated in Los Angeles, he kept out of pictures while his father was winning fame and fortune. He attended Hollywood High school and then a business college, intending to adopt commerce as a career. Only the death of his father moved him to carry on the fame of the Chaney name.

May 21, 1933

"Oh, Susanna" Their Theme Song
—Telling on Hollywood—

CREIGHTON CHANEY owns Sutter's Mill— the gold strike of '49

JACK HOLT joined the Klondike gold rush

June 26, 1933

Chaney Reduces

From Hollywood comes a note on how Creighton Chaney lost twenty pounds in a little more than two weeks, and still kept fit, too.

One full meal every other day and a mixture of sauerkraut and tomato juice five times daily. And a ten mile run every day—just to keep his muscles hardened. This is the diet that he introduced to Hollywood, but it is doubtful if anyone outside of that miracle city could ever stand up under such strenuous exercise with so little food. (S. W.)

July 12, 1933

Noah Beery Jr. (right), **Dorothy Davenport Reid,** former screen star and widow of Wallace Reid, with **Lon Chaney Jr.** at the film industry reunion celebration. Young Beery and Chaney are starting screen careers in emulation of their famous fathers.
—*A. P. photo.*

March 18, 1935

Lon Chaney's Son Will Use Father's Name

HOLLYWOOD, Jan. 5. — (P) — Creighton Chaney, 28-year-old son of the late Lon Chaney, movie "man of a thousand faces," has changed his mind. He will be billed on the screen as Lon Chany, Jr., after all.

Two years after his father's death in 1930, Creighton entered pictures and at the time he attracted considerable attention for his steadfast refusal to use his famous father's name in his own career.

To-day, admitting he expected criticism, he explained his new decision.

When he began in films, deserting active participation in a water-heater company in which he still holds an interest. Chaney said, he did not feel that a "mere beginner" should presume to use a famous actor's name.

"Now," he went on, "after two years I think that some day I may be a good enough actor at least not to discredit the name professionally."

Chaney is married and has two sons, Lon, 6, and Ron, 4.

January 5, 1935

Son Of Lon Chaney Is Divorced At L. A.

LOS ANGELES, July 25.—(P)—Mrs. Dorothy A. Chaney won an uncontested divorce to-day from Creighton Chaney, son of the late Lon Chaney, motion picture actor.

She charged Chaney drank excessively, stayed away from home and was sullen. Her attorneys said a "very generous" property settlement had been made, in which Mrs. Chaney "got nearly all" the community property.

Custody of two sons, Lon, 8, and Ronald, 6, was placed in Mrs. Chaney's hands.

July 26, 1936

Lon Chaney, Jr., like his father, finds magic in a make-up box. The picture shows him "as is" and in a recent characterization as a sinister bad-eyed human derelict.

Chaney's Son, Makeup Wizard, Following in Dad's Footsteps

Famous Parents' Secrets Help Lon, Jr., in Screen Characterizations; Only 29, Has Been Married Ten Years; Shuns Gay Life

HOLLYWOOD, Nov. 9 (AP).—The little black box from which the late Lon Chaney evoked the weird characters he made famous on the screen reposes now in the local film museum.

But from another box, converted from its intended purpose as a large container of fishing tackle, Lon Chaney, Jr., has begun to draw characters which he hopes will keep alive the screen significance of his name.

In two productions already the younger Chaney has essayed characters similar to those for which his father was famous before his death in 1930. In "Shadow of Silk Lennox" young Chaney portrayed a gangster leader, and in "Scream in the Dark" he played a dual role, first as a young detective, then as a sinister, bad-eyed, scraggly-bearded human derelict—in reality three roles, for the young detective is required to impersonate the other character.

Knows Dad's Secrets

Like his father, Lon, Jr., is his own makeup man. He is studying the art intensively, devoting three hours daily to practice in transforming his personality through the use of makeup and character study.

"My father," he says, "knew things about makeup that no one else did, and I learned two or three of his secrets. But he always said, and I agree with him, that the important thing in a characterization is what you do after the makeup is on. My father had so many tough knocks in his life that he acquired early a knowledge of human character. He made things easy for me, but I am studying all the time—trying to get behind every unusual face I see, copying photographs of odd people and trying to work them out as characters."

It was last year that Creighton Chaney, who was in the water heater business before he came into pictures as a character juvenile, was persuaded to assume the name of Lon Chaney, Jr., and attempt characterizations like those of his father. From the beginning he had preferred character work to "straight juveniles," although he could qualify for those, too.

Doesn't Like Gay Life

"Like father, like son," applies in the younger Chaney's off-screen life as well. The late actor, remembered for such films as "Phantom of the Opera," "Hunchback of Notre Dame" and "He Who Gets Slapped," never participated in the "gay life" of the film colony, but was a family man always. Lon Chaney, Jr., has been married to Dorothy Hinckley, his schoolday sweetheart, nearly 10 years, and at 29 is the father of two sons, Lon and Ron, aged eight and six, respectively.

November 10, 1935

. . . testimony that Creighton Chaney, son of the late Lon Chaney, drank to excess and remained away from home, won Mrs. Dorothy Chaney a divorce decree in Los Angeles courts. She was awarded custody of their two sons.

July 29, 1936

Movie Scrapbook

LON CHANEY, JR.

PLAYED WESTERN LEADS AND IS A TRICK RIDER.

BOUGHT A HIVE OF BEES FOR HONEY —CLAIMS HE GOT STUNG.

PLAYS CHARACTER AND HEAVY ROLES.

RAISES CHICKENS, PIGS AND GOATS.

Heir to a famous name, Lon Chaney, Jr., decided to carry on the tradition after his father's death ... A child of the theatre, he was born in a dressing room in Oklahoma City 25 years ago ... Spent his first six years on the road with his parents who were then stock company actors ... His father wanted him to be a banker, but he tried the movies—with little success till he turned to westerns ... Played leads and learned trick riding ... Now under contract to 20th-Fox and works steadily, playing character and "heavy" roles ... Hasn't had an opportunity to use his father's makeup kit which he still owns ... Present ambition is to make enough money to buy a 1000-acre ranch and raise cattle ... Married and has small chicken farm ... also raises a few pigs and goats.

March 21, 1938

December 20, 1938

SUIT DECIDED

Creighton Chaney

Mrs. Dorothy Chaney

Star Dust

★ *Fame a Handicap*
★ *Come-Back at Seven*
★ *Gang O. K's Marlene*

—— **By Virginia Vale** ——

IF THE public likes Lon Chaney Jr. in "Of Mice and Men" he's going to be one of the happiest young men in Hollywood. For he's severely handicapped in trying to carve a career for himself. As the son of a famous father he is expected to be better than average; what would be success for somebody else is just a passing grade for him.

He tried out for the lead in "The Hunchback of Notre Dame," and didn't realize how lucky he was not to get it until he saw a revival of the film recently. "It made me realize more sharply than ever how good my father was," he remarked. "And what a tough time anybody will have trying to live up to the part. Anything I might have done would have been a pale carbon copy." Yet he had the courage to

LON CHANEY JR.

try to get that role, which many people consider one of the greatest screen performances his father ever gave. Lon Jr. is hoping that, as "Lennie" in "Of Mice and Men," he can take a long stride forward on the path that leads to success as great as his father's.

Lennie in Mufti

Lon Chaney Jr., who plays the halfwit giant, Lennie, in the Geary success, "Of Mice and Men," as he looks off the stage. In his right hand is his famous father's old makeup kit. He will be a Press Club guest tonight.

April 29, 1939

October 19, 1939

April 1, 1940

A HOWLING SUCCESS: A more or less imaginary scene from "The Wolf Man," the horror film due Wednesday at the Orpheum. You may recognize Maria Ouspenskaya, Lon Chaney Jr. (as the "Wolf Man"), Evelyn Ankers, Claude Rains and Warren William in the crowd.

January 11, 1942

APPENDIX 4:
SUMMER STOCK DRACULA
WITH J. EDWARD BROMBERG

Role Assigned In 'Dracula'

J. Edward Bromberg To Play Van Helsing Part At Robin Hood Theatre

J. Edward Bromberg, stage and screen character actor, arrived in Wilmington yesterday to begin rehearsals at the Robin Hood Theatre in Arden for "Dracula" in which he is to play the central role of Van Helsing.

The thriller, which opens next Tuesday evening for a week's run at the Robin Hood, is rarely revived in summer theatres because of the many technical difficulties, according to Director Windsor Lewis. The theatre regards "Dracula" as one of the high points of its summer season, Mr. Lewis said, pointing out that the staff has been working on the many complicated production details almost since the beginning of the season.

The theatre considers itself especially fortunate to obtain the services of Mr. Bromberg, Mr. Lewis said, as the actor rarely makes summer theatre appearances. One of the main reasons for Mr. Bromberg's coming to Arden is the fact that his son is a production assistant at the Robin Hood.

Mr. Bromberg appeared in Group Theatre productions of "Awake and Sing," "Both Your Houses," "Gold Eagle Guy," "Waiting for Lefty" and "Men in White." He has been seen in more than 40 screen productions in recent years, including "Son of Dracula" in which he played the same role he will portray next week at the Robin Hod.

Mr. Bromberg's recent Broadway appearances have been in "Jacobowsky and the Colonel," "Toplitsky of Notre Dame" and last season's Clifford Odets drama, "The Big Knife," in which Cynthia Rogers of the Robin Hood company also appeared.

Robin Hood Actor

J. Edward Bromberg

August 4, 1949

In *Son of Dracula*, J. Edward Bromberg portrayed Prof. Lazlo, a character clearly influenced by Prof. Van Helsing in Bram Stoker's 1897 novel *Dracula* and in Tod Browning's 1931 film. Six years later, in Arden, Delaware, Bromberg officially played Van Helsing in a summer stock version of *Dracula—The Vampire Play*. The following clippings are from that 1949 production.

Man About Town

J. E. Bromberg In 'Dracula'

Well Known Stage And Screen Actor Joins Cast At Robin Hood Theatre

THE STAGE and screen star, J. Edward Bromberg, has so many years and so many plays and/or movies to his credit that there is no doubt about his place in the theatre world.

This week, the Artist Theatre group summer-stocking the Robin Hood in Arden is more than lucky to have Bromberg as a guest member of the company for their production of "Dracula."

Of course, there is a motivating influence: Bromberg's son Conrad has been with the Robin Hood group all summer, gaining experience and training as a member of the production staff, and trying out his stage legs in occasional small parts.

With all this as background, it was interesting to talk to the senior Bromberg about his son and his plans for Conrad in the theatre.

"I have none," the actor said casually. "I have not at any time suggested the theatre to him or encouraged him to set his sights toward the stage. It is up to him to decide what he wants."

Well, wadyknow! Most parents we know make some attempt, in greater or lesser degree, to influence sons toward their own vocation or one of the parents' choice.

"Conrad starts his first year at the University of North Carolina next month," the actor said—which prompted a Duke alumnus in the conversation to remember the rival school is only 15 miles distant from his alma mater.

"Chapel Hill, eh? Oh, yes, they have the Chapel Hill Players, and a topnotch course in theatre. When I was there Paul Green and Professor Koch were heading it."

Mr. Bromberg didn't look the slightest bit interested. Not in that subject; his eyes lighted as he asked about the University of North Carolina's swimming pool and tennis courts.

"Conrad is a crackerjack swimmer, and a better than average tennis player," the elder Bromberg said, not without an undertone of pride.

He was extremely interested in hearing about the outstanding swimming and tennis facilities at Carolina, but not a word about the players. His son picked the Chapel Hill institution himself.

A young mother of several sons looked archly at her husband as Bromberg continued his conversation with Director Windsor Lewis.

"That's my idea of a swell father," the lady said, in a tone that suggested more than just general comment.

The well known stage and screen character actor, J. Edward Bromberg, will make his first summer theatre appearance in one of the few revivals in recent years of "Dracula" opening tonight at the Robin Hood Theatre in Arden.

Mr. Bromberg will play the central role of Van Helsing, the same part he took in the motion picture "Son of Dracula." Mr. Bromberg consented to come to the Arden theatre because his son, Conrad, is a production assistant at the theatre this year and because the group of young Broadway actors and technicians known as Artists Theatre is operating a theatre similar to the one in which he launched his career.

With Provincetown Players

That beginning occurred with the now-famous Provincetown Players, the experimental theatre group which first gave a hearing to such writers as Theodore Dreiser, Edna St. Vincent Millay, Paul Green and Eugene O'Neill.

After playing in numerous productions with Eva LeGallienne's Civic Repertory, Mr. Bromberg joined forces with another famous theatre organization, the Group Theatre, which during the Thirties was one of the most vital forces in the American theatre. He appeared with that company in Clifford Odets' first plays, "Awake and Sing" and "Waiting for Lefty," and in "Both Your Houses," "Night Over Taos" and "Men in White."

In 40 Films

In recent years Mr. Bromberg has appeared in over 40 films, the latest being "Arch of Triumph" and "A Song is Born." Last season he was seen on Broadway in another Odets play, "The Big Knife," starring John Garfield.

The title role in "Dracula" tonight will be played by John Drew Devereaux and others in the cast are Gayne Sullivan, Martin Brooks, Laura McClure, Robert McBride, William Whedbee and Cynthia Rogers.

Mr. Lewis stated yesterday that advance ticket sales for "Dracula" indicates capacity houses and advised that early reservations will secure the best selection of seats.

August 8, 1949

August 9, 1949

'DRACULA' CHILLS ROBIN HOOD FANS

Eerie Vampire Drama Opens At Arden, Makes Audience Lose Hot Weather Blues

THE CAST

Jonathan Harker	Martin Brooks
Wells	Cynthia Rogers
Dr. Seward	Gayne Sullivan
Abraham Van Helsing	J. Edward Bromberg
R. M. Renfield	Robert McBride
Butterworth	William Whedbee
Lucy Seward	Laura McClure
Count Dracula	John Drew Devereaux

Bats fly, dogs howl, and the vampire chills the blood of the watcher as he thrills in horror to this week's offering at the Robin Hood Theatre. "Dracula" is on stage.

Last night it was a toss-up between acting and scenery for applause. The illusion of old stone castle, with its curving stone staircase, it huge fireplace and heavy firedogs, its mysterious pictures, its flying bats, moving chairs, deep windows and draperies, its wall-hangings and surprising bookcase—all these were excitingly done. But when the tomb scene produced the feeling of great depth below the house, one bowed to the ingenuity of Jack Knisely and his crew for a job superbly done.

On these sets are J. Edward Bromberg and John Drew Devereaux, sharing honors as they battle to destroy each other. Previous work of Mr. Devereaux has been noted with more than passing interest, but it is even more interesting to watch him create the tense atmosphere of this play with his spectacular appearances and disappearances. One of the real achievements in his role is that it begins with suggestion (make-up is excellent) and develops into active menace nicely peaked for gasping climax.

Smoothly, dominately, Mr. Bromberg makes the audience believe the reality of the story and his own efficacy. He breathes confidence and assurance; he looks as one expects the eminent Dr. Van Helsing to look. The Artists' Theatre, Inc., is lucky to have him within its fold this week.

Gayne Sullivan is in sharp contrast to the strong character of Van Helsing. As the weaker, skeptical physician-father, he is an excellent foil both for Mr. Bromberg and the third of the battling crew against evil, Martin Brooks, who plays the fiance of the stricken Lucy.

Frequently Mr. McBride is on the amusing, dizzy side in the roles he plays, but his Renfield is both menacing and pathetic as well as crazy, proving once again the versatility of this favorite player.

As Lucy Seward, the current victim of Dracula, Laura McClure arouses pity and horror and a bit of spine-tingling, handling the part quietly and very effectively.

Teamed with the touched but pretty maid, William Whedbee is good for some laugh lines, accompanied by smooth action and an accent that is as delightfully followed through as his business. The role of the maid (Miss Rogers) gives the lady little opportunity for lines, though she makes the most of them.

Excellent entertainment for those who like thrillers and for those who are hunting a way to cool off, "Dracula" will chill your spine.

C. L. J.

August 10, 1949

ROBIN HOOD THEATRE
Grubb-Harvey Rd.
Arden, Del.

NOW PLAYING

The Famous Thriller
DRACULA
With
J. EDWARD BROMBERG
JOHN DREW DEVEREAUX

Phone: Holly Oak 6686
CURTAIN AT 8:30

August 12, 1949

The Vampire Strikes

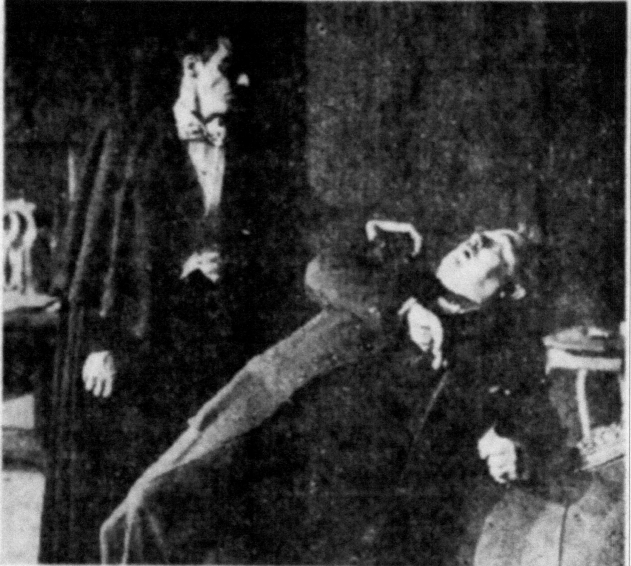

John Drew Devereaux (left) as Count Dracula, and J. Edward Bromberg as Professor Van Helsing, are shown in one of the many moments of suspense in "Dracula," on the Robin Hood stage at Arden this week.

August 10, 1949

APPENDIX 5:
"IN DEFENSE OF THE GHOULS":
1946 ARTICLE BY CURT SIODMAK

A PUBLICATION OF THE
SCREEN WRITERS GUILD, INC.

THE SCREEN WRITER

FOR FEBRUARY 1946

IN DEFENSE OF THE GHOULS

CURT SIODMAK

AMONG the products the industry is turning out to satisfy the immense market are "prestige pictures" — expensive, artistic shows, made to create respect for Hollywood, and to please the highbrows. Sometimes these creations reward the head offices by sending home an unexpected barrel of cold cash. But if not, they send home "prestige."

In the meantime, the bookkeepers in Wall Street whose money is tied up in this gigantic industry carefully study the reactions of the greater mass of American people.

"Last night we showed a honey of a picture called Jeepers Creepers," writes a theatre owner in Muddy Creek, New Mexico. "It cleaned up. Also ran Midsummer Night's Dream."

Author of Donovan's Brain, a classic horror-novel, and numerous others, CURT SIODMAK has applied his talents in this field of writing to motion pictures.

1

The greater part of the studio payroll is met by pictures like Jeepers Creepers, very much to the distress of many genuinely creative people of the industry.

There is a rigid class distinction in the choice of picture material. First, of course, come the great works of literature. Second are famous and successful books and stage plays, and then special material for the great stars. At the bottom of the list, half a notch above the run-of-the-mill Westerns, are the Horror Pictures. No Number One producer will ever touch these stories intentionally, although the industry gladly accepts the money they make — like a father who pays the rent with the ill-gotten gains of his disreputable daughter.

Sometimes these lowly subjects try to get into the respectable class. Mr. Henry Myers talks about the intelligent "Lewtons" (The Cat People, etc.). But the Frankenstein monster, lumbering down the hill toward the unhappy village in Transylvania, the Wolf Man who watches anxiously the moon that changes him into a four-legged beast, and Dracula who sleeps in his coffin during the day to become a vampire at night — these are still the really gilt-edged moneymakers.

Years ago Lord Byron, Percy Bysshe Shelley, and Mary Wollstonecraft amused themselves in the little North Italian town of Lerici by writing horror stories. Miss Wollstonecraft created Frankenstein, or The Modern Prometheus. It was the story of a "thing" put together with parts of human corpses and brought back to life; a very sad, bewildered monster chased and murdered by intolerant natives. It did not want to harm anybody, only wanted to live.

The Wolf Man — another scary character — is a human being stricken with a dreadful curse. When the moon is full he changes into a murderous wolf, only to repent and suffer after his time of trial is over and he resumes human form again. He wants to die to escape his fate.

So these ancient tales are once again but the fight of good and evil in the human soul, sin and repentance. The evil takes the graphic form of an animal, the repentance a human form. In religious pictures of saints, hell and purgatory, the evil is shown in the shape of dragons, monsters, and other devilish creations. The motion picture uses the same pattern but with variations. Dracula, the Hungarian count who rests in a coffin filled with his native soil during the day, to rise with other undead during the night, appeals by its deep sex implications. Vampires feed on the blood of their victims who, in turn, become their slaves. Primitive sadistic and masochistic tendencies are expressed in this yarn and its countless imitations.

Our emotions always react precisely, never making a mistake. Only reasoning leads us to false conclusions. Against our logic, these abstract tales of monsters and Draculas, the influence of the moon on our fate, the phenomena of the sky and mysteries of the night, touch atavistic memories from a dim antiquity when our ancestors huddled in caves and dreaded the unknown dark.

Thus, these horror stories, as uncomplicated and simple as they appear on the screen, are based on complex and fundamental wishes and desires which probe deep into the subconscious. Our ancestors, defenseless but for a bow and arrow, a sharpened rock or club, wished to be as strong as the strongest animal of their respective countries. In Europe the wolf was the most dreaded and ruthless killer. So men wanted to change into wolves — werewolves with supernatural power. In India stories are told about the tiger-men, in Africa about the leopard-women, and in the Pacific Islands about people who turned into powerful snakes. The hearts and livers of these animals were eaten to make man equally strong and steel-hearted, and the warriors, so fortified, became Lycanthropes, possessed by wolf-madness. The medical profession today uses this name for a certain kind of mania in which the patient imagines himself to be a wolf, a name based on a mythical King Lycaonids, ruler of Arcadia, whom Zeus changed into a wolf when Lycaonids offered him human flesh to eat. Werewolf stories have their historic roots in tales of Greek mythology.

Pathologically, our emotions can be traced back to their source. Freud, Adler, Jung base their theories on the presumption that every reaction has its root in frustration. In appealing to frustration, the basic emotions will respond.

3

T H E   S C R E E N   W R I T E R

The writer of horror pictures cannot, of course, base the effect of his stories on experience alone. Despite all experience, no writer can produce stories which will assure anticipated reactions to the public in the way a mathematician is sure of results when compounding certain formulas. A writer cannot detach himself from his own emotions. He can only hope that the public will respond the same way he did while writing his horror scenes. Though reactions follow laws, they can only be analyzed after the reaction has occurred.

A classic scene of horror was created by DeWitt Bodine in his Cat People: A girl in a swimming pool is threatened by the presence of a wild animal. The surrounding water impedes her movements — a nightmare we all have experienced, — she wants to run away from danger but her arms and legs respond slowly, increasing the feeling of frustration and terror and transferring that feeling to the audience.

In The Spiral Staircase, a mute girl is menaced by a murderer. She tries, in her despair, to telephone for help, hoping against hope that the impact of fear will loosen her tongue. The agony of her frustration transmits itself terrifyingly to the public.

Or Cary Grant carrying a glass of poisoned milk to his wife. The spotlight plays on the white liquid, increasing the impression of a deadly drug. Slowly, inexorably he walks up the stairs while Miss Fontaine is waiting for him in deadly frustration . . . Anticipating a scene, knowing the inescapable solution, rooting for the hero at the same time, creates that feeling of terror for which the scene has been written and primed to get the desired effect.

Supplant the murderer with the ogre who slowly walks up the stairs to kidnap the fair heroine, the glass of milk with hands grown into animal claws. The effect will be the same.

The complaint is universal that the intelligence of the average moviegoer is that of a twelve-year-old child and that pictures callously cater to that undeveloped taste rather than take the trouble to educate the public. This, in the experience of the writer and of all those seriously concerned with films, is a basic myth that is a long time dying. Intelligence and emotion do not have a common

4

IN DEFENSE OF THE GHOULS

root. The intelligence of most people increases with the years, but their emotional reactions stop growing at the end of childhood. Entertainment seldom appeals to the intelligence. It wants to entertain and therefore addresses itself to the emotions.

A terrific upsurge in the demand for horror pictures took place during the war. It was against all logic. There was enough terror and fear in the world — why then did people flock to see the ghouls rise from the graves? Again the mass audience was looking for a release from its fears, created by death, destruction, atrocities, fear for imperiled loved ones. No one who can read and hear can escape the constant impact of terror. Though fear can be controlled by logic, it still accumulates in our subconscious, searches for outlets, reveals itself in our dreams. Like sickness being fought with toxins of the same virus, people flocked to see horror pictures, to find release from their nightmares, though they were frightened at the same time.

Motion pictures with a war background increased this subconscious terror. They were too close to actuality, something that existed, and the impact of which nobody could escape. War pictures left the audiences depressed and unhappy. The synthetic happy endings, when a lonely plane sank an entire enemy fleet, or a soldier with a machine gun wiped out a whole army, only put them into a state of mistrust and doubt. But seeing the monster kidnap the hero's bride — a monster personifying fear — made them shriek and at the same time laugh with relief. That ogre on the screen did not exist at all. He was abstract, detached from their lives. They were not personally involved in the synthetic plot.

Horror stories were entertainment for which people gladly paid their money. The antitoxin had its wholesome effect. It made them happier than any comedy could. Beside the thrill of primitive excitement they could still ridicule the fairy-tale ghouls who scared them as instinctively as the same monsters had actually terrified their ancestors.

Fairy tales as old as the oldest religions voice our ancestors' fears and hopes. The bad witch who personifies the Winter hexes Sleeping Beauty into sleep until the young prince, Spring, wakes

5

T H E   S C R E E N   W R I T E R

her with a kiss. Little Red Riding Hood is swallowed by Winter, the big bad wolf. The dashing hunter, Spring, rescues her. In Snow White and the Seven Dwarfs, the bad stepmother, Winter, poisons her with an apple, and again the young prince, Spring, brings her back to life.

Much fright and horror is buried in these age-old tales; the fear of the dead, of hunger and of cold. But there is also a hope that the sun will eventually shine again to dispel the ice and snow and bring warmth and life back to the suffering people. Horror pictures are built on stories which appeal to the subconscious. When, to quote the manager of a big theatre, "people line up around the block and the house is full of escapists," you will know they are just reacting to primary instincts of fear and pity — emotions as vivid as love and hatred.

Almost every melodrama contains scenes of horror, though the A-Plus producer would never accept that term for his million-dollar creation. When horror enters the gilded gate of top production it is glorified as a "psychological thriller." But a rose by any other name . . .

★   ★   ★

APPENDIX 6:
HANS J. SALTER INTERVIEW
BY WILLIAM H. ROSAR

Music historian William H. Rosar has given us permission to publish *for the first time* his 1975 interview with famed film composer Hans J. Salter. We reproduce it here from its original typewritten copy.

AN INTERVIEW WITH HANS J. SALTER

by

William H. Rosar
(additional questions submitted
by Clifford McCarty)

Transcript revised by
William H. Rosar and
Hans J. Salter
April 28, 1975

ROSAR: According to Clifford McCarty, you did film work in Europe.

SALTER: Yes. I worked for the European branch of Universal among other producers. I worked with Henry Koster, as director, Joe Pasternak, as producer, and with Felix Jackson as writer.

R: When was this approximately?

S: That was in the late twenties and early thirties.

R: How did you get into the movies?

S: My first connection with movies goes back to the early twenties. I was employed by various theaters in central Europe, conducting operas, operettas, musical comedies, and even stage plays like Shakespeare's "A Midsummer Night's Dream", with the music by Mendelssohn. During the summer months there was no activity. They usually closed around April or early in May. So, during the summer months until the end of the summer season, about September or the beginning of October, I conducted in movie houses. They had what they called "film operettas". It was the invention of somebody in Germany, whereby he had a regular silent film with interpolated songs. At the bottom of the screen they ran the "lead line" and there was a bar in the center, and as the note hit that bar it was supposed to be in sync with the actor on top -- which it wasn't. But after a while, if you watched it, you could get a fairly close sync. You had four singers, in the pit, and an orchestra, and you played this operetta two or three times a day depending on the size of the theater. I did that for about two years, with great success, I must say. We travelled in Vienna around to different movie houses, and I had to rehearse the orchestra, and I had the singers with me. It was a group that I had rehearsed, and they knew the songs. That was my first contact with the movies.

R: How did this all seem to you at the time? Like Vaudeville, or did anyone take it seriously?

S: No, nobody took it seriously. It was nice entertainment. People were not too sophisticated in these little theaters. I went to Berlin in 1923 and was conductor at different opera and operetta houses and was then engaged as a conductor of silent films. In the late twenties I accepted a very tempting offer to lead the large orchestra in one of the biggest movie houses in Berlin.

R: Was there anything else to your job other than conducting?

S: Yes, sometimes I also had to write a few scenes if I couldn't find the right thing in the library. It wasn't too often, but it happened once in a while. When sound came, I moved right away into sound film. Sound came in '31 or '32.

R: I see from your resumé that you were associated with UFA.

S: Yes, I started at UFA in 1928 or early '29 and when sound came in, I switched to production, and was assigned as musical director and composer to some of their first attempts in this field. UFA was one of the first companies to buy Western Electric equiptment from America, and bring it over. Nobody knew how to handle it, but they experimented and they were very successful because nobody else in Central Europe had it.

R: Did you have other jobs at UFA besides composing and conducting?

S: Well, I had to do everything. The technique of underscoring was still in its infancy. Actually, the continuation of a silent picture approach, until by trial and error, some new ideas were born and established. The thirties was UFA's boom period. Even when Hitler came to power they were still going great guns, until after the war, I think. Then they started to fold up, more-or-less. But they are back in business, as far as I know.

R: Did you by chance know Franz Waxman when he was at UFA in the thirties?

S: Sure, I knew him long before that, when he was pianist in a little jazz band called of all things, "The Weintraub Synkopaters".

R: Did you go to work for Universal in Europe before or after sound came?

S: After. I would say from '32 on I worked exclusively for films.

R: Did you work for anyone other than UFA and Universal in Europe?

S: Since I was free-lancing, I worked for a number of film companies, such as Gloria, Matador, Elite, Omesto, Emelka, Alliance, and Terra, where I wrote the music for a fine picture starring Conrad Veidt, among others, which was called THE MAN WHO COMITTED MURDER. The director was Curtis Bernhard, who later became well-known in Hollywood at Warners and M.G.M.

R: When sound came, how much music was usually written for a picture in the beginning? Was there scoring under dialogue?

S: Well, if the picture was a musical -- and most of them were musical comedies of some kind -- you wrote three, five, or even six songs, plus some source music where needed, and used them thematically throughout the film. In dramatic films, you employed music sparingly, and mostly during silent streches since dubbing under dialogue was very complicated and still in its experimental stage.

R: Was your film work in Europe exclusively in Germany and Austria?

S: No, I did some pictures in Hungary for Universal, and also in Prague, but they were all made for the German market, sometimes in two versions, like French and German, or English and German. About '36 or the end of '35, this unit of Universal's European production moved over to America. That was, first Pasternak, then after a while Koster followed, and then Jackson. I saw the war coming in Europe and tried desparately to get out. But their (Koster, Pasternak, and Jackson) position was not too strong at the time, so they didn't encourage me to come over. But I came anyway, on my own, and it took me six or seven months until I was put on the payroll at Universal.

R: When did you arrive?

S: In '37, I think in September.

R: Would you say that by the time you left Europe you were fairly proficient at film scoring?

S: I would say more than competent.

R: So then, when you left Europe you came to the U.S. with the intention of applying for a position at Universal?

S: Yes, it was my only hope! It was practically impossible at that time to get a job. It was the end of the depression and jobs were hard to come by, and were so actually until the war started in '41. My first jobs at Universal didn't last for more than two or three weeks maybe, and then they laid me off again.

R: What were your first jobs?

S: I did some orchestrations for Frank Skinner and for Charles Previn. For example, I orchestrated Skinner's score for SON OF FRANKENSTEIN. I also did a lot of those track jobs. You see, in those days Universal was pretty close to bankruptsy. You expected any day to find the gates closed. So, they only scored the top pictures -- Deanna Durbin pictures and others with outstanding casts -- and the others were just tracked. We used music from a picture that was done two or three or even five years previous, and out of five or six different pieces from different pictures, we arrived at the underscoring of a scene. In some instances, this was just as good as if the music had been specially composed for the scene. It was a time-consuming process, and you had to have a certain knack for that type of work, and I was pretty good at it.

R: In making these scores, on what basis did you choose any
given cue? Were you familiar with the material in the music
library?

S: Of course I studied most of the scores, and in time was
very familiar with the library. The librarian, Nicholas
Nuzzi, helped me sometimes in locating certain cues.

R: How did you annotate what was to be used in these track
jobs? Would you jot down that so many measures of a cue
would be used, or was it done in minutes and seconds? I
ask this since I assume that you could alter the tempo
of a piece, and tailor to some extent that way.

S: Well, I wrote out some kind of scenario. More than ever
it was a combination of new composition with old material.
I sketched in the melody line of the old cue that had to
be copied and the timing.

R: Would you use click track for any of this kind of work?

S: Yes, click tracks were of great help in cases where in-
tricate synchronization between picture was required. I would
ask the music editor to give me a complete bar breakdown
describing the action in detail, and that would enable me to
catch cues which in free-timing might have been very time-
consuming. Of course, you had to have a great skill as a
composer to avoid a certain mechanical feeling that could
creep into your music. In other words, you had to write
around the clicks.

R: What was going on when you arrived at Universal?

S: YOU'RE A SWEETHEART was the picture they were working on
the first day I came on the lot. Charlie Previn was in charge
of the music department, and other than myself, Frank Skinner
and Charlie Henderson were the only other composers.

R: That must have been about a year or so after the studio
was sold by Laemmle to Rogers.

S: Rogers was in charge at that time, but he didn't last very
long.

R: What sort of musician was Skinner at that time?

S: Skinner was a dance band arranger, basically. He grew up
in the dance bands. He was a trombone player originally, and
he made dance arrangements -- stock arrangements -- for Robbins,
and they were very, very good, and very successful. They played
all over the world. Robbins brought him out to Hollywood in
'37 to work on a big musical at M.G.M. When that was finished
he wanted to go back to New York and continue working for
Robbins, but for some reason he decided to stay here and he
got a job at Universal, orchestrating vocal and dance band
arrangements for musical production numbers. Later, he became
quite proficient and knew his way around larger orchestral
groups, although in later years he rarely orchestrated himself.

R: Did Previn conduct?

S: Yes, in the beginning he conducted almost everything, except the pictures that I worked on. Skinner didn't have any ambitions to conduct, and he was a poor conductor anyway. So, Previn conducted all the pictures that Skinner worked on, which gave Skinner an advantage, because Previn liked to be the guiding light behind every score. Charlie Previn was a very nice and very likeable fellow. I was very fond of him, and he was very nice to me. In the beginning he was sort of aloof, and felt afraid that I was after his job, because he didn't feel too sure himself in that position. He didn't know much about film music, either. In those days everybody had to work on every picture, practically. We hardly had any Sunday to ourselves. We used to work six days a wekk. On Saturday, they stopped production around two or two-thirty. If you were fortunate to get off on a Saturday afternoon, that was really something! Sundays we usually worked too. In the first year I don't think I had more that maybe three Sundays off.

R: So it was practically your whole life!

S: Yes, everything! You see, Charlie Previn was a bachelor, and he had no other interests, and he assumed that since he was interested in helping put Universal back on their feet, that everybody else shared the same interest.

R: On these track scores, it seemed that Universal re-used the original recordings to a point, until around 1939, and then they started re-recording the music. For example, the first Flash Gordon serials, that is, FLASH GORDON (1936) and FLASH GORDON'S TRIP TO MARS (1938) used the original music tracks. They in FLASH GORDON CONQUERS THE UNIVERSE (1940), they re-recorded the old music. Do you know why they stopped using the old tracks and recorded new ones?

S: The Musician's Union put a stop to using the old recordings, and they couldn't do that anymore. So, they had to re-record it. But I wouldn't be surprised if sometimes if the playing wasn't too good in the new recording, they might have supplanted it.

R: As I wrote you, I heard a story where the Union came into a recording session where some old material was being re-recorded, to make an inspection. Everything seemed proper, but as it ended up, they decided to use the old tracks, and not what they had recorded!

S: It might have happened. But later every track had code numbers on it, and they checked those numbers to make sure they didn't use the old tracks.

R: Were there regular inspections?

S: Not regular, but once in a while when they were suspicious
they did check. You see, in those days there were no contract
orchestras. When I came to Universal there was the so-called
quota system in practice. That meant a musician could earn
only a certain amount of money each week. To give you a figure,
let's say a hundred dollars. When he reached two hundred dollars,
he couldn't accept anymore jobs. In this way they spread the
work around among more musicians. Later, after the war they
started to have studio orchestras again. Universal had to have
thirty-six men under contract for the whole year. Whether they
used them or not, they had to be paid fifty-two weeks in a year.
That lasted until television came in, and then they discontinued
it.

McCARTY: Going back to your arrival at Universal in 1937, do
you remember the title of the very first picture you worked
on?

S: The first picture was RAGE IN PARIS. I remember it because
I got my first check, which I kept for a while before cashing
it. The film starred Fairbanks Jr. and Danielle Darrieux. It
must have been in '38, because it was long before they put me
on the payroll. I wrote one sequence in that, a rather long
one, lasting about three and a half minutes or so, which I
orchestrated and conducted myself, caught every cue, and became an instant success. I'll never forget that, because up
to that point they treated me like an outsider, more-or-less.
And then they gave me the chance and let me write that one
sequence, and that broke the ice completely! From that moment
on I was accepted. There was general enthusiasm, and hand-
shaking, and embracing. Right after this sequence was played,
the orchestra gave me an applause, and the strings players
beat their bows on their instruments, and was henceforth a
member of the family, so to speak. But then the thing that I
had least expected happened. A week later they let me go!

R: I bet that was a surprise!

S: They said, "We have nothing for you -- we'll call you
back as soon as we do." You must realize that Universal was
in very dire financial straights at that time.

R: How long were you unemployed?

S: For a few weeks or a month. But they called me back, and
then I did a small picture called DANGER ON THE AIR. I wrote
the main title and a few short cues, and the rest was track.
Hayes Pagel was the music editor who did these track jobs
at the time. Next came YOUNG FUGITIVES for which I devised a
system of using different cues from old scores, following the
action in detail like a new score would, all orchestral parts
written out. I wrote the main title and some connecting bridges
and it all worked very well. This sytem was later used by others
and was called "Salterizing". All thru this period I helped in
different ways -- sitting in on recording sessions, monitoring,
watching sync on stage (Deanna Durbin requested my presence),
attending meetings with producers, directors, etc.

R: Did you work on more than one picture at the same time in those years?

S: Sure. Don't forget on top of that we had to go to these screenings. As soon as a picture was in first cut, they ran it for the different departments. Sometimes there were two or three screenings in a day. So, this was time-consuming, and then we had to work on all these pictures, because man-power was very limited.

M: Who assigned pictures - Previn? On what basis were you or Skinner or someone else chosen?

S: Yes, Previn assigned pictures, but the individual pro-ducer could also voice his preference. Let's say over the years a certain producer would admire a composer's treatment or approach to his pictures. He then would seek this composer's advice, pertaining to music on future productions. That usually also meant the final score, if the composer was available. But in the beginning, in the late thirties, we had to work on all pictures. Universal produced about seventy films a year in those days, and there were only three composers on the staff. So, we had our hands full.

R: Did you do any orchestrating for Henderson?

S: No. Henderson didn't do much composing. He was mostly a vocal arranger, and he worked on those Durbin pictures. He didn't last very long, either. He and Charlie Previn didn't get along too well. I think at the end of '38 or the beginning of '39 he left. I think he went to Fox later, and stayed there for quite a while.

R: Was George Parrish there at all after you came?

S: Yes. Whenever none of us were available, George Parrish came in and did some orchestrating.

R: So you orchestrated SON OF FRANKENSTEIN. What kind of sketch did Skinner give you?

S: He gave me a good sketch, a pretty full sketch. It was on three lines I would say, sometimes four.

R: Did he indicate orchestral coloring?

S: Once in a while. You see, with this score especially, we worked under terrible pressure. I remember the last two or three days before the recording, we didn't leave the studio. We just stayed there, and Frank worked on a piano there back behind the library in a room in the old building where Hitch-cock now has his office. In back of the recording stage there's a bungalow a little higher up. That was the music department. The library was in the second half of the building, and behind the library there was another office and that's where we hid in those days. So, Frank would write a page or two, and I would take a nap in the meanwhile. Then I would orchestrate and he would take a nap. We stayed in our clothes there, for two or two and a half days.

R: What did you think of the end product?

S: I thought it was a good score. But we were not conscious of creating masterpieces out of anything.

R: How aware was Skinner of the musical world? Was he aware of contemporary music at all?

S: Not very much. You see, Skinner was at that time in the process of acquiring a certain knowledge of music. As I told you, he was a dance band arranger. He had very little schooling.

R: Did you help him at all?

S: Well, whenever it was neccessary, I did help him.

R: As I mentioned in my letter, it seems strange, but some of the material in SON OF FRANKENSTEIN score sounds somewhat like Florent Schmitt's "La Tragedie de Salome".

S: That's right. Well, he was a great admirer of French music. He mentioned a few times chord progressions in Gounod, and in Bizet, and so on, and he was also a great admirer of Cesar Franck. He probably studied these scores on his own, quite a bit, and developed while he was working. He learned while he was composing.

R: So he was probably experimenting to some extent.

S: Yes. His style didn't change too much, basically. He reached a certain plateau, and then he stayed on that. His harmonic vocabulary was rather limited, I would say. But he had a certain knack for writing film music, as it was required in those days.

R: All things considered, I would say the SON OF FRANKENSTEIN score was quite effective.

S: Oh yes. Most of those scores, I would say for the time, were tops. When I orchestrated for Skinner we had discussions about certain orchestral passages. He took advice from me.

R: I remember in a number of the mystery and horror film scores, the novachord was used.

S: Yes, they didn't have electronic organs in those days, although they had an organ on the stage at Universal, but at that time it was out of order I think.

R: Previn conducted SON OF FRANKENSTEIN?

S: Yes.

R: Did you usually conduct your own scores? What about
Skinner-Salter collaborations?

S: As a rule, I conducted my own scores. But in the fifties,
Joe Gershenson instituted a new policy, whereby he would
conduct everything, while at the same time trying to establish
a speed record. The Salter-Skinner scores were mostly in that
period, I think. But before that change, after Previn left,
I conducted some of Skinner's music, or he did it himself.

M: Was Gershenson a composer or just a conductor?

S: A conductor only.

R: After Universal made SON OF FRANKENSTEIN in '39, they
made a picture called TOWER OF LONDON, the same year. The
score consisted of what amounted to a rehash of the material
in SON OF FRANKENSTEIN, although the melodic material was
altered. The harmonic and orchestral fabric remained basically
the same. On the cue sheets, Skinner gets credit, but shares it
with a Ralph Freed. Was Freed a composer?

S: The story of the TOWER OF LONDON score is quite interesting.
Originally, Charlie Previn wanted to treat that picture differently. He thought by using music of the period, recording on
old instruments like recorders, alto flutes, oboe d'amore,
viola da gamba, harpsichord, etc., he could create the right
atmosphere. So, I adapted and orchestrated the music of
Dowling, Purcell, and others, but the front office disliked
that thin, tinkly sound thoroughly, and it was all thrown out.
Then, we had to substitute the SON OF FRANKENSTEIN music, since
there was no time left to write a new score. Ralph Freed was
a lyric writer, and whenever he collaborated with Skinner on
a song, he shared in the credit, even when the music was used
instrumentally only.

M: You and Walter Jurmann are credited with a picture called
THE GREAT COMMANDMENT (1939). How did you happen to go this
- on loan-out from Universal?

S: I did that film early in '38, before I signed a contract
at Universal. The producer was Cathedral Films, and 20th
Century-Fox bought it later, but I'm not sure when they released it. It was a good-sized score of about thirty-eight or
forty minutes. I recorded it at General Service Studios with
a free-lance orchestra. Most of them were the same group I
used at Universal, so I felt right at home. I also remember
another picture I did at that time called MIRACLE ON MAIN STREET,
to which Walter Jurmann contributed some songs.

R: Do you remember working on THE WOLFMAN?

S: Yes.

R: The screen credit on that picture lists you, Skinner, and Previn as composers. That's about '41, I think.

S: Previn wrote a sequence or two once in a while, just to keep his fingers in the pie. He picked some simple things, and he wrote them. But the bulk of the score was always written by Skinner and myself, whenever we collaborated.

R: How did collaboration usually work anyway? Did you break it up into cues and then decide who would do what?

S: Well, the way we did it later on -- I don't remember whether we did it already then -- we devised some basic themes. Skinner maybe wrote a theme, and I wrote a theme, and maybe I wrote a third theme, and then we exchanged them, and we all used them. Let's say we had three themes in a picture. The way it worked was usually by reels. Let's say he got reel one, and I got reel two, and so on. Once you see eye to eye on the treatment of a score, and since each one of us knew his business at this --that is, later on, I'm not talking about the first few years -- it worked pretty well, I would say.

R: So much material was reused, I would think it would become a little tired after a while.

S: Oh yes. There came a moment when we couldn't use certain cues anymore, because they were overused. It was always a question of time, as you know. You see, if you had only let's say ten days to score a picture, you didn't have much choice, and you took the way of least resistance to get a picture out. But later on, when they had a little more time and their release dates were not so close together, I asked for say four weeks. There I had a little more time and leeway, and I could organize myself better, which worked to the advantage of the picture.

R: I would think so.

S: You didn't have to use any material that had been used before, you used all new material.

R: Do you recall the first picture which you got to do by yourself?

S: I remember one of the Durbin pictures on which I did all the underscoring, I think it was probably the first one, and Skinner orchestrated the songs, if I remember correctly. It was a picture called SPRING PARADE, and it was either 1940, or '41. But even before that, I did quite a few on my own, but they were smaller pictures. SEVEN SINNERS was one of the first pictures I did, but that was with Skinner. It was a picture with Marlene Dietrich and John Wayne. BLACK FRIDAY I think was also one of the first ones I did by myself.

(Courtesy of Rich Bush)

R: MAN MADE MONSTER was fairly early.

S: Yes, I did that, I think, all by myself. INVISIBLE MAN
RETURNS was another I did myself.

R: Did you have to cook up your inspiration or did you
actually respond to the pictures you scored at all?

S: Well, that's the difference between an amateur and a
professional. An amateur has to wait for inspiration, whereas
a professional has to create it. If he is in command of his
senses, then he functions well.

R: How many times would you usually view a picture before
scoring it?

S: Well, as I said before, there was usually a showing for
all of the departments, when the picture was in first cut.
Then, I ran it with the producer or director, or just the
producer and just the director, and then the head of the music
department, and we decided where to put music and where not
to put it.

R: Did the producers and directors have anything to say about
the scoring usually?

S: It varied. Some of them had definite preconceptions.

R: I know that the Siodmak brothers were invovled with some
of those pictures, and I would think them somewhat above
the average Universal personel.

S: Oh yes. As a matter of fact, I had already done one picture
for Robert Siodmak in Germany, on which there were other people
invovled whom you might know. For example, Billy Wilder. Wilder
was already here at Paramount when I arrived in '37. I knew
Fritz Lang very well, too, from silent pictures. I conducted
a picture of his called WOMAN IN THE MOON, that was in '28,
I think. I also did a picture of his at Universal called
SCARLET STREET. We got along very well.

R: He's Viennese, isn't he?

S: Yes, he is. He was a painter originally. He once told me
his whole life story. While he was at Universal we used to
have lunch together, and spoke about these things.

M: Your biographical sketch states that you became a U.S.
citizen in 1943, but the ASCAP BIOGRAPHICAL DICTIONARY gives
the year as 1942. Which date is correct?

S: 1943 is the correct date. Frank Skinner was one of my
witnesses.

R: On some pictures, there seems to be a combination of reuse and new material, although that new material was sometimes a new treatment or development of old material. Was this because of time limitations, budget, or what?

S: It was usually the old devil time that forced me to do it. The studio had to meet certain release dates that were set in New York, and when they gave you five or six days to score a film, you had to make short cuts, and still do everything possible to help the picture.

M: Who orchestrated your own scores over the years?

S: In the beginning, George Parrish and others, but starting in 1945 or '46 mostly Dave Tamkin, who was then chief and only orchestrator at Universal. On my assignments away from Universal for independent producers, I usually orchestrated myself.

M: Apparently Paul Dessau, Eric Zeisl and Mario Castelnuovo-Tedesco wrote some music for three of your films:

HOUSE OF FRANKENSTEIN – Dessau
INVISIBLE MAN'S REVENGE – Zeisl
UNCLE HARRY – Dessau and Tedesco

How did they happen to work at Universal, though apparently not much?

S: They were called in a few times to help me out when I couldn't finish a score in time, but I usually had to rewrite most of their cues!

M: Was your leaving Universal in 1947 occassioned by the merger with International Pictures? What prompted your return three years later?

S: My contract ran out in 1947, and since I was not too happy with my assignments at that time, I decided to try it as a free-lance composer. After the death of Milton Schwarzwald in 1950, Gershenson became head of the musical department, and he made me an offer which I could not turn down.

R: One of the things which seems to stand up the best in those Universal films of the forties is the music, which I feel contributed a good deal in many ways. At times, the music was the most interesting thing going on!

S: The music was somehow a little above the picture, and
it lifted the picture to a higher plane. When we saw these
pictures first they were <u>nothing</u>. They were nothing, and it
was an interesting challenge to the composer to make sense
of this whole thing, and sort of bind it together and clean
up certain psycholgical quirks in it. My chief aim was --
and still is -- to put some depth or perspective into a scene
to be scored and add some meaning to it. What is the director
trying to tell us at this point I ask myself and then I proceed to bring out the strong highlights and soften the weak
ones in a given scene. That was the big challenge, to me at
least.

R: And perhaps to put in drama where there simply wasn't any
to start with!

S: That's right. Often there was no drama, no horror, no
suspense, there was nothing there! Really, it's a fact.
The music saved a lot of these pictures.

R: I guess it had been the story of Universal since it
began making films, ~~they~~ they had interesting ideas, but
didn't have the wherewithall to really make the best of
them.

S: Well, it's a matter of dollars and cents. If you only
have so much money to work with, you can't afford to hire
better brains and better craftsmen to lift your product
to a higher level. So they had to do the best they could
with the resources they had at their disposal.

M: Your biographical sketch says that you have free-lanced
since 1952, yet most of your films since then have been for
your old studio, Universal. Is this because you have maintained close relations through the years, although not under
contract?

S: Yes, that's right. I always considered Universal City my
home town, so to speak.

M: In the fifties, when other studios usually assigned a
single composer to a picture, Universal often put two or
three composers on one film. Why was this done, and who made
the decision?

S: Well, it was always a question of time, and meeting a release date. That means it was physically impossible for one
composer to deliver a big score in the time alotted.

M: You have scored so many films that you must sometimes run
out of ideas. Do you ever use something from an old score
in a new one when this happens?

S: No. Every film inspires me in some way. Some of them send
out stronger vibrations than others. But whenever a musical
problem presents itself, I always find the right solution for
it. You might call it "inspiration". As far as reuse is concerned, I have probably re-used parts of cues that were not
used in a picture whenever it was recut after the preview,
and some of the sequences hit the cutting room floor. But
that happened in only a few instances. I might have patterned
a theme after one of my previous scores, if that treatment
proved highly successful. But generally, I always tried a
new approach.

R: What would you regard as your best efforts?

S: Of my dramatic scores, I like best MAGNIFICENT DOLL,
THUNDER ON THE HILL, and BEAU GESTE. Among comedies, my
favorites are COME SEPTEMBER and BEDTIME STORY. Among
the many westerns I did, BEND OF THE RIVER with Jimmy
Stewart had a fine score. My best efforts in the T.V.
field would be MAYA, a series for M.G.M., THE LAW AND
MR. JONES for Four Star, and WAGON TRAIN for Universal.

M: What other film composers and film scores do you particularly admire?

S: I think Miklos Rozsa is in a class by himself. I especially
admired some of his scores in the late forties and early fifties,
like SPELLBOUND and LOST WEEKEND. I also liked Jerry Goldsmith's
earlier efforts, which showed a lot of promise.

* * * *

DRACULA
NEVER
DIES

**WATCH OUT
FOR HIS
RETURN!**

chastain

APPENDIX 7:
SEQUEL TO DRACULA
BY MANLY P. HALL

In 1939, Bela Lugosi's friend Manly P. Hall wrote a treatment for a sequel to Tod Browning's 1931 film version of *Dracula*. Universal expressed interest, but no film was ever made. What follows is reproduced from an original carbon copy used by Hall's representative Stanley Bergerman to solicit interest in it.

(Left) A make-believe movie poster for the never-made *Wolf Man vs. Dracula*, created for this book by artist **George Chastain**. You can see other examples of George's amazing art at his website, egorschamber.com/portfolio/

SEQUEL TO DRACULA

Story synopsis

by

MANLY P. HALL.

In the ruined chapel of Castle Dracula stands the ancient crumb-
ling sarcophagus of the vampire. On the front is an armorial crest
of Transylvanian nobility and the word DRACULA cut in great, deep
letters.

Van Helsing and four other men are tugging frantically at the
heavy stone lid. The last rays of the setting sun are filtering
through broken casements and are shining upon the massive tomb. The
vampire must be destroyed before the coming of night. He is mortal
only while sleeping through the daylight hours on the earth of his
native land.

At last the heavy lid gives way and the five men gaze down upon
the body of the vampire horrible in sleep. Van Helsing resolutely
grasps the sharpened wooden stake. As he stands over the body of
Dracula, the last ray of sunlight fades from the face of the vampire.
Dracula awakes, leering hideously. It is now night and he is immortal.

Without a word Van Helsing drives the stake through Dracula's
heart. The vampire howls with fiendish glee and shams death.

Their work done, the five depart.

When the last sound of their footsteps has faded away, Dracula
opens his eyes. "Too late, you fools," he hisses, "the sun has set."

Slowly the form of the vampire turns into a shimmering mist in
which only the head remains visible. The weird plasma oozes over the

SEQUEL TO DRACULA   -2-

side of the sarcophagus and vanishes into the dim corridors of the
castle.

>   For thirty years the vampire
>   sleeps in his tomb, allowing
>   old age and death to destroy
>   his enemies one by one.

In the ruined chapel, fallen into still further decay and spun
with webs and filled deep with rubbish, a strange demented creature
stands by the side of the sarcophagus and whispers into the crack
under the lid: "Master, Van Helsing is dead. It is safe to come out
now."

The lid of the great sarcophagus rises by some mysterious mech-
anism. The gruesome hand bearing the ring of Voivode Dracula appears
and the vampire slowly rises. He has had no blood for many years,
therefore he is now a whitehaired man, aged and bearded. His face is
hollow with the sleep of years and his clothes are rotted about him.

By the light of a single candle in a grotesque stand, Count Dracula wearing a long black robe is seated in his study writing a letter
with an ancient quill pen. The envelope is addressed to Senora Martinez, 14 Plaza de la Republic, Buenos Aires, Argentina. The paper, aged
and yellow, is emblazoned with the count's heraldic arms. The letter
announces to the Senora that she is to prepare for his immediate arrival to renew a past acquaintance. It is signed with a medieval flour-
ish, "Count Dracula".

SEQUEL TO DRACULA   -S-

Buenos Aires is the most beautiful city on the American continents, combining all that is new and modern with the grandeur of Spanish palaces and great flowered estates.

The home of Senora Martinez is an imposing mansion in the midst of rose gardens. In spite of its beauty there is an air of mystery and fear about the entire establishment.

Senora Martinez is a cultured, sensitive woman approaching 60. She has spent the last several years of her life in a wheelchair.

Lord Godalming is her alter ego; he is an aging Englishman with handlebar mustaches and a monocle, a sort of perpetual guest most frequently found in slippers and jacket smoking a big meerschaum. For many years he has been silently and pathetically in love with Senora Martinez.

The third member of the household is Senora Martinez' son Quincey, an attractive young man approaching thirty who is hopelessly in love with Mercedes, one of the belles of the upper social set in which the family moves.

There are servants whose stoical attitudes reveal little of what is going on between and behind their black Indian eyes.

Quincey and Mercedes are on one of the broad porches of the house when a scream is heard from within. Rushing through Venetian doors, they find Senora Martinez unconscious on the floor beside her wheelchair. Lord Godalming enters through another door and kneels beside the prostrate form, his heart in his eyes. He sees the letter clenched in one of her hands. A look of terror comes into his face, but he does

SEQUEL TO DRACULA -4-

not communicate his impressions.

Later Senora Martinez and Lord Godalming are seated in front of a great chest elaborately carved and painted in the Florentine manner. Lord Godalming opens the chest with an old massive key. The box is filled with books, bundles of papers, and oldfashioned tubular phonograph records. These documents are the diaries and stories concerning Count Dracula. They include Dr. Seward's notes, Jonathan Harker's journal, and Dr. Van Helsing's Diary.

From her wheelchair Senora Martinez asks for a book carefully wrapped and tied. There is a sad conversation in which she acknowledges that she has known all these years that Count Dracula was not dead. She has been a widow more than twenty years, but carefully has kept the story from her son lest it blast his life also. Knowing that the influence of a vampire cannot extend across water, she has put the Atlantic between herself and Dracula, but now he is going to come to her with his boxes of earth.

In the private offices of Justice Jose Gonzalez, Senora Martinez tells her whole story, pleading that the Argentine authorities will prevent the landing of the sinister count. She opens the carefully wrapped book and shows it to the justice. It is Bram Stoker's <u>Dracula</u> and in the author's hand is the inscription on the flyleaf: "To Mina Harker with the sympathy and understanding of Bram Stoker." The justice who is a friend of the family, hardly knows whether to be impressed or amused, but when Mina shows him the letter that has just arrived from Transylvania, he accepts the gravity of the situation.

As Lord Godalming wheels Mina out, Justice Gonzalez presses some of the buttons on his desk. Clerks and officers enter. The justice gives orders to watch for the boxes of earth that will announce the arrival of the count. He also instructs that any strange craft that enters the La Plata River is to be stopped.

Several nights later there is a mist upon the river. Through this fog suddenly appears a magnificent black streamlined yacht bearing the name <u>Nemesis III</u>. The yacht enters the south basin slowly, approaching a dilapidated pier in the worst part of the city docks which is called the <u>boca</u>.

The harbormaster immediately announces the arrival of the strange ship. A group of detectives head for the dock. When they arrive they find the yacht moored to the dilapidated pier. Jumping aboard, they enter the captain's cabin and see that officer apparently studying his charts. When they shake him, however, he rolls out of the chair, dead. The second officer is dead also, roped to the wheel. The crew is dead. There apparently is nothing alive but a great black cat that hisses violently at them. In the storeroom are several great boxes.

Leaving two men on guard, the others depart to make their various reports and to notify the quarantine officer. The two detectives standing beside the gangplank have not noticed the long black dray that has drawn up, nor do they see the shadowy figure that jumps from the underpiling of the pier to the deck of the yacht. This figure creeps along the deck and enters the door of the principal salong, a room of considerable size with an ornate flooring of inlaid wood. In the dim light, the central panel of the floor slowly rises, and the hand of Dracula with

SEQUEL TO DRACULA   -6-

its signet ring appears. The same half-crazed being that was seen at the tomb is crouched in the corner of the room. It whispers hoarsely; "Come, master, everything is in readiness."

The detectives on the dock are uneasy. The great black cat has walked across in front of them -- an ill omen. Suddenly one of the detectives hears a slight sound and turns to see the demented creature that was on the yacht jump back to the under part of the pier. Cautioning the other to watch the gangplank, this officer crawls down under the pier, trying in vain to catch up to the elusive shadow.

The other detective who has been shivering slightly, turns up the collar of his coat as though the night had grown cold, and with a gesture of reassurance lights a cigarette.

Suddenly two pale, gruesome hands encircle the inspector's throat.

The second officer has failed to catch the slinking figure under the pier. A powerful black automobile has just disappeared into the night. The detective sees a loading van containing several great boxes slowly pulling away.

The arrival of Dracula causes an immediate change in the personality of Mina Martinez. Lord Godalming is obviously worried. His dogged devotion to the woman he has loved since his youth is now mingled with the most terrifying forebodings. He knows that Dracula has come to claim his bride according to the blood-pact made thirty years before.

After Mina has retired, Godalming goes to the great chest, takes out Van Helsing's diary and settles down by the fireplace to review

the incidents that it contains, and to equip himself for the new fight.
The last words of the diary read: "Thus, thank God, Count Dracula is
dead."

A strange mist has gathered in the room. As Godalming closes
the diary he looks up full into the face of Count Dracula who leers
hideously at him from a great chair on the opposite side of the fireplace. Dracula remarks that it is a pity that Dr. Van Helsin is no
more -- he was a worthy adversary.

At this moment the main lights of the room are turned on. Quincey and Mercedes enter laughing. Mercedes drops her wraps and seats
herself in the very chair that Dracula is occupying. The vampire vanishes.

Seeing the anguish in Lord Godalming's eyes, Quincey approaches
and asks for an explanation. The Englishman tells the strange story
of Dracula and finishes with the statement that the vampire is even
now within the house. The young people are stunned. So this is the
secret that his mother has kept all these years. Godalming lays out
a program of defense. He appoints Quincey to watch his mother, and
warning Mercedes of her danger, prepares in his own desperate but
uncertain manner to fight the sinister force at work in their lives.
Returning the diary to the locked chest, he prepares for an all-night
vigil at the foot of the stairs that leads up to Min'as room.

In the days that follow, Mina slowly turns into a vampire. By
day she is bound to her wheelchair, but with the setting of the sun
she rises to obey the mental impulses of her infernal master. Lord

SEQUEL TO DRACULA   -8-

Godalming is forced to watch the woman he adores slowly transformed into a loathsome creature that tries to destroy even him. Count Dracula leaves death and destruction in his way. He has descended as an evil blight upon the city.

Mina turns upon Mercedes. But Dracula wishes the young girl for himself. The two vampires fight like beasts of the underworld.

Against this infernal conspiracy, Lord Godalming, a man willing but not brilliant, and Quincey impulsive and daring but lacking organization, fight valiantly. They discover several boxes of the earth which Dracula has brought with him, and destroy them by casting the earth into water, according to the old legends. They are heckled and interfered with by Dracula's half-crazed servant. But in spite of every effort, they cannot find the hiding place of Dracula himself.

At last the end comes for Mina. Dying, she regains for a short time her normal reason, and exacts from Lord Godalming the promise that after she is dead he will drive the stake through her heart and release her from a vampire's fate. The broken-hearted nobleman promises. Mina then lapsing into a stupor, dies trying desperately to get to Dracula.

A few days later Godalming and Quincey open the grave. Lord Godalming drives the stake through her body, and her face regains its beauty and dignity. Lord Godalming falls brokenhearted over her body.

Dracula and his half-crazed menial now turn their attention upon Mercedes, determined that she shall join the ranks of the undead.

Lord Godalming and Quincey use all of the skill and courage that they possess, and for a time succeed in disconcerting the vampire. During the day they still are searching for the body with the box in which it must rest.

At last Dracula's hiding place is discovered. He had brought some of his earth, and destroying the records in the great chest, had taken up his abode right in the house.

That night Lord Godalming leaves Quincey to protect Mercedes, and removing the earth from the chest pours it down a well on the property.

He returns to find Quincey unconscious on the floor and Mercedes gone.

Notifying the authorities, he converges with them to the black yacht which still is moored to the dock. They find Mercedes in a sort of somnambulism, wandering towards the boat, stumbling over the broken planks and beams. On the black deck of Nemesis III stands Dracula. At his feet grovels his mad servant. The officers fire at him without result. Suddenly Lord Godalming stops and points towards the east. Dawn is breaking. Dracula also sees it and with a howl of fury rushes into the cabin. The black yacht moves out into the river with the madman at the wheel. Count Dracula lies in his box of earth underneath the floor.

Mercedes released by the dawn finds Quincey waiting for her; while Lord Godalming sadly but thankfully returns with them to the house of tragedy.

ACKNOWLEDGMENTS

The authors express gratitude to the staff members at the following institutions, who assisted in the research for this book: the Billy Rose Theater Division of the New York Public Library, the Harry Ransom Center at the University of Texas at Austin, the Louis B. Mayer Film and Television Study Center in the Doheny Library at the University of Southern California, and the Margaret Herrick Library of the Academy of Motion Picture Arts and Sciences in Beverly Hills.

The authors also extend sincere thanks to the following individuals who assisted with research and images: Mike Bannon, Buddy Barnett, Marty Baumann, Ronald V. Borst, Ryan Brennan, John Brunas, Mike Brunas, Ross Clark, Michael Copner, John M. Cozzoli, Frank Dello Stritto, Jack Dowler, Beau Foutz, Fritz Frising, Scott Gallinghouse, Kerry Gammill, Christopher R. Gauthier, Douglas Kennedy, Hal Lane, Prof. Murray Leeder, Scott MacQueen, Mark Martucci, Kathleen Mayne, John McElwee, John Morgan, Lynn Naron, Constantine Nasr, Robert Neill, Henry Nicolella, Susan Oka, Gary L. Prange, Frederick Rappaport, Donald Lee Rhodes, Phyllis Ann Rhodes, Alan Rode, Mary Runser, Gary J. Satterlee, David Schecter, Rich Scrivani, Robert Singer, John Soister, Sally Stark, Russ Sumner, Marlisa Santos, Laura Wagner and David Wentink.

The authors' deepest appreciation to a small number of individuals who did so very much to see this book come to fruition. They include William Armstrong (who provided the reissue pressbook for *Son of Dracula*), Rich Bush (for invaluable research on *Son of Dracula* music), Bill Chase (for sharing photographs), George Chastain (for creating such memorable artwork), Ned Comstock (for locating the original pressbook for *Son of Dracula*), Kristin Dewey (for sharing photographs), Bill Kaffenberger (for scouring archives in search of clippings used in the appendices), Gregory William Mank (for allowing us to reprint his Louise Allbritton biography) and William Rosar (for sharing his unpublished interview with Hans J. Salter). We are vastly indebted to John Antosiewicz for opening up his still collection.

Artist: Marty "The Astounding B Monster" Baumann

CPSIA information can be obtained
at www.ICGtesting.com
Printed in the USA
BVHW012002100719

552885BV00027B/132/P